# NORWICH CITY

# The Eighties

## Edward Couzens-Lake

AMBERLEY

First published 2015

Amberley Publishing
The Hill, Stroud,
Gloucestershire, GL5 4EP

www.amberley-books.com

ISBN 978 1 4456 3871 3 (print)
ISBN 978 1 4456 3888 1 (ebook)

British Library Cataloguing in Publication Data.
A catalogue record for this book is available from the British Library.

Typesetting and Origination by Amberley Publishing.
Printed in Great Britain.

# Contents

# Introduction

It's Tuesday 1 January 1980.

Pink Floyd are, somewhat unfeasibly, at number one with 'Another Brick In The Wall' whilst a nation, dozy with torpor at predictable festive excess is settling down for yet another night in front of the television with the first ever episode of *Hi Di Hi* due to be shown on BBC1 at 7.30 p.m. – lucky old Britain! *Match of the Day* wasn't on, sadly – but Barry Norman was, with *Films Of The Year* at 11.10 p.m., looking back at some of celluloid hits of 1979, including *The Deer Hunter*, *Apocalypse Now* and *The China Syndrome* – decent films all so maybe something worth sitting up if you weren't too hung over and haggard after the previous evenings celebrations.

Worth waiting up for or worth getting back home in time for? Good fortune had certainly blessed those TV devotees amongst the Norwich City faithful travelling back to Norfolk after their New Year's Day game at Crystal Palace. They'd almost certainly miss *Hi Di Hi* but would be able to, if they wished, doze off in front of Barry, dreaming, perchance, of the day and game they'd just witnessed at that most salubrious of all English stadiums Selhurst Park, the San Siro of South London.

It had not been a particularly exciting game, motions having been gone through on an icy pitch, one that John Bond, the Norwich manager had deemed, pre-match, as being too dangerous to play on. Referee Darryl Reeves thought differently though, declaring that the match would go ahead. The almost inevitable 0-0 draw that followed summed up the cautious approach both teams subsequently employed in conditions that would almost certainly see a match called off today. A point apiece then, but, for Bond and Norwich, fury followed at its conclusion, not at Norwich's performance or the result, but the fact that Canary striker Alan Taylor had, after a collision with self-appointed Palace hardman Jim Cannon, been stretchered off the pitch with a knee injury, one which the state of the pitch had more than likely played a contributory factor.

Norwich's hard-earned point, their fourth consecutive draw in the league elevated them up to fifth place in the Division One table that New Year's Day evening. The Canaries are, to coin a well-used and, even then, irritating cliché, 'flying high'; they're just eight points shy of league leaders Liverpool and have, the injury to Taylor notwithstanding, plenty of cause for celebration on that New Year's Day.

Fifth in Division One. A playing squad that boasts the likes of, amongst notable others, Justin Fashanu, Jimmy Neighbour, Graham Paddon, Martin Peters and Kevin Reeves. One is a World Cup winner with England, another is destined to play for England, a third, yet to arrive, will also play for England as a Norwich player, becoming, when he does, the fifth Canary to wear the three lions on his shirt in around a decade. The club also boasts a popular and charismatic boss in John Bond – a popular and respected figure within the game and a 'name' the club can call their own. He might not be their first ever 'name' but certainly their first of the rich and all-encompassing media age that the game was, over a decade before Sky Sports and its Super Sunday, already spiralling into.

Norwich City, in short, have made it into the big time, something they'd already more than ably demonstrated in the first half of that 1979/80 season with some remarkable results against some of the games more esteemed names-this included a 4-1 win over Manchester United at Carrow Road, a 4-0 triumph over Tottenham, 3-1 against Nottingham Forest-Clough, Shilton and all, the reigning European Cup holders. Norwich fans can also look back on a 4-2 win at Everton and more than respectable 0-0 draw at Liverpool, one of only six games Liverpool had failed to win at home in the league that season and one of just two league games played at Anfield that season which had seen them fail to break down the visiting sides defence, one which featured, in this instance, the venerable Kevin Keelan in goal, thirty-eight years old and as reliable and passionate about himself and the club as ever. Good times.

Days of footballing pomp and circumstance which, truth be told, would not and could not have been dreamt about a decade earlier.

Norwich's first competitive match of the 1970s was an FA Cup third-round tie at home to Fourth Division Wrexham. And, whilst their league form under recently appointed manager Ron Saunders had not exactly been scintillating, the Canaries were placed in a lowly sixteenth place in the Division Two table prior to kick-off. Saunders' team were expected to dispatch their lower league opponents with few problems along the way but this did not turn out to be the case and, 2-0 up at half time, Wrexham held on a vaguely surprising but perhaps not altogether unexpected victory, despite a second-half goal for Norwich from Trevor Howard that hinted at a possible comeback.

It was the fourth time that the Canaries had exited the tournament at the first stage in seven years. There was, clearly, a lot of work for Saunders to do, providing a demanding Norwich Board of Directors, set on top-flight football with a single minded zeal, gave him the time and space to do so. Others had tried and failed. Indeed, since Archie Macaulay had moved onto bigger and better things at West Brom back in 1961, four men had come and gone in around seven and a half years charged with the onerous task of taking Norwich to Division One. All had failed. As would be the case with Saunders, and quickly, if there were any more afternoons like that chilly one of 3 January 1970. Fortunately for both him and the club, he was given that time and consequently delivered his hard-working, fast-moving and occasionally physically uncompromising Norwich side to Division One by the end of the 1971/72 season, his third in change at Carrow Road.

You can read all about that and what followed in this books companion volume, *Norwich City: The Seventies*, also by Amberley Publishing.

Saunders therefore was the master of discipline that got Norwich in amongst the elite in the first place, Bond is the man who, after a mid-decade wobble, got them back again in 1975 and kept them there for a further five seasons after that, a club record for top-flight longevity he shares with Dave Stringer, one that will need a gargantuan effort from any future Norwich manager to match, let alone beat. Five consecutive seasons in the Premier League and all under the same man in charge? It might, of course, have happened under Mike Walker, just as it might have done under Paul Lambert or Chris Hughton – but 'might' is a big word in football.

The problem that over-achieving clubs have at the top level is, just as it was with Bond, the men who play a part in keeping there can, all too easily, be lured away by bigger clubs with deeper pockets, just as it happened with Bond and Lambert. Over three decades span their respective departures to Manchester City and Aston Villa, a near aeon in modern football – yet, despite all the changes that the game has seen between those managers leaving of Carrow Road one aspect of it remains deeply constant – the small will get picked upon by the big, the poor by the rich. Was, is, and forever will be.

Yet as we have seen, the evening of 1 January 1980 sees Norwich City in a good place, a very good place indeed. Surely Bond has no intention of being lured away, surely he sees the rich potential at the club and values the quality of both his playing squad as well as the tolerance and occasional indulgences of his Chairman?

He won't be going anywhere anytime soon. Will he?

Edward Couzens-Lake

# Foreword

I remember being sat on my arse at home in Southampton in the build up to Christmas in 1982. Things weren't going too well. I'd been released by Southampton that summer and, after a difficult month at Newcastle I was playing part-time for Bobby Gould at Bristol Rovers. I wasn't fit, I wasn't getting the best out of myself and I wasn't enjoying life in the Third Division. It all seemed over.

Then the phone rang. Bobby said that Ken Brown had asked him if I might fancy another crack at the First Division and, if so, would I give him a ring?

I didn't have to think too hard about it! Gouldie knew that I wasn't enjoying my football so I phoned Ken. He just told me to get myself up to Norwich because they didn't have too many attacking options and we could work on a month by month basis. That was good enough for me – I'd managed to prang my car and could only get hold of a Mini for the long drive to Norfolk but it was worth the effort.

Ken Brown is a smashing bloke and he said I could carry on training part time if I wanted to, but I wasn't going to make that mistake again. I'd learnt that if it was worth doing, it's worth doing properly so I said I'd give it a real good go. The next thing I knew, I played well enough to make an impression in the East Anglian derby on Boxing Day, we won and I never looked back.

What a great time it turned out to be. I loved every minute and owed City everything for extending my career in such a lovely environment. I was in my element. I more or less did as I pleased and although my legs had gone, I could still play a part and influence games and the kids alongside me were instrumental in that. They all had plenty of talent and with Mel Machin as their coach, they came on in leaps and bounds. I loved it. Every one of them makes me smile.

Paul Haylock, Peter Mendham, Dennis van Wijk, Mark Barham and especially Louie Donowa. I gave him so much stick but I thought the world of him. A smashing lad who could be magic one minute and awful the next – and I told him every time!

Then we had a bit of class. Chris Woods was a good lad and an exceptional goalkeeper; Steve Bruce was all action and very brave and then there was Dave

Watson, who I thought was top class. They were all young and all went on to achieve so much with England, or in Brucie's case, Manchester United. I got on great with John Deehan who was a real threat up front plus Asa Hartford, who joined after me. Asa is one of my best mates and made a real impact. Then there were other lads who I still remember with a smile. Keith Bertschin was one of the hardest blokes I ever played with and Greg Downs was a real pro, a good lad. I was very proud to have played my part amongst them.

Everyone mattered at Norwich City. It was like a village green team, with the tea lady, the apprentices and the fans all feeling involved. The fans especially were great to me and I was so happy when they had their big day at Wembley. And winning the League Cup there with Norwich was incredible. I was thirty-six, Asa was thirty-four and we never thought we'd get a chance of playing at Wembley again. How many clubs would allow one of their players to have his lad in the dressing room as well as sitting on the bench for a major cup final? That's what Michael did as a ten-year-old, and he even joined us on the lap of honour.

Norwich City is a special club and I look back on my two and a half years with great affection. I wasn't there for long and only ever signed a rolling, monthly contract but they gave me free rein to enjoy my football.

I can't thank Ken, Mel, the players and most importantly the fans enough.

Great days.

'On The Ball City!'

Mike Channon

# CHAPTER ONE

# Goodbye, Mr Bond

*At least the game gave Bond the chance to get Royle back onto the pitch for his first game for nearly a month but, when he did eventually come off the bench and into the action, it wasn't, as you would have expected, for Muzinic but for the unfortunate Ross Jack who at least offered some threat in attack, whereas Muzinic offered no threat to anyone other than his overworked translator.*

There are probably better places in the world to be in the early evening of any day than Selhurst Park, the dank and singularly unremarkable home of Crystal Palace Football Club. More so on the evening of a New Year's Day, especially when you've spent most of it working; most of everyone else's holiday come to that working or training; selflessly missing out as you do so on all the traditional excesses so easily accessible to most at that time of year.

Such is the lot of the professional footballer at Christmas.

It's not as if the Canaries have ran themselves into the ground with regard to the number of games they've played over this particular festive period. The 1979/80 season saw Norwich play four league games in eleven days – hardly an over strenuous commitment by any stretch of the footballing imagination, especially when compared to the days when a full league programme was played right over and including the holiday period. Take the 1930/31 season for example, which saw Norwich play the same number of games in just eight days-including consecutive matches on Christmas Day, Boxing Day and 27 December, three games in three days with nine Canaries playing in every minute of that testing trio of games.

And people say today's players are as fit as they've ever been.

Not that there were any shirkers in the Norwich squad over the Christmas and New Year holidays nearly half a century later. Of those four league games played in that eleven day period, seven Canaries played in all of them – Kevin Bond; Roger Brown; Greg Downs; Kevin Keelan; Graham Paddon; Martin Peters (at thirty-six one of the oldest players in the top flight) and John Ryan. The last of that quartet of games, that prickly 0-0 draw at Selhurst Park meant that Norwich finished that run of four games league unbeaten – albeit via four draws. But, as New Year's Day 1980 drew to a close, it had proved enough to life them into fifth place in the Division One table, level on points with fourth placed Southampton; Ball, Boyer, Channon and all, and eight points adrift of league leaders and eventual Champions Liverpool. The team, the squad and football club that John Bond has built in his own image, flamboyant, unpredictable and with a tendency for the unexpected, are performing well and looking good; the prospects of the Canaries repeating or even surpassing their previous best ever finish in the top flight of English football (10th in the 1975/76 season) growing ever more probable with each and every game played.

The Norwich players now had a quick break before an FA Cup third round tie at Yeovil Town, then sat in a comfortable tenth place in the Conference and on a bit of a barren run as far as league form was concerned with one draw and four defeats in their previous five matches. Two of those had been home defeats (Worcester City, 0-2 and Weymouth, 0-1) at the Huish, famous for its eight foot side to side slope, one that First Division Sunderland couldn't get to grips on in a fourth round game back in 1949, and were sent back to Roker Park on the back of a 2-1 defeat, a match that still ranks as one of the biggest giant killings in FA Cup history. Hungry Somerset eyes now lingered on Bond's side, confident that the prosaic surrounds of their untidy yet well-loved little ground would help see the Canaries off in much the same manner.

The two sides did have a bit of FA Cup 'previous'. Norwich had, as a Division Three South side made the long trip cross country to Somerset in 1953. Naturally enough, their own relatively humble status at the time didn't excite the locals as much as the visit of Len Shackleton and co. had four years earlier. It was, however, a chance for Yeovil to kick-off another cup run, and at the expense of opponents who they might reasonably have thought they had a good chance of beating. Norwich were, after all, no Sunderland, and they certainly had no players of the calibre and fame of Len Shackleton to call upon. The Canaries did have Johnny Summers though, a small and quintessentially tricky winger who made metaphorical hay upon the Huish mud, scoring both goals and being generally unplayable in Norwich's comfortable 2-0 win, a result that was perhaps more of a shock to the wider footballing world than a Yeovil win might have been?

Two motives for Yeovil Town on the day then. A chance for their current players and management to create a little bit more FA Cup history at the expense of a top flight club whilst also having the chance to put one over Norwich, the side that had, against popular expectation, swatted them aside in their previous meeting, extinguishing, in the process, more FA Cup dreams in the West Country before they'd even began.

All the ingredients, as everyone was saying, of an FA Cup shock. A non-league team at home to one from the elite, a sloping pitch, lots of mud and a hostile, extremely partisan home crowd. Television coverage of such a game was naturally a given with the BBC sending Barry Davies and the *Match of the Day* cameras down to record a possible upset, that and for Davies to get his own Ronnie Radford moment, onfield small boys clad in parkas optional. But it was not to be as the spoilsport Canaries, clad in an unfamiliar all yellow strip, shattered the dreams of both Yeovil and the footballing nation by winning 3-0 with Graham Paddon, Keith Robson and Justin Fashanu scoring the goals. Paddon's opener perhaps best summed up the Norwich domination on the day; Robson and Mendham combining well on the Yeovil left before the latters floated ball into the penalty area saw Paddon strike it home first time with all the confidence and conviction you'd have expected from one of English footballers most criminally underrated players at the time.

Job done.

Thus Norwich eyes must have been smiling on the long trip back to Norfolk. Those smiles would have been even wider a week later after a 1-0 win over Coventry City at Carrow Road, a goal on the stroke of half time by the effervescent

Keith Robson enough to secure the win and propel the Canaries into the relatively dizzying heights of fourth place. Their points total of twenty-eight would, even now, have been enough to have kept them safe from relegation at the end of the previous season, thus, barring a disaster of 1957-type proportions,[1] Bond and Norwich could already look forward to and plan for another season, their sixth in succession, at the top table come August 1980.

Little wonder therefore that the Norwich board were so determined to secure John Bond to the club for as long as possible. This had included the offer to him of a ten year contract at one point, a staggering and hitherto unknown act of faith for any football club, indeed, any business to offer to any one employee, given the risk of paying it off should things have gone wrong early on. The offer was on the table though and, clearly mindful that it would help make him financially comfortable for the rest of his life no matter what the outcome, Bond saw no reason not to sign it, even going as far as to suggest if he was having one then his assistant, Ken Brown, should certainly be offered the same terms. At this point, Arthur South, the no-nonsense Norwich Chairman baulked. 'No, no John, that offer is for you and you alone, we value and respect what you have done for us at the club and this contract is our way of showing just how much faith we have in you as our manager.' But Bond, presciently mindful of how high his stock was rising in the game wasn't having it.

'Sorry Mr Chairman, but if you won't offer those terms to Ken, then I don't think I'll be signing it. We are a team and I would hope you would also have realised and accepted that.' Needless to say, a few days later South called Bond into his office again and said that the club were now, after all, willing to offer the same contract to Ken Brown. manager 1 – Chairman 0. It doesn't happen often. But it did then for John Bond at Norwich. His status at the club was virtually untouchable; he was Norwich City, so much so that his nickname in and around the club was 'King John'. A popular story goes that after one game, when the Rt Revd Maurice Wood, Bishop of Norwich from 1971 to 1985 and a fervent Canary fan popped his head around Bond's office door, Bond asked him if he would '... put in a word for me at HQ?' to which the canny Bishop replied, 'I'm ahead of you Mr Bond, I already have.' God was in his heaven. And John Bond, 'King John', was in his office at Carrow Road. From 5 January 1957, Norwich's league record in Division Three South read as P20, W3, D5, L12 – the Canaries finished bottom of the table and had to apply for re-election to the Football League.

Following their win over Coventry City, Norwich, along with most other league teams in England found themselves and their season affected by the weather, a particularly wet and icy few weeks from mid-January onwards causing many games to be postponed, often on more than one occasion. It wasn't bad enough to stop the Canaries from tumbling out of the FA Cup at the 4th-round stage, a fine

1-1 draw at Wolves on 26 January being followed up by a 3-2 defeat at Carrow Road in the replay. That result and defensive performance that accompanied it led to Bond recalling David Jones for the clubs next home game on 9 February against Liverpool, a match that not only announced the arrival of a great and natural footballing talent onto the national stage but also, less prominently, saw another great talent make the last of his 673 appearances for Norwich City.

A dull but crisp Carrow Road afternoon greeted the two sides as did, again, the BBC *Match of the Day* cameras, Barry Davies now headed east in order that his three day journey from London to Norfolk might be rewarded with another Liverpool win as they sauntered their way to another Championship. Norwich were therefore billed as the unfortunate fall guys, the beleaguered locals coming up against a gladiator elite, a Liverpool that was remorseless, blood red shirts and an attitude that either stirred or chilled the blood, depending on your affiliation. And no messing about with squad rotation or feeling a need to rest key players either, they were all there and on display. It was an autograph hunter's delight that included Clemence, Neal, Hansen, Dalglish, McDermott – one hell of a five-a-side team there, the problem was, there was six more of them.

Bond opted, unsurprisingly, to fight fire with fire with the busy and competitive Peter Mendham, a midfield terrier who could also play the sweetest of passes accompanying Graham Paddon in midfield. John Ryan and Martin Peters provided the width and, in the case of Peters, considerable guile whilst, in attack, Norwich had a duo who were, potentially, as good a striking partnership the club had ever had with Justin Fashanu and Kevin Reeves, twenty-two and seventeen years old respectively and as raw as their youth suggested. Reeves had been one of Bond's chance signings, one of many from Bournemouth, his former club. Initially signed on loan, he had also attracted the attention and subsequent interest of Terry Neill at Arsenal. It was perhaps Arsenal's growing interest in him that led Bond to take the plunge, signing Reeves permanently for just £50,000, having initially awarded him his first team debut, whilst still a loanee, at, of all places Highbury on 15 January 1976. Reeves had since been a relatively slow burner in the Norwich squad, his talent and potential unquestionable as he ended his first season at the club with eight league goals from twenty-one league games.

By the time he took his place and the Number 8 shirt for the Liverpool game, he'd made a total of 114 league appearances for the Canaries, scoring thirty-five goals. That average of around a goal every 3.25 games was hardly of the free scoring variety but then Reeves had never been bought with that in mind. Bond saw him as a similar sort of player to another Bournemouth old boy-cum-Canary, Phil Boyer. 'Charlie' as he had affectionately been known in and around Carrow Road was a very capable forward in his own right, but, importantly for the team, was more than willing to let his intelligent running plus his ability to drag his markers out of position in order to let his strike partner benefit. Reeves, similarly fleet of thought as well as foot, therefore took up the same role alongside Fashanu as Boyer had for MacDougall – to run for him, create space, get the knock downs and generally be his wingman. It was a partnership that Bond hoped would swiftly gel and be as effective at the highest level as Boyer and MacDougall, scorers of thirty-nine goals between them during the 1975/76 season had been.

If Reeves was the cutting edge therefore, then Fashanu was the irresistible force. His size, strength and power were part of a formidable all round armoury, honed from a childhood spent training to be a boxer and, in doing so, getting as far as the British Schoolboys Heavyweight Boxing Final in 1977. Boxing's loss became football's gain September of that year however when Justin signed for Norwich as an apprentice. Now, a little under two and a half years since he had joined the club as an uber-confident sixteen year old, he was a first team player with thirty-nine league goals and eleven goals to his name with, everyone was sure, a lot more to come.

So, for all of the reputation that they brought with them, a defence that had, the previous season, conceded just sixteen league goals in forty-two games, with just four of those at Anfield, Liverpool held no fears for Fashanu and he would have been his usual loud and confident self in the dressing room prior to kick-off. A confidence that, to be fair, would have been shared by his Norwich teammates which was reflected in the Canaries taking the lead after just two minutes with Martin Peters characteristically ghosting in to score from a close range header. Good news and bad news for Norwich for, whilst it was always a great confidence booster to get an early lead in any game, this was Liverpool, the best team in the country and probably in Europe who they were playing. So it presents a problem. Do the Canaries look to hold onto their lead, albeit for eighty-eight minutes of what would be continuous pressure, or did they look to score more?

Silly question. This is a John Bond team, remember?

Thus the puffed up Canaries looked to increase their advantage straight from the kick-off. Not the wisest of moves, indeed, maybe scoring hadn't been the most sensible thing they had done either. Two minutes from the end – yes, but two minutes after kick-off? A sure and certain way of rattling their opponents gilded cage and so it proved when a now snarling Liverpool equalised through David Fairclough. Then, barely a quarter of an hour later, the Reds went ahead, Fairclough making it 2-1 and, with it, seemingly restoring the natural balance of things. It was already turning into a game that had the makings of a classic. All the ingredients were there-feisty underdogs, crackling atmosphere, heavy pitch and illustrious opponents experiencing, for them, a difficult afternoons work already. In fairness, they should have known what to expect. The corresponding fixture at Anfield back in September had ended in a 0-0 draw with Dalglish expertly kept on the fringes of the action thanks to a stolid man-marking job by Phil Hoadley, once of Crystal Palace and the Orient. Liverpool had much of the ball and, not surprisingly, most of the action took place in the Norwich penalty area, but, with Kevin Keelan revelling in the big stage and a crowd just short of 45,000, the Canaries had held onto that point. The question now was a simple one: would their perceived failings in that game at Anfield provoke Liverpool onto seek some kind of retribution here or would their performance on the day inspire Norwich to do it all over again and at least secure a point, even if their defence was showing a couple of changes from that Autumn game with Greg Downs and Roger Brown stepping in for Hoadley and John McDowell.

Despite being in some illustrious company, Fairclough was the main threat in red. He'd long had the reputation with Liverpool as being their 'super sub', back in the days when clubs could only name one man for the bench. Liverpool, being Liverpool, invariably had a forward sitting there, biding his chance-either to steal a goal if they were struggling (unlikely) or to give Bob Paisley the opportunity to rest either Dalglish or former Ipswich striker David Johnson who were their usual first choice duo in attack. This game was both his and Sammy Lee's first start of that campaign and they had combined well for Fairclough's equaliser which came down the Norwich left. His second was even better, the move starting with a powerful run from Hansen (atoning for his 'shocking defending' for the Norwich opener when he had wafted a leg in the general direction of scorer Peters in a less than half-hearted attempt to stop him); Fairclough's shot from his subsequent pass was an exquisite curling effort that gave Keelan no chance.

It was genuine end to end stuff as first one side and then the other threw caution to the wind and charged, Light Brigade like, onto the massed ranks of an opposing defence. Norwich's reward for their continuing bravado came after thirty-three minutes when Reeves bundled the ball home from a Paddon corner. It was by no means the final significant action of the first half but it was the final goal of an enthralling forty-five minutes and, when Mark Scott brought it to a reluctant end, the terraces heaved to the sound of people reliving what had just gone before them before they fortified themselves with Bovril and a Wagon Wheel in preparation for the second chapter.

The second half of the game is, of course, best known for the goal scored by Justin Fashanu to bring the scores level again, this after Fairclough had completed his hat trick after a long and penetrating run down the Norwich right from Dalglish had split the Norwich defence wide open. With fifteen minutes to go and Liverpool now 3-2 up, you might have been forgiven for thinking that was it and that Liverpool would merely put the shutters up to ensure there would be no more sloppiness on their part and that the victory that had not only come for, but fully expected, would be theirs for the taking. A good game, yes. But not yet a great one and a game, at that moment, free from a really special moment or flash of genius.

No more than five minutes had passed since Fairclough had put Liverpool ahead for the second time and, as expected, they'd proceeded to slow things down a bit, trying to take some of the sting out of the game – they were, in effect, bringing in the deckchairs after a long hot day on the beach was coming to a close. Except that no one had told the team in yellow and green it was time to go home. Instead, Norwich pressed forward again as Greg Downs fed a quick pass to John Ryan as Norwich made progress down the Liverpool left. Ryan, an underrated and very intelligent player had been aware of the lurking Fashanu and, whilst barely breaking his stride fed the ball onto the Norwich striker, continuing his run in full preparation for the return pass, one which never came as Fashanu used the pace and direction of the oncoming ball to work a chance for himself, flicking the ball up before hitting an exquisite volley into the top left hand corner of the Liverpool goal. It was a strike that not only had both the Norwich crowd and Barry Davies in raptures, Davies' voice rising to its characteristic excitable tone as he eulogised the goal he had just seen; '... Fashanu ... oh ... oh WHAT a goal ... oooh, that's a MAGNIFICENT goal ... didn't seem to be the room between Ray Clemence's hand and the post ... as the crowd applaud surely one of the best goals they've seen at Carrow Road this season ... a really sweet turn by the tall man and curling high up, just away from Ray Clemence's hand and just inside his far right hand post for 3-3 ...' One of the best goals seen at Carrow Road that season? It was, and remains, one of the best goals that has ever been scored at Carrow Road, the resultant sight of Fashanu turning around and walking back to his own half in response, a finger raised to the air in modest acknowledgement at what he had just done one of those endearing and very iconic ones of that whole footballing era, a modest and understated response from a man who, right there and right then had the football world at his talented feet. In his laudable biography about Fashanu, writer Nick Baker recalls how, on the day before that game, Fashanu had gone out to lunch with two of his friends, one of which was his Norwich teammate Dave Bennett.[2] The talk had invariably been about the forthcoming match the following day with Bennett suggesting that, if Fashanu had scored, he should flap his arms out in celebration whilst his other friend had disagreed saying he should merely stick his finger in the air as it would be 'cool'. Whether or not Fashanu recalled that conversation as he walked away after his goal is open to question, but the fact that he chose to celebrate one of the most spectacular goals in English footballing history in much the same way as he might have acknowledged a tap in during a training session was not just cool, it was just about as cool as it gets, a wonderful strike and unforgettable response from a man who, in an instance, had made himself the most coveted player in English football.

Such is the legend that has risen as the result of Fashanu's goal that many people prefer to forget that Liverpool went onto win 5-3, courtesy of two late goals from

Dalglish and Jimmy Case or the part that they had played in a remarkable match, one that Liverpool's legendary manager Bob Paisley described afterwards as '... a superb, open game ... most teams will try to close it down against us but Norwich didn't – there was no way they were going to settle for a point'. Liverpool captain Phil Thompson was equally effusive saying it was the best game he had ever played in whilst referee Scott concurred, saying not only had he never refereed a better game, he didn't think he ever would.

Plaudits all round for the Canaries then. It wasn't the first, and most certainly wouldn't be the last time that a game they had featured in else a result or performance had caught the eye and attention of the nation rather than just the hard-core support in and around Norfolk. And that was all very well and good – but it came with accordant problems, all of which the club had to address. Fashanu's goal had heightened his profile sufficiently enough for other clubs to step up their interest in him and, with strike partner Kevin Reeves also attracting the attention of others, few Norwich games were now played without a phalanx of scouts from other clubs in attendance, each desperately trying to look as inconspicuous as possible. But they were there, spotted, no doubt, at first by their peers from other clubs as well as some of the more savvy Norwich fans who were able to pick out an unfamiliar face with ease amidst a mass of more familiar ones. Fashanu and Reeves were, as far as John Bond was concerned, the striking duo on which he was going to build his team around. The Canaries had struggled to replicate anything like the sort of partnership that Ted MacDougall and Phil Boyer had brought to the club for much of the previous decade. They had proven themselves to be one of the best forward partnerships the club had ever had, something which arguably remains the case to this day. So replacing them was going to be a challenge and Bond had gone his utmost to do so, bringing in the likes of Viv Busby, Roger Gibbins, Keith Robson and Dave Robb, all with varying degrees of success early on, but none of them long term solutions but players who were a stop gap, representing a need for the here and now rather than the future. Reeves and Fashanu, as it turned out, were both very much about the future-the problem now was whose future were they going to be a part of? Fashanu's profile and rise to national prominence was now peaking after his goal against Liverpool whilst Reeves had already attracted the interest of Arsenal manager Terry Neill. It seemed sadly inevitable that neither player would be at Carrow Road for very much longer.

This must have frustrated the hell out of Bond. He was an ambitious man and wanted more for Norwich City than mere year on year survival in the, as it was known then, First Division. Since he'd led the Canaries back to the top flight in his first full season at the club in 1975, they'd had respectable finishes of 10th (one that has only been surpassed on three occasions in 113 years), 16th, 13th and

16th again. Respectable yes – but that was about it. Bond wanted more than that, he wanted a team that would challenge at the top of the league as well as in the two domestic cups. He'd laid down his marker almost as soon as he'd arrived at Carrow Road in 1973, revamping the clubs schoolboy and youth set up as well as the manner and style in which the club played the game-the clubs reputation of being one that 'like to play good football' is all down to Bond. Yet respectability and a reputation for playing good football weren't enough for him. He wanted success, he wanted trophies. The problem was that now he looked as if he was piecing the sort of squad together that might stand a chance of doing that, the leading sides looked as if they were going to spirit away two of the clubs best players, leaving him with no alternative but to start planning all over again.

He also, in the wake of the Liverpool game now had the additional problem of wondering quite how the club were going to cope with the loss of long serving goalkeeper Kevin Keelan. He'd originally left the club the previous year, choosing to sign for the New England Teamen in the US, returning to Carrow Road on loan after his replacement, Roger Hansbury had broken a leg in pre-season. Thus, on 18 August 1979, Keelan took his place in the Norwich side for the trip to Everton, the seventeenth consecutive season he had started with the club and the sixteenth which had seen him as first choice. Norwich had won that game 4-2, their first away win in the league in forty-two attempts and now, twenty-five league and nine Cup matches later, he really was, at 39, about to take his leave from Norwich for the second and final time.

It was a shame, perhaps, that his last game had ended in defeat, one that had seen him concede five goals; it was also, perhaps, a shame that the headlines and the glory after that remarkable game had gone to Fashanu and Fairclough. Not that it made, or makes, the slightest bit of difference to the legacy and legend of Kevin Keelan, Ron Ashman's 'bargain of the century' when he signed from Wrexham in 1963 and now, 673 competitive appearances later, a man who had played in goal for Norwich City during the '60s, '70s and '80s.

Bond now had the onerous task of wondering who he was going to replace him with-if, that is, he could ever be replaced. What with Keelan on his way back to the USA, where he lives to this day, as well as having to prepare himself for predatory bids for his two young strikers, Bond was going to have his work cut out to do anything more than get to the end of the season as comfortably and with as less further upheaval as possible before contemplating another assault on the top division that Summer.

He wouldn't have been any happier after the Canaries next game, a fortnight after the epic encounter with Liverpool that saw Norwich take on Wolves, again at Carrow Road – and an expectant Carrow Road at that. Norwich may have lost the game to Liverpool. But it hadn't stopped people talking about the part they'd played in the match, the attacking football and the sheer verve of their play – showing, as Paisley had commented, no fear of Liverpool whatsoever. The Reds had only conceded three goals in a league game once before that season (at Southampton) and only once during the entire 1978/79 campaign. So they either had the meanest of defences or were so good in midfield and attack they weren't accustomed to teams having a go at them in the way that Norwich had. In truth it was a combination of both. Their back four at Carrow Road was Phil Neal, Phil Thompson, Alan Hansen and Alan Kennedy: a formidable barrier ahead of the even more formidable Ray Clemence. All of them bar Kennedy were full internationals – with Kennedy set to be picked by England himself a few years later. That defence ended up conceding just eight goals in their twenty-one league games at Anfield that season and only twenty-two in the same number of away league games, easily the best in the league. The fact that Norwich had breached it three times – twice from corners and once from a piece of magic – didn't so much count against Liverpool, as for Norwich and both the players that Bond had in his squad, the way they played and what he felt they were capable of. The Canaries had risen up to fourth in the table prior to the Liverpool game and level on points with Arsenal so there would almost certainly have been talk at Carrow Road of another top ten finish and maybe even a push for one of the European places, something which Bond hoped might keep the likes of Reeves and Fashanu at the club for a bit longer. Unfortunately for Norwich the 1-0 win over Coventry on 12 January that had seen them end that weekend in fourth place was followed by a gap of four weeks before their next fixture which was the Liverpool game, the inclement weather not serving them well whilst their opponents were able to get some more league games in whilst Norwich only managed to play four from 1 January to 23 February meaning, though it was through no fault of their own, they had slipped down the table to 11th by the time Wolves arrived at Carrow Road on 22 February. With a fourth consecutive league fixture at home to Middlesbrough to follow four days later, Bond would have been expecting two wins and the four points it would be worth to propel the Canaries back up towards the top six.

But he was to be disappointed.

He would probably also had been disappointed with the attendance (17,063, over 8,500 down in the Liverpool gate) for that game. Hadn't Norwich just taken part in a thrilling league match against the top side in England, if not Europe, standing toe to toe and given them the sort of match and fright that had drawn them praise from both their opponents as well as the wider footballing world? Hadn't they got some of the most promising young footballers in the country in their ranks – Reeves and Fashanu stood out – but there were others, players like Peter Mendham, twenty, a local lad born in King's Lynn, a hard-working midfielder but with a little more to his game than that as he was also not short on skill and technique, equally as able to play a forty yard pass to the feet of a colleague as he was a four yard one.

Norwich also had Greg Downs, a striker turned full back who'd made his debut in, of all games, an East Anglian derby game against Ipswich two years earlier – a proverbial baptism of fire for any teenage footballer – yet he had acquitted himself well, stayed in and around the first team and was now beginning to look at a run of games and permanent place in the team. Then there was Kevin Bond, the manager's son, one who had, as you would expect, endured a tough start to his Norwich career with some fans questioning his right to a place in the team. He'd more than won them over mind, with some commanding displays at right back, playing in all of the Canaries league games the previous season and impressing throughout this one.[3]

Still only twenty-three and with England B honours to his name already, he was another name to be reckoned with and another reason for his manager to be confident of a prosperous time ahead with his current squad – providing, as I have already alluded to, he could keep them all together. With such a quartet of promising youngsters allied to the undoubted and proven class of Martin Peters, Graham Paddon and David Jones, no one would have been blamed for sharing the manager's optimism.

Optimism that, for some, would have been blown clean out of the water following Norwich's game at home to Wolves which was a one sided and dismal affair with the visitors winning 4-0. Bond had made just one change to the starting line up from that which had faced Liverpool, drafting in yet another young tyro who had come through the ranks, twenty year old winger Steve Goble who'd made his league debut for the club earlier that season at home to Manchester City, following that up by scoring the opening goal in the following weeks 4-2 win at Brighton. With Goble bringing pace and excitement to the left handed side of the pitch and Peters bringing guile and that unerring ability of his to 'ghost' into goal scoring positions from the other, coupled with the threat of Reeves and Fashanu in attack, it had the makings of a youthful (six players were aged twenty-two or under), almost exuberant side in nature but one that was tempered with the wisdom of the ages in someone like the evergreen Peters and certainly one that, with confidence supposedly high should have been no match for a Wolves side that had won only two of their previous eight games.

Along, as the expression amongst Canary fans goes, come Norwich. To say that Norwich capitulated against Wolves would be an understatement. They did so much more than that, lying down and surrendering from kick-off, allowing their modest opponents to make hay, scoring three goals in a one-sided first half and going onto lose 4-0 in a thoroughly miserable display all round. Two of the Wolves goals had come from penalties, courtesy of rash tackles from the normally reliable centre-back pairing of Roger Brown and David Jones, Kenny Hibbitt scoring on both of those occasions with Mel Eves and John Richards doing the honours from open play, simple penalty box goals, tap ins that illustrated just how badly disorganised Norwich had been on the day. It had been one that was particularly disastrous for Roger Hansbury, recalled to replace the USA bound Keelan for his first game since the end of the previous season. Hansbury had originally made his league debut for Norwich back in September 1974, conceding four as Fulham had romped to an easy 4-0 victory at Craven Cottage. Now, here he was again, back in the side in place of the now departed, rather than injured Keelan – with four goals going past him again being the end result. Replacing Keelan in the hearts and minds of Norwich fans was always going to be an near to impossible task for anyone – Bond could have signed Ray Clemence or Peter Shilton and it wouldn't have been any easier – but, for Hansbury it must have been very difficult indeed. The question remained as to whether he would be able to establish himself in the team for the long term, one question of many that would have swirled around in the minds of both players, fans and the Coaching staff after this game, one inarguable fact now being that, in just two home games, Norwich had conceded nine goals, hardly the form of a team looking to finish in the top six and look to push on the following season.

It would have come, post-Wolves, as a surprise to no one if Bond wasn't already beginning to take the team as far as he could, as far as he could, that is, without a massive injection of cash to bolster a squad that clearly needed both an injection of class and top flight experience at the back. The manner in the way in which some cash was, eventually, made available to him might well have made him look to question his long term future at the club even more. The Canaries faced Middlesbrough just four days later, a game that, inevitably saw Bond make changes to his starting line-up. Hansbury retained his place but three paid the price for the glaring defensive failings against Wolves with Downs and Brown removed from the back four in favour of Richard Symonds and former West Ham man John McDowell. Goble was also, after having just one game to make an impression, his place going to another player brought up from the youth ranks, twenty-year-old Mark Halsey who had made quite an impression himself in his Canaries debut against Newcastle United two years earlier when he had been sent off. Bond now felt he was deserving of a second chance, hoping, no doubt, that Halsey's competitiveness in midfield would enable Norwich to win the ball more often and dictate the play. That and the other changes did make Norwich more organised and harder to break down-but, so too, were their opponents with a dull 0-0 draw the end result, an injury to Fashanu adding to the clubs steadily accruing woes.

Norwich's next opponents were Manchester City who'd they'd shared an entertaining 2-2 draw with at Carrow Road back in October. They'd been struggling for form, points and goals throughout the season and were winless in their previous nine games leading up to this one, scoring just eight goals in the process and shipping in four in games against Brighton, Southampton and Nottingham Forest in that time. manager Malcolm Allison was, therefore, under a tremendous amount of pressure to turn things round at Maine Road – or face the inevitable consequences. He had, as far as Bond would have been concerned, a playing budget that anyone would have been envious off. Steve Daly had been signed from Wolves for a British record (and strangely exact in these days of 'undisclosed amounts') fee of £1,437,500 whilst Mike Robinson had arrived from Preston for £750,000 – a wildly speculative fee for a player who, at the time, had no top flight experience and had made just forty-eight league appearances for Preston in four years.⁴ Over £2 million on just two players. How Bond must have dreamed of those sort of financial resources at Norwich. The most he'd ever paid for a player remained the £145,000 paid to Bournemouth for Phil Boyer – around 10% of the fee Allison had paid for Daly – and that had been over six years previously. Now Allison and Manchester City were casting covetous eyes on Kevin Reeves, signed by Bond, also from Bournemouth for just £50,000 and, he had hoped, to play up front for Norwich alongside Boyer – something which had happened just the once, in a 1-0 defeat at West Ham in April 1977. Boyer left Norwich that summer, at a loss, meaning that Bond was never able to see how well the two might work together in attack – not in the yellow and green of Norwich City anyway.

Norwich battled their way to another 0-0 draw at Maine Road, a third consecutive game for them without a goal. With Fashanu injured, Alan Taylor, the scorer of two goals for West Ham in the 1975 FA Cup Final against Fulham stepped in, but he was clearly not fully fit and struggled, as did, to an extent, Reeves, who, for all his energy and penalty box prowess, needed another striker firing on all cylinders alongside him. Fashanu eventually came off the bench but it was to no avail and Reeves, by now aware of Allison's interest in him, must have felt he had failed his very public audition.

To Allison and Manchester City it mattered not that Reeves hadn't performed at his future home and they pushed ahead with the deal, their offer of £1 million for a player who had cost Norwich just 5 per cent of that, at the time, eye watering total, too good for the Canaries to refuse, money that even Bond would have to admit, would do a great deal of good at and for the club over the next few years, even if the clubs biggest signing that came from that sudden influx of cash turned out to be one of the Canaries most disastrous transfer purchases in their history. With Reeves gone, having signed off with a goal in his final game, a 2-2 draw against Brighton at Carrow Road, the Canaries proceeded to shuffle their way to a thoroughly unconvincing and low key end to the 1979/80 season, winning just four of their remaining twelve games of the season, post-Brighton, one of them being an impressive 2-1 win over Arsenal at Carrow Road, all the more as it came after the Gunners, spear headed by Alan Sunderland and Frank Stapleton with the added spice of Liam Brady and Graham Rix in midfield had gone ahead, through Rix, after just nine minutes. Norwich equalised through the increasingly impressive David Jones before Arsenal won a penalty after Hansbury was adjudged to have brought down Brian Talbot. That could, and maybe should, have been that but Hansbury had no fear in facing Liam Brady, saving his spot kick with some aplomb. The unexpected miss deflated Arsenal and it came as no surprise when Norwich scored a winner, Paddon setting up Fashanu for his eighth of the season.

Bond had, by now, been able to spend a little of the money brought in from the sale of Reeves, making the surprising but very welcome signing of forward Clive Woods from Ipswich Town. Woods, a massive Norwich fan was born in Norwich, yet, despite impressing at Norwich based Eastern Counties League side Gothic FC, the Canaries were slow in making a decision about him, finally offering Woods a trial when he thought that, having already been involved with Wolves, Ipswich and Scunthorpe United (where his house mate was none other than Kevin Keegan), he was maybe worth a little more, deciding, eventually, to go for a more committed offer from Ipswich, later admitting that the Canaries '... always seemed reluctant to give terms to local players'. This was certainly true and in the case of his future Ipswich teammate Trevor Whymark, another Norfolk born player who the Canaries missed out on. Woods cost Norwich £120,000, a not insubstantial sum for the Canaries (it was their third highest ever transfer pay-out) and, in the short time he spent at Carrow Road, he reminded the Norwich fans what it was like to have an old fashioned winger burning up and down the touchline again, his pace and trickery having not quite diminished with age, even though he was, at the time of signing, thirty-two. He cemented his place back in the hearts of his home City (and Norwich really was that – during the eleven years Woods had spent with Ipswich, he had commuted to the club from his Norwich home) with a goal before the end of the season, his first for the Canaries also being the clubs fifty-eighth and final goal of the 1979/80 campaign, their fourth in a convincing 4-2 win over Derby County at Carrow Road that also saw Keith Robson, Justin Fashanu and Graham Paddon finding the target. Norwich finished the 1979/80 season in twelfth place with 40 points from their forty-two league games. It was, at the time, the second most successful league season in the clubs history. They'd only missed out on equalling their tenth place finish in 1975 by one win, and over their seven year history in the top flight, their average finishing place in that league had now dropped from 16.1 to 15.5, an all-time high. It had not, all things taken into consideration, been a bad or even a disappointing season – even though one of its absolute highpoints had been the display and post-match acclaim after that 3-5 defeat to Liverpool.

Only five more clubs in the league had scored more goals in their twenty-one home games than Norwich's 38 (Southampton, 53, Liverpool, 46, Nottingham Forest, 44, and Manchester United and Ipswich, 43). With only three having lost fewer at home than the Canaries' 3, (Liverpool, 0, Manchester United and Nottingham Forest, 1.) What was a little more frustrating was that Norwich had lost three games after initially being in front – against Liverpool at Carrow Road plus the away games at Tottenham and West Brom. Had they held on to win all of those, their finishing points total would have been eighth – and just one point short of a place in the following seasons UEFA Cup. All if's, but's and maybe's of course – after all, had Norwich lost the three games they went onto win after initially being behind, they would have found themselves in a relegation battle, the table was, that season at least, that competitive.

All in all therefore, John Bond should have been, professionally speaking, a contented man on 3 May 1980. The Canaries had, once again, proved themselves to be more than capable of holding their own in England's top division, this had been their fifth successive campaign there, one that probably earned them their status as an 'established' club at that level – a thought and possibility that would have been far, far from the thoughts of the clubs hierarchy, players and fans just a decade earlier when the Canaries had finished the 1969/70 season eleventh in Division Two, ten points adrift of promoted Blackpool in second place as well as early exits from both domestic cup competitions. That season had been the first at the club for Ron Saunders, the man charged with getting the club to the top flight for the first time in its history, something he achieved two years later. Yet Saunders had lasted only another year and a bit after that success, frustrated maybe at the lack of resources and even ambition at a club whose own hopes and aspirations either did not or could not (or, more probably both) match his own. He'd quit on the spot after a home defeat to Everton but, such was the reputation he'd got for himself during his time at Norwich, he more or less walked into another top job, being appointed as Manchester City manager within a few days of his leaving Norwich before, far more significantly, going to Aston Villa who he led to First Division title success in 1981.

He'd seemingly felt he couldn't achieve what he wanted to do in the game at Norwich City, was there a chance that, as the 1980/81 season grew ever closer, John Bond might, after seven years at Carrow Road be getting his own version of the seven-year itch and wondering if he might have to follow the lead of his predecessor and find a club whose resources and ambitions more closely matched his own?

If he did, then there was no sign of anything for Canary fans to worry about during the summer of 1980. There had, admittedly, been some other partings of the way at that time. Alan Taylor took his leave of Norwich, Norfolk and the country as a whole to start a new life in Canada playing for the Vancouver Whitecaps whilst another striker, Phil Lythgoe left for Oxford United. Lythgoe, the son of former Canary Derrick had signed for the club as an associated schoolboy after an initial trial with Bolton Wanderers. Following a tour to Holland by the club to play in a youth tournament in 1977, his profile grew as he was voted the best player at the tournament with, unsurprisingly, calls soon following for him to be fast tracked into the first team, making his debut against Manchester City in January 1978, a month after his 19th birthday. He made seven more appearances that season, scoring once, in a 3-1 home defeat to Manchester United that April. That proved to be his only goal for the club and now, two seasons and just four more appearances later, John Bond had decided to let him go. It was a disappointing – but perhaps inevitable – parting of the ways, not only for Lythgoe, but also those Norwich fans who liked to see young players, either those who had come through the clubs schoolboy and youth system else had been picked out and away from other clubs for relatively nothing, make it into the first team and ultimately be successful – something the club itself also liked to see. For Norwich to compete financially in an age when there were no massive television or sponsorship deals in place, the surest way to keep the club afloat and heading in the right direction was to either raise them or bring then in cheap-before eventually selling them on at a high price! Fifteen players had turned out for Norwich during the 1979/80 season who fitted into that category and, whilst some would indeed go on to do just that, for every Kevin Reeves and Justin Fashanu, there was always, sadly, a Phil Lythgoe, Doug Evans or Mark Nightingale.

The club suffered two more considerable losses on the playing front with exits of Martin Peters and David Jones. World Cup winner Peters, a man who ended up making more league appearances for Norwich than Tottenham Hotspur, the club he is most closely linked to, had arrived at Carrow Road for just £50,000 in the spring of 1975. No one had dared expect that he would have had the impact on the club that he did, captaining it in the wake of Duncan Forbes' departure, going onto make 232 League and Cup appearances with the Canaries with, at one point, the demands for him to be recalled to the England squad whilst he was at Carrow Road coming from fans and critics of the game from all over the country, not just in and around Norwich.

There is no doubt that, during his time at Norwich, Peters was one of the best players in the country, one who would have fully merited a recall to the England squad, especially at a time when players like Tony Towers and Brian Greenhoff were being selected ahead of him, as was Ian Callaghan of Liverpool who, at thirty-five years of age and eleven years after his previous appearance for England, was selected again whilst Peters was shunned, the reason given for his omission being that he was 'too old' and that England needed to build for the future. Why pick Callaghan then, especially as he was eighteen months older than Peters. Big-club bias, when it comes to international matches is not, as this case illustrated, something which is exclusive to the modern age, something further illustrated by the fact that Graham Paddon, as good a creative midfielder as there was in England during his two spells with Norwich was never picked for an England squad, something which irks me to this day as he should, most definitely, have been the first Canary to play for England.

Peters' departure to take over as Player manager of Sheffield United (had he stayed with Norwich for just a little while longer, he might have had the opportunity to have the same role with the Canaries) somewhat overshadowed the decision of Welsh international defender David Jones to retire from the game due to injury. Jones was another Bournemouth old boy at Carrow Road, albeit one who had come via Nottingham Forest for just £50,000 in 1975. He had, during his time with Norwich, proven himself to be a more than capable replacement for either Duncan Forbes or Dave Stringer, bastions of the Canary defence for so long until his arrival, his final total of 132 League and Cup appearances for Norwich a shadow of what they might have been, had he been free of injury, a player who, had that been the case, could well have served for a decade or more at the heart of the Norwich defence.

Football managers are, of course, very fond of adjusting or even completely rebuilding their playing squads prior to every new season commencing. More often than not this accompanies talk of 'revamping' or 'improving' the squad that has just finished the previous season, shipping out, in the process, some players who might have been brought in to 'revamp' or improve' it twenty-four or even twelve months earlier. Failings at any level are always attributed, first and foremost to the content of the clubs playing resources and the man in charge with the first step usually to ship a load of players out in order to ship a new load in. This often ignores the fact that the most successful teams are often those that do very little in terms of personnel change, introducing new players only when they feel a specific position in the side can be improved by the acquisition of a new player who is better than the current one with that Liverpool side of the 1980s being an example of the more calm and considered approach. When, for example, Kevin Keegan left Liverpool for Bundesliga Hamburg SV in 1977 for a fee reported to be £500,000, Liverpool manager Bob Paisley didn't instigate a wild and all-encompassing approach in spending the money on several new players, some of whom might not have been good enough, as Brendan Rodgers did for the money the club received for Luis Suarez in the summer of 2014, choosing instead to spend a little under that amount on a straight replacement for Keegan, in this instance, Kenny Dalglish.

One class player out, one class player in. Sensible management and a good use of club resources. It also, you feel, would have left him feeling he was coping with a situation that, seen at ground level, could have been a negative one for the club-the loss of one of their best and most influential players, and after they had won League titles and a European Cup. Bond now found himself in a similar situation with Norwich, albeit on a lesser scale. The loss of Jones meant he would need to find a new centre half, not an easy task for any club, but, not only that, he had to replace Peters, something which would be a lot more difficult. Peters had been the heartbeat of the club for five years, its heart and soul almost, and someone who was, without question, an inspiration to his teammates. Talking about Peters in 2013, another former Norwich Captain, Kevin Bond said of Peters, 'I found myself just watching him, observing what he did in training and how he conducted himself in training and at the ground, before matches, during them and afterwards. Whatever he did, you couldn't help but follow.'[5]

Praise indeed. And you can bet whatever you like that his father and manager would have been telling him to do it anyway. Clubs often find it difficult to replace a player who has been more than that, someone who galvanises team spirit and acts as both a role model and inspiration to the other members of the squad. Norwich City have found it as difficult to replace other players who have been at the club with that sort of reputation and standing, for example, Kevin Keelan, Darren Huckerby and Grant Holt. And, as far as the Norwich City that was preparing to start the 1980/81 season was concerned, with the jury still very much out on Keelan's potential replacement Roger Hansbury, the fact that they now had to consider replacing the irreplaceable a second time with Peters now leaving might have made John Bond consider leaving Carrow Road on a high and in a good place to secure his next role in the game whilst leaving those onerous responsibilities to his successor?

He did, of course, have access to some of the £1 million that the club had received for Kevin Reeves – or, rather, a percentage of what they had already been paid by the financially embarrassed Maine Road club with nothing like that fee originally passing from one club to another in exchange for Reeves services. Bond wasn't one to let money burn in his pocket and he bided his time (much, you suspect to his Chairman's relief!), eventually bringing in just the one player in time for the club's opening fixture, the man in question being Joe Royle, the ex-Everton, Manchester City and England centre forward joining from Bristol City for £60,000, primarily as a replacement for Reeves but also, Bond would hope, to act as a new 'wise old head' in the squad to the likes of Fashanu and all the other young players in it. There were some Norwich fans who questioned the signing, there usually are. But they would have felt their arguments were worth hearing. Royle was thirty-one when he'd signed, hardly a veteran, but, even so, not someone who would be able to give the club many years' service or merit a likely profit when he moved on. He'd also not been in the best of goal scoring form for Bristol City, netting just eighteen times in 101 league appearances for the club – an average of a goal every six games, a total that would equate, over one league season of forty-two games of just seven goals, a return that Kevin Bond had surpassed during the 1979/80 season – and he was a right back!

Royle, wearing the number nine shirt, made his Norwich debut in their opening game of the 1980/81 season, a potentially tricky home clash trip against Stoke City. Stoke were, like Norwich, in the process of learning to live without the services of a key player – Norwich had lost Kevin Reeves the previous March, now Stoke were having to do the same without Garth Crooks who had moved to Tottenham. They were still a side packed full of both attacking and creative talent with an attacking spearhead of Adrian Heath and Lee Chapman as well as the midfield nous of Paul Bracewell – players who would, in due course, go onto win five league titles between them as they eventually went onto bigger and better things themselves.

One sign that the times were certainly a changin' for Norwich City at this time is when a comparison is made between the team selected for the Stoke game and that selected for the opening fixture of the previous season with only five players – Kevin Bond, John McDowell, Tony Powell, Justin Fashanu and Graham Paddon starting both whilst four had moved on, Jimmy Neighbour having joined West Ham, the final member of a rather famous four (Keelan, Reeves and Peters were the others) now permanent absentees from the Canary ranks. All four were, unquestionably, players who would be hugely missed and with Royle the only addition in the summer, the Norwich fans in the rather modest attendance of 14,616 might have been excused for coming to the game with more of a sense of hope than expectation about them. As things turned out, any fears those fans might have had were swiftly and joyously blown away as Norwich took a 4-1 lead into the interval, going onto win the game 5-1 with Fashanu, who scored a hat-trick in just under twenty minutes, devastatingly effective and a very constant and awkward presence throughout, his first goal, hit from fully twenty-five yards out conjuring up memories of his form and goals from the previous campaign – particularly the one he had scored against Liverpool! By 4.45 p.m that Saturday afternoon therefore, with Fashanu having hit the first hat trick by a Norwich player for nearly four years and Norwich top of the table as a result, everything in and around Carrow Road was looking veritably rosy. It came as something of a shock therefore when Norwich proceeded to lose their next four league games, a miserable run of form that saw them ship in eleven goals at the wrong end whilst only scoring three themselves.

Hmm. Clearly not as rosy as everyone had first thought.

Bond knew his team needed another figure like Peters to help steady nerves and, in doing so, help gel the team in the same way he had done for the previous five years. The bit of business the club had done in signing Peters arguably remains the best bit of business that they have ever done on the transfer market – but it was real 'lightning in a jar' stuff, something which only happens in football once, at best, in a lifetime. There were, of course, options available. Stan Bowles might have been one. Bombed out of Nottingham Forest by Brian Clough that July, you might have thought Bond would have been the perfect manager for him to play under – Bond would have indulged Bowles and, in all likelihood, Bowles would have responded. Yet the only side who came in for him was Orient, who signed the wayward but potentially brilliant maverick for just £100,000. Then there were the more experienced, seasoned players and internationals who'd seen it and done it at the top level. Someone like Gerry Daly for example, still only twenty-six, a vastly experienced and talented midfielder who had proved his worth at Manchester United and Derby County who were now looking to move him on. Daly ended up joining Coventry City for £150,000, an excellent piece of business for the Sky Blues. Had Norwich been aware of his potential ability, or that of Bowles? Both seemed just the sort of players that Bond would have loved to have signed – big characters with no shortage of talent, players with the ability to turn games with one pass, one flick of the boot or run. Then there was Barry Silkman, another talented and experienced midfielder who'd played for, amongst others, Crystal Palace and Manchester City. Yet he went to Brentford for just £50,000 before being deemed good enough by Terry Venables, a manager with a similar eye for a player to Bond, for QPR.

Were Norwich ever in for these players and others like them, all of whom made moves from June to August 1980. Colin Barrett, two times a European Cup winner with Nottingham Forest moved to Swindon Town on a free. Then there was Tommy Cassidy, who moved from Newcastle to Burnley for £180,000. He, like Barrett and all the other players mentioned were the sort of individuals you could see playing under Bond, and prospering. Cassidy, another midfielder, went onto win a third division title with Burnley yet he was far too talented a player to be stuck at that level of football. An opportunity, it seems, missed, just as all the others were. Bond and Norwich's lack of action on the transfer market at that time was surprising to say the least. Four key players had moved on but only one had been brought in. It wasn't as if players weren't available – the Football League recognised sixty-nine player moves in June and July alone with another forty taking place in August.

Yet only one of them saw the Canaries as a buying club. That opening day win over Stoke had papered over the cracks only, the truth of it was that the squad was weak, both in terms of playing numbers and, especially with Keelan, Reeves and Peters all missing, on quality. Sheffield United, it should also be said, enjoyed a great start to their Division Three campaign under Peters, winning their first three games without conceding a goal, with Peters himself scoring in the first two games. Letting him go when he might easily have been retained with the promise of a coaching position or even the job as manager himself as and when Bond moved on (something which many people now thought inevitable) now seemed like an extreme act of footballing folly. When Bond did, eventually, wield the chequebook again, he did so in considerable style, breaking the clubs transfer record in the process. But that was to come. Mindful that, with the loss of Keelan ad Peters, Bond was initially looking at players who, he felt, had the background and reputation that the younger players, particularly the younger ones in the clubs squad, could look up to. Yet, in acknowledging that, he also knew he couldn't replicate the Peters deal, that lightning wouldn't strike twice and that a current or even past England international would, in all probability, be out of his and the clubs range.

He had, admittedly, tried to sign Alan Ball for the Canaries when Peters' World Cup winning teammate of 1966 had left Arsenal a decade later but had lost out with Ball making no secret of his wish to join Lawrie McMenemy down in Southampton. He'd even tried to sign Bobby Moore for the Canaries at one point, going as far as to make an enquiry about him when Moore, an old West Ham colleague, had left West Ham in 1974 only for Moore to turn him down,[6] citing a preference to stay in London and joining Fulham-not that it had stopped Bond trying again when Moore left Fulham three years later. A Norwich side that might have contained Moore alongside Duncan Forbes at the back with Ball and Peters pulling the strings in a midfield that also contained Graham Paddon is a tantalising thought – but no more than that. Even by the beginning of the 1980s, both transfer fees and players expectations with regard to wages was beginning to spiral out of reach to clubs like Norwich, something which made operating at the top end of the British transfer market, with some exceptions, a little more competitive than it had previously been. So, mindful of the success Tottenham had achieved with Osvaldo Ardiles and Ricardo Villa, as well as Ipswich with Arnold Mühren and Frans Thijssen, Bond opted to look abroad for his new man and ended up doing his shopping in Yugoslavia.

The man who ended up costing the Canaries £300,000 was midfielder Drazen Muzinic of Hadjuk Split. He was, at twenty-seven, reckoned to be at the peak of his career as a player, one who had won five domestic cups and four league titles with his club as well as making thirty-six appearances for Yugoslavia, representing his country at both the 1974 World Cup (he'd played in Yugoslavia's 0-0 draw against Brazil in their group match) and the 1976 European Championships before being named the Yugoslav Footballer of the Year in 1977 – no mean feat when you consider his peers at the time were players like Safet Susic and Dragan Dzajic. An illustrious footballing CV therefore and a player who Bond hoped would, in time, have as much influence, both on and off the pitch, on the Canaries as he had done with Hadjuk Split, a side who had won the Yugoslavian league title on nine different occasions, one that, therefore, with such a history and reputation, would expect its players to thrive on that constant pressure to achieve. Bond wasn't bringing Muzinic to Norwich for him to win league titles with them, but he did now expect his side to push on domestically by looking to finish in the top six as well as make a reasonable challenge in one of the cup competitions with the Canaries, the clubs recent record in the FA Cup being particularly poor – eight third round exits in the previous ten years. Peters later revealed in his autobiography *The Ghost Of '66* (Orion, 2006) that, after he left Sheffield United he'd hoped to be invited back to Norwich to join the coaching staff, going as far as anonymously calling the local newspaper to reveal Cardiff City had made him an offer to join them as a player, hoping that the Canaries would pre-empt that offer and ask him to return to Carrow Road. Sadly for both Peters and Norwich, nothing came of it and, as he wrote, '... nothing came of my devious plan.'

Make or break therefore for Norwich and their manager. They'd started the season well only to be overwhelmed by that disappointing run of defeats, one that had eventually been halted with a scrappy 1-0 win over Southampton, Canary old boy Phil Boyer included, at Carrow Road on 13 September, Muzinic making his debut and, according to one report, showing some 'nice touches'. The fact that he wore the Number 9 shirt in that game when he clearly wasn't a centre forward or goal scorer of any repute (thirteen goals in his 283 league appearances for Hadjuk Split perhaps hinted at that) remains a puzzle to this day – although, it could be that, with Royle missing with an injury, he simply wore the shirt that Norwich's more traditional centre forward wore for that game, squad numbers still being a long way from being introduced into the game. He also, it was noted, had little to no command of the English language, needing someone to translate Bond's team talks to him, something that was hardly conductive to getting a clear and simple message across. Thus, for a while at least, 'man on' became 'Ман Он'; 'keep it simple' was 'бити једноставно' and, no doubt, 'Drazen, it's your round son' became 'Дражен, то је твој син круг.' Not an ideal situation as you can imagine, especially as the man who had more than doubled Norwich's record outlay for one player showed absolutely no inclination whatsoever to learn English, preferring to leave his translator, who'd been hired from the University of East Anglia, to communicate on his behalf – even on match days.

But this was not the only problem surrounding Norwich's new star man. It soon turned out that no one at the club had even seen him play a game and that he had not, even once, been watched by one of the members of the clubs scouting team. One of the reasons for this was probably the fact that the clubs hierarchy didn't feel it could justify the costs involved in sending a scout all the way to Split to watch a player with flights, accommodation and all the other expenses involved. So they didn't. Or, rather, they simply wouldn't. With video technology still in its early stages and, in this case, something that would not have been available anyway, the club therefore made the decision to sign Muzinic on his reputation alone, accepting that his playing CV, both domestically and internationally, was enough for them to make the decision, something they pushed ahead with despite the fact that they had absolutely no competition from any of the other leading clubs in either England or Europe for his signature something which, with hindsight, you think might have been considered unusual for a player with such an illustrious footballing CV to his name.

A quietly effective debut for the record signing then. But not that it was the major talking point of the day, either pre or post-match. Rumours had abounded around the ground and City that Manchester City had approached John Bond about the possibility of him taking over as their new manager, something which both he and the club would have, at least publicly, have given little time or credence to as, at that time, Malcolm Allison was still in charge at Maine Road. The only problem with that was, certainly as far as the Manchester City fans were concerned, was that he had already outstayed his expensive welcome as his team of expensive signings with egos to match were not living up to what was expected of them – which was a whole lot more than the start they had made, Kevin Reeves included, to the 1980/81 season. They'd met Nottingham Forest at the City Ground on the same day as Norwich had played, and beaten, Southampton, losing 3-2, despite being 2-1 ahead at half time. Reeves had, at least, found the net on two occasions during their first six games, a run that consisted of three draws and three defeats-unacceptable at just about any club in the top division even back then. But bad enough to warrant dismissing their manager? Perhaps not. Their chairman at the time, the notoriously demanding Peter Swales kept his power dry and the gossip connecting Bond with the job faded, at least for a little while.

It wasn't that Bond had nothing else to worry about. By the time the Canaries travelled up to Middlesbrough on 4 October, he was still having problems fitting Muzinic into his side as well as life in Norfolk as a whole. Muzinic still relied exclusively on his translator in order to communicate with his club mates, manager included and it soon became clear that one of the things he had failed to communicate in any way, shape or form, is what he felt his best position is, or where he should be used in the team – he turned up for training and matches, was selected for the latter and pretty much did his own thing, much to the growing exasperation of his teammates, one of whom, Justin Fashanu came out with the legendary quip 'I don't think we got Muzinic. I reckon they sent his milkman'.

For Fashanu to feel confident enough to make such a public quote about a fellow professional and teammate sums up about what his colleagues must have been thinking at the time. Muzinic would have been one of, if not the most highly paid player at the club, one who had arrived with a massive reputation and playing history that included lining up against Brazil at the World Cup. 'Fash' and his fellow professionals, not surprisingly, were expecting a whole lot more than they were getting. They, as had Bond, had expected a confident, skilful and tactically aware player, someone who would have seamlessly slotted into the side, becoming, in the process, as much its fulcrum as Peters had been for five wonderful years. Instead of that, they got a quiet, occasionally moody and socially withdrawn individual who looked out of place (according to long-time Norwich fan Paul King, Muzinic '... always looked out of his depth') and out of step with both football and life as a whole in Norwich. Yet he had cost the club £300,000. So he couldn't be dropped. Norwich had to persist with him. And persist they did. For that trip to Teesside, Muzinic started for the fourth consecutive match, again wearing the misleading Number 9 on the back of his shirt. The game was, with the BBC's *Match of the Day* cameras present, an opportunity for both Norwich and Muzinic to finally make their mark on the season, to make an impression in a good way and in front of the watching millions at home, just as they had against Liverpool the previous season. If only. The Canaries were 2-0 down at half time, ending the match on the wrong end of a 6-1 thrashing, one characterised by a dreadful defensive performance – as well as more mediocrity, bordering on sheer anonymity from Muzinic. At least the game gave Bond the chance to get Royle back onto the pitch for his first game for nearly a month but, when he did eventually come off the bench and into the action, it wasn't, as you would have expected, for Muzinic but for the unfortunate Ross Jack who at least offered some threat in attack, whereas Muzinic offered no threat to anyone other than his overworked translator. You can be sure that it would have been a very long, quiet and reflective coach ride back to Norfolk for all concerned, fans included. But possibly no one more so than Bond who would have been absolutely devastated at the display and result, but, more than anything, the continuing failings of his most expensive signing.

The teams coach driver, by the very nature of his job, would have been privy to much of what was going on at the club. Players rows, fights and fall outs might often have come to a head on a long and tedious coach ride to or from a game, breaking the tedium for some but, at least, for others, providing a chance to get long held frustrations and grudges out into the open. It would be naive to think that a group of twenty-five to thirty young men, fighting fit, ambitious and with testosterone to burn would all get along with one another, especially if the sole intent of some of them, particularly new signings, would be to take someone else's place in the team. Chris McGregor drove the Norwich City team Coach from 1976 to 1982, working, at the time, for Cullings Coaches who were based in Claxton. For Chris, it was his dream job, the opportunity to drive a brand-new luxury coach and staying, as part of the job, at a five star hotel every week – with meals provided!

'Because of Norwich's geographical location, the first team always travelled to a match the day before it took place, even games at Ipswich. We'd typically leave the old training ground at Trowse at whatever time we needed to go in order to arrive at our hotel at around 6.00 p.m. on the evening before. So, for example, if it was a game at Ipswich, we'd leave at 5.00 p.m., or, for somewhere like Liverpool or Newcastle, about midday – there weren't so many bypasses in those days! We'd arrive at the Hotel and everyone, myself included, would go up to our rooms, change and get down for the evening meal at around 7.00 p.m., with every player expected to be back in their room, for the night, by 9.30 p.m. No alcohol was allowed for 48 hours before any game.

'On the morning of the match I'd drive the coach down to the stadium so we could get the kit there as well as take a look at the pitch. We'd have a little ritual then – I'd score three goals against the physiotherapist (from 1980 this would have been the much-liked and respected Tim Sheppard) before he took his turn and scored three goals against me – so I can honestly say that I've scored a hat-trick at just about every Premier League club ground! Then it would be back, with the coach, to the team hotel for lunch, which, in those days would be a choice of either fillet steak or Dover sole for everyone, me included.

'The manager would then give his team talk before we all headed back to the ground, together with a police escort. If the coach was parked near the ground, I'd join everyone in the dressing room pre-match as well as joining all the other club staff on the bench during the game itself.[7] Straight after the game had ended, I'd pop back on the coach to get all the other football results before heading back to the dressing room to collect up all of the dirty kit and get that back onboard before sitting and waiting for the manager and his staff, as well as the players to come back.

'If it had been a good match with a good result, they'd all go into the players' lounge afterwards, we'd then leave a little later, say about 6.00 p.m. If, on the other hand, it had been a bad match, the players would all be back on the coach and ready to go back by 5.30 p.m. Whatever the result though, the coach would always be loaded up with plenty of alcohol for the journey home, that was very much the order of the day, the players wanting to make the up for all of that abstinence before the game. John Bond always sat on the table seat at the back of the coach with John Sainty (first team coach) and the other card players whilst Ken Brown (assistant manager to Bond) sat at the front.'

Work done and with the potential of a Saturday night ahead of them if the trip home was not a particularly long one, both management and players would expect Chris to do his best to get them back to Norwich so they could, if at all possible, enjoy whatever was left of the evening in and around the pubs and clubs in the City.

'The homeward journey would be like a Formula One race, full speed ahead and back as soon as possible – via the nearest convenient town to stock up on fish and chips. I'd get served first so, as soon as I was finished eating mine, the last one to be served from the team would be back on the Coach and we'd be ready to go again. Big Dunc (Duncan Forbes) would, every time, ask for the same thing, the words booming out in his deep Scottish accent, "Crocodile sandwich please, and make it snappy." One day, whilst we had stopped off in Grantham, the girl in the shop said it before he did – and that was the last time we ever heard Dunc use that line! But, like I said, once everyone was back on board it was go, go, go! I knew that, if the players were not holding on as I went round a bend, then I was going too slowly. Sometimes the television would be put on, so, of Norwich were on, everyone could look and see where it had gone wrong! The card schools were all consuming from the time we left, and, inevitably, cards and booze sometimes didn't mix and it would kick-off a bit but it never lasted and was usually a good atmosphere. As soon as we arrived back at Trowse, they'd all rush off the bus and into their cars and off to the night clubs if there was still time. I'd then have to clear up the mess they'd left behind and clean the coach, inside and out before returning the kit on the Monday morning.'

Mixing with the team meant that the players treated Chris just as they would have any new recruit to the team, looking after him and generally giving him advice when needed about the etiquette of away games.

'The first time I was away with the team I came down for the evening meal on the night before the match, me, just a working class lad with no previous experience of staying in posh hotels. I sat down with the menu in my hand, just looking at it with some awe, wondering what to have, given what was on it and the price. Kevin Keelan noticed me doing this and said, "Are you worried about ordering?" I said that I was and was thinking that maybe I'd have beans on toast in order to keep the costs down, only for Kevin to put me at my ease by saying, "Forget about what's on there and just look at the cost. Order the most expensive thing in each section and then just work your way down the menu." But I also have some great memories of being at the games as well. In one game at Spurs, one of their players went in and made a really bad tackle on one of our lads which really upset Mel Machin. He jumped up in protest, hit his head on the dugout roof, cue a string of swear words; sat down again, not realising it was a flip up seat, falling on the ground in the process – more swear words whilst everyone sat around him was crying with laughter at him – which caused yet another string of swear words.'

Driving the coach back down from Middlesbrough that Saturday afternoon after the 6-1 humbling at Middlesbrough must have been a sobering experience for all involved, a game and result that was, quite possibly the Canaries worse ever performance under Bond. Would he, as usual, have joined the card school at the back of the coach, laughing and joking with his players over endless games of three card brag as they looked back over the game and ahead to the next one, traditional formalities and divisions relaxed for what was, after all, 'down time' at the end of their working week, time when the cards, a little gentle banter with the boss (plus the chance to take a few quid off him) and numerous cans of beer were the order of the day rather than tactical briefings, endless repetitions of set piece moves in training and lap after lap of the training pitch? Probably not. It would have been a long, tedious and quiet journey, one that might have livened up as Trowse grew ever closer and frustrations, lightened by too much alcohol, boiled over.

But, as Chris has already sad, tempers often flared, cross words would be exchanged; maybe, on some occasions, punches would be thrown. But it would all be forgotten by the start of the next working week, another game to prepare for and a chance to put this, like any other bad result, to bed, gone and forgotten.

Not, on this occasion, as far as John Bond was concerned. Maybe he'd been questioning his position at the club since the beginning of the season and the inactive summer that preceded it. He was, he had been, determined to build a side that could contend and be in and around the top six to eight in Division One. Ipswich had long established themselves as one of the leading sides in the country with resources that were surely that not greater than those available to him at Norwich? They'd done well because they'd been able to keep the core of the side together for a prolonged period of time, something which encouraged consistency, progress, results and success. Even when they'd struggled in the league, during the 1977/78 season, they'd still gone onto win the FA Cup before finishing sixth and third in the following two seasons with players like Alan Brazil, Eric Gates, Paul Mariner, Arnold Muhren, Russell Osman and Frans Thijssen becoming household names – without having to leave Portman Road to do it. It is very likely that had any of those players been at Norwich they would, soon enough, have been whisked away somewhere else, just as Kevin Reeves had been and just, as it looked more and more probable, as Justin Fashanu also would be.

When you're looking to punch well above your weight in football it isn't the prolonged success of the big clubs, the then elite that hurt. It was any prolonged success by clubs you would otherwise have deemed your equals – an Ipswich, West Brom, even a Nottingham Forest. They were all at a level that Norwich had not yet reached and, in fairness, did not look like they were ever going to reach. And, for all the job security he had at Carrow Road, for all the adulation of the fans, the respect of his players and the indulgences that his board regularly offered him, John Bond knew his time at Norwich was at an end; there was, quite simply, nothing more the club could do for him and nothing more he could do for the club. It was over.

Less than a week later, Manchester City, who had eventually grown weary of Malcolm Allison's financial excesses yielding no apparent reward, made a formal approach to the Norwich City board to talk to Bond about their managerial vacancy. This had had finally come about after his dismissal on 8 October, four days after their 3-0 defeat at Liverpool, one that had seen them drop to one place off the bottom of the table with just four points to their name. Bond was, almost immediately, installed as the favourite for the job with all of the leading football writers of the day predicting his name was as good as on the door to the manager's office at Maine Road.

Three days later, on 11 October, Norwich entertained Wolves at Carrow Road in a Division One fixture with no sign of Bond at the ground, word soon getting around the crowd of just 12,995 that he was at the Hawthorns, watching his prospective new side lose 3-0 to West Bromwich Albion, their seventh defeat in eleven league games that season. Whether or not he was at that game is open to question; what was, however, no longer open to question, was which football club he was about to be named manager of with Manchester City confirming his appointment on the following Friday, 17 October 1980, Bond becoming the second consecutive man to walk out on the Canaries for the perceived bigger club and bigger challenge that awaited him (as well as far greater playing resources) at Maine Road. For the Canaries, with their own season, new as it still was, in danger of coming apart at the seams with ten games so far played for only six points, it was imperative that they were able to find a new man themselves as soon as possible, one who now had the unenviable task of following in the enormous and very forward thinking footsteps Bond had trodden into Norwich City history during his six years at the club.

CHAPTER TWO

# The Nice Man Cometh

*If John Bond knew the worth and importance of making sure his Norwich side was populated with a few wise old heads, then Brown was going in the opposite direction, signing two players who were 'young and hungry' before the phrase had even been invented, building, as he did, the backbone of a Norwich side that would grow along with those players, players who would, eventually, earn the club a great deal of much-needed money as they eventually left for bigger and better things.*

Whatever reasons John Bond might have given, either publicly or to himself in private as justification for leaving Norwich City, it didn't stop there being a tremendous lot of speculation as to who might eventually take over from him at Carrow Road.

The Canaries would certainly have been an attractive option to any young and ambitious young manager looking to take his next step up the footballing ladder. Both Ron Saunders and Bond had come to the club from the lower divisions (Oxford United and Bournemouth respectively), going onto more than prove themselves and their coaching capability at Carrow Road, so it wasn't beyond the realms of possibility that the club would look, for a third consecutive appointment from a lower league club. Overtures had already been made to Bobby Moore, recently installed in charge at Oxford City, only for Moore to, admirably, reject the Canaries interest. Flattered? Yes. But inclined to walk out on the club that had just put their faith in him, even though they were non-league? No. There were other candidates, all of whom fitted into the, as it is known today, 'young and hungry' bracket. Gerry Summers for example, a friend of Bond, indeed, someone whose Coaching ability Bond greatly admired was working wonders at Oxford United. Then there was Jimmy Bloomfield, still only forty-six, who'd done remarkably well at Leicester City before taking over at Orient who, incredibly, he'd led into the Division Two promotion race that season. Another possibility might have been John Docherty who, like Bloomfield, was overachieving at a smaller club, namely Cambridge United who were also looking to be in the Division Two promotion shake-up at the end of that season.

Plenty of candidates, most of which, you have to say, would probably have been more than receptive to a phone call from Canaries Chairman Sir Arthur South. Bond was now expected to appoint long-time assistant Ken Brown as his number two at Manchester City, perpetuating, in doing so, a working relationship that had seen them play alongside one another at West Ham and Torquay United as well as at Bournemouth and Norwich as manager and assistant manager. Yet, with Norwich rumoured to be ready to offer another member of their coaching staff, John Benson the top job at Carrow Road, Benson surprised everyone by upping and joining Bond, leaving Brown, somewhat unexpectedly, seemingly high and dry back in Norwich. Bond's surprising decision not to invite Brown to join him at Maine Road thus marked the end of a playing and coaching partnership between the two former friends that had commenced in 1953. Yet, if Brown felt let down by his old friend and colleague that feeling wasn't going to last very long, as Sir Arthur South made the most of what turned out to be a great error of judgement on the part of Bond by inviting Brown to replace him at Carrow Road with Mel Machin promoted from his coaching role to become his assistant. Those appointments drew a line under what had been a torrid couple of weeks or so at

Carrow Road but at least things could now settle down with the new managerial team no doubt keen to get their players' minds off all that had been going on over that time and back down to the football. One fixture in particular would have already been brought to their attention, the pending trip to Maine Road and an encounter with their former manager on 1 November. If ever there was a fixture that Brown would have been desperate to win, then it would have been this one. But the same would have applied to Bond. It was therefore set to be a fascinating encounter between the two sides, and, much more so, the two managers; one that saw Bond come out on top in a tense encounter that saw him put one over his old side with a 1-0 win, the goal coming from Paul Power.

The Canaries had gone into that game on the back of four league matches that had seen one win and two draws, the sole defeat coming at Arsenal on 21 October, the day Brown and Machin's full time appointments had been confirmed. Norwich had looked good for a point for much of the match, one in which Mark Barham, revelling in his more attacking role on the right flank top off a superb individual performance with a well taken equalising goal, his first for the club which had brought the score back to 1-1. Norwich were, however, eventually undone by two late Arsenal goals with Brian McDermott and Kenny Sansom scoring in the 84th and 89th minutes respectively. That defeat and the manner of it would have troubled Brown, the all too obvious vulnerabilities of the Norwich defence once again proving to be their undoing, one shorn of confidence and, since the departure of Keelan and diminished role of Forbes, one that was definitely lacking in leadership.

Brown knew that these defensive deficiencies had to be addressed and would have determined very early on that the club needed to re-establish the strong spine that had characterised it during much of Bond's time at the club, that of Keelan, Forbes, Peters and Reeves. With three of those players gone and one, Forbes, now very much on the fringes of the first team, there was clearly some very important team rebuilding to be done and players of both ability and character to bring in. But would Brown be able to get the ones he wanted, especially with the Canaries not only struggling but, in having lost Bond, now without the man whose presence was often enough to tempt a new player to the club on its own? Brown would also, as it turned out, have another Bond to deal with soon enough, in this case, the ex-manager's son who had since gone public in the local press claiming that the club, and, in particular, Sir Arthur South, had badly treated his now departed Father.

One early casualty of the Brown regime had been club record signing Drazen Muzinic. With Bond seemingly reluctant to want to take the Yugoslav international with him to Manchester (something, you suspect, the Norwich board as well as most of the team would have been happy to see happen), he remained resolutely at Carrow Road, his loyal translator by his side, the unfortunate student from the local University now having to mug up on how best to tell his employer that he'd been dropped from the first team. Brown had left him out of the side for the Coventry game and it would be ten games until Muzinic got some first team action again, coming on as a replacement for Mark Barham in the 2-1 win at Leicester City on 29 November. His gradual reintroduction into the first team continued with another appearance from the bench a week later, as he replaced Mick McGuire in a 2-2 draw against Manchester United at Carrow Road, Brown now seemingly confident enough to decide that, if the Canaries record signing had a future at the club, it would be as a defensive midfielder. He continued to show his renewed faith in Muzinic by awarding him his first start under his management at Crystal Palace on 13 December, hopeful, no doubt, that the match against the division's bottom team would prove to be a platform for Muzinic to settle back into the team and a role that had been clearly defined to him. It would have been no accident that Palace were the team he chose for Muzinic's return either. They'd won just three of their twenty-two league fixtures so far that season, including a current run that had seen five defeats from their last six games. It was as good a chance as Muzinic was ever going to get to prove he had what it took to succeed in the English game; a platform, Brown and Mel Machin hoped would see him finally assert himself and look every inch a £300,000 international player rather than a three bob pub one.

Unfortunately for Norwich, their visit to Selhurst Park coincided with the first match back at the club of former Manchester City manager Malcolm Allison, the man Bond had replaced at Maine Road. Allison had previously been at Palace from 1973 to 1976 where, despite winning no major honours with them during that time, he had, much as Bond had done when he first joined Norwich, rebranded the club from top to bottom, raising both it and his own media profile with a mix of his own outgoing and colourful personality as well as a somewhat visionary approach to the clubs overall profile. He changed their kit for example as well as amending their rather homespun nickname of Glaziers to that of their present moniker, the Eagles. In short, and despite going through two relegations during that spell, he put the club, for so long the runt of the London footballing litter, well and truly on the map. He did have some football success with them, primarily taking the rebranded Eagles to an FA Cup semi-final in 1976, something that Archie Macaulay, a man with a considerably smaller public profile, had done with Norwich in 1959. Now Allison was back and, no matter what might have gone on before, including their dire league run up until this game, Selhurst Park was positively rocking and rolling as only it can, in anticipation of Allison's return. He'd already inflamed the sensitivities of both Manchester City and Canary supporters by virtually dismissing John Bond's managerial capabilities in an interview with ITV's Brian Moore at the end of the preceding month, saying,

'It's an amazing game football. All of a sudden, John Bond is a genius, he's bought three players and made Manchester City play. I wonder why he could never do it before in twelve years of management.'

Surprised at the criticism, Moore, one of the great commentators and observers on the game then, and at any time, points out that Bond had some success at Norwich, including taking them to a League Cup Final as well as First Division respectability, a great achievement for anyone at, as Moore says, a 'provincial' club. But Allison is having none of it, replying, 'One League Cup final?' before reeling off a list of other 'provincial' clubs then in the First Division as if to emphasise there really was nothing special about Bond's achievements at Carrow Road. He then concludes, with an air of finality, that the whole scenario and Moore's defence of Bond is 'nonsense'. Clearly someone was going to pay for all of this impertinence at his expenses. The problem with that, as far as we are concerned, is that the team lined up to play them on his return was the Canaries.

Another of Brown's first actions upon taking over at Norwich had been to drop the beleaguered Roger Hansbury in favour of his understudy, North Walsham born Clive Baker. Baker, who'd made his Norwich debut under Bond and, again at the expense of Hansbury in April 1978, returned for the home game against Sunderland, a game that saw only the Canaries third defensive clean sheet of the season. It was enough to earn him a run of games that had included a much needed win against Leicester as well as that impressive 2-2 draw against Manchester United. Baker and his Norwich teammates would therefore have been confident of another good performance as they travelled down to South London, including the recalled and starting Drazen Muzinic who would now be wearing the Number 4 shirt rather than the Number 9, the latter, perhaps fortunately, now back with Joe Royle. Allison's return to Selhurst Park did indeed turn out to be the triumphant one that most of their supporters thought it would be as well as the man himself. And certainly his players who performed like a top six side, defeating the Canaries, the 'provincial' side so casually dismissed by Allison by four well worked goals to one, the lone Norwich effort coming from Royle, his fifth of the season. All in all, it was a dismal effort, not as bad, maybe, as the feeble surrender at Middlesbrough, but not far short of it. Brown was so appalled at Norwich's performance in that game, that he made four (out went Greg Downs, Tony Powell, Mark Nightingale and Mark Barham; in came Mick McGuire, Phil Hoadley, John McDowell and Peter Mendham) changes to the starting XI for Norwich's next game, a home clash with Coventry on the Saturday before Christmas. That fixture ended up seeing the appeal of doing some last-minute shopping of anticipation of the pending holiday overtake any desire to go to the football for many, with just 12,630 in attendance for the game against Gordon Milne's side, one who weren't having the best of times themselves, sat in lower mid table and in need of points just as much as

Norwich were. Astonishingly, Drazen Muzinic retained his place in the starting line-up, albeit now wearing the Number 3 shirt as Brown,[1] desperately tried to find a role in the team for the despairing Yugoslav, his return and prominence in first team affairs only, you suspect, in place because of pressure from the club board to pick him and try to get some sort of return on the fee spent. The spectacular failure of Muzinic to perform now meant that It would probably be some considerable time before the club pushed the financial boat out so far again with every player, from now on, no matter where he came from, being considered without suitable due diligence being carried out by the Canaries scouting network. Lessons had been learnt, as that rather tired and predictable contemporary saying is ever fond of reminding us. And how. With the clubs limited resources pretty much exhausted by the Muzinic deal and low gates doing little to change that anytime soon, Brown would have to do his absolute utmost to, just as his predecessor had done, to ensure that he shopped for bargains and did his fair share of wheeler dealing. It certainly seemed as if there would be no more big name and big money signings at Carrow Road for a while.

At least there were signs of improvement during the Coventry game. Baker was solid enough in goal whilst a side that included plenty of competitive players like McGuire, playing against his former club; Powell and, of course, Justin Fashanu. The latter was now beginning to be as prominent in the front pages of the newspapers, as he was in opposing team's penalty areas. And no wonder. The media loved him. He was young, brash and full of self-confidence; a Barnardo's boy who'd found both himself and his younger brother John fostered out to an elderly couple in Shropham, a small and unassuming village around twenty miles or so from Norwich. Justin, or Fash, as both his teammates and the Norwich fans referred to him could quite easily disappeared, and through no fault of his own, into quiet obscurity in the heart of rural Norfolk. But he was never going to accept that, he wanted to shine, to excel, to be someone. And, as an outstanding young sportsman from his schooldays onwards, there was little doubt that he wouldn't. He excelled at both boxing and football, choosing the latter as his sporting priority when Norwich scout Ronnie Brooks asked him if he wanted to try out for the clubs youth team in 1976. From that moment on, 'Fash' wanted to be a top-class professional footballer and now, a little over four years later, he was all that and more, someone who Leeds United had already tried to sign only to pull out of the deal at the last moment. There was little doubt that Fashanu would go onto bigger and better things – and certainly bigger and better than Leeds United. The only questions were with whom and when? As far as a lot of people were concerned, it would be at Manchester City where he would not only work with John Bond again, but resume the promising partnership that he had with Kevin Reeves who was already enjoying working alongside Bond and John Sainty again.

Fash certainly did his job in the game against Coventry, allowing himself to be effectively shackled by Gary Gillespie and Paul Dyson; giving that formidable duo so much to do and worry about with his busy and rumbustious presence that other Norwich players were virtually neglected. This ended up giving Joe Royle and Graham Paddon time and space to get themselves into the game and the goals; one each to be exact, with Norwich full value for that 2-0 victory. In terms of the league table, it kept the Canaries out of the bottom three by a margin of three points, with only three more separating them from Middlesbrough in twelfth place and the sort of security in mid-table that had, in the end, not been enough for John Bond. For Ken Brown, that sort of anonymous mediocrity would have been everything that he would have wanted for the club right now, and with nineteen league fixtures to go until the end of the season, he set about adding some new players to the squad to not only help stabilise the club's current position but look to be part of better times ahead. It had, in all honesty, already been a season to forget for Norwich. Keelan, Peters and Reeves were still missed. That was inevitable. What was unforgivable was that not one of them had been adequately replaced with doubts already being raised about Roger Hansbury and Clive Baker in the Canaries goal and whether, to be brutally frank, if either of them were up to the job? If that sounds unfair then it isn't meant to be. The real problem with both players wasn't anything to do with their ability. Hansbury, for example, went onto play for Burnley, Birmingham and Cardiff City, succeeding David Seaman, no less, at St Andrews whilst Baker went onto make over 300 appearances for Barnsley from 1984 to 1991, twice winning their Player of the Year award. So both were, unquestionably, very good and more than capable goalkeepers. The problem was that they both had to live and work with the large and ever present reputation of Kevin Keelan hanging over them.

How do you follow a player like that?

Norwich had similar problems attempting to replace Duncan Forbes, centre half, leader of men and a man extraordinaire. He'd signed for the Canaries in 1968 and had even, eight years later, been sent out on loan to Torquay United when he was thirty-five, the Norwich hierarchy, no doubt, seeing the move as the beginning of the end of his illustrious career at the club with both Tony Powell and David Jones able to play in his position. They were, at that time, Norwich's future whilst Forbes, loved and revered as he was (and remains) was part of the club's past. Yet it was he, at thirty-eight years of age, who'd been called up by the club to fill a yawning defensive gap for games against Liverpool and West Brom earlier that season.

He'd ultimately and brutally been shown up in the West Brom match and was especially given the proverbial run around by Cyrille Regis who Forbes, frustrated beyond belief, eventually resorted to wrestling to the ground in his own area. He simply had no other way of dealing with the strong and athletic striker, a player who he would, have no doubt about it, had in his pocket for the entire game even five years earlier. Forbes should never have been selected for that game, the fact that he was, and struggled, perfectly illustrated how Norwich had never adequately replaced him and that, four years after it first seemed that time and tide were contributing to seeing him take his final leave from Carrow Road, one of the options that the Canaries had in their squad as a potential replacement for Forbes was Forbes himself. He was, on that occasion, withdrawn not long after half time with Greg Downs replacing him. Big Duncan made just one more appearance for the Canaries after that match, a 1-1 draw at Carrow Road against Wolves on 11 October. His presence on that day would have been as much for his qualities of leadership and strength of character as much as anything at a time when, with John Bond set to quit, both the players and staff remaining at the club would have felt unsettled and unhappy at how events were turning out.

You had to feel for Ken Brown. He'd barely started his reign as Norwich City manager only to realise that one of his first, and most pressing priorities, was to finally replace the irreplaceable; to find and secure the signatures of three players who would, for at least the next few years, replace the Holy Trinity of Keelan, Forbes and Peters in the hearts and minds of Canary fans. But not only that. These would need to be players who were no short term fix, ones who would quickly become an integral part of the club's long term footballing aspirations. It is, therefore, to his extreme and lasting credit that, even with a club that was clearly struggling and a playing budget that was probably the smallest in Division One, that Brown did manage to replace the three players in question. He not only did that but managed to find two who would go onto play for England whilst they were at Carrow Road whilst the other would become the very first Norwich City player to appear in the final stages of a World Cup.

Brown's first signing for Norwich ended up being, arguably, his best. The man in question was, in the great tradition of the club, learning his trade and gaining vital experience by playing regularly for Liverpool's reserves, one who knew he would have to bide his time for a first team chance, such was the calibre and star quality of the players ahead of him far as a place in the starting XI was concerned. When you consider that the two players who occupied his position were Phil Thompson and Alan Hansen, then you start to realise why nineteen-year-old central defender Dave Watson took note when Liverpool manager Bob Paisley asked him to call in at his office one chilly November morning. Paisley had news for Watson and good news as it turned out. Another club had asked about him but not only that, a club that were also in the First Division. Would he like to travel down and meet their representatives? The Canaries need for a young and imposing centre back had seen Doug Livermore and Dave Stringer sent to watch Liverpool Reserves play at Aston Villa with their target rumoured to initially be Liverpool's Colin Irwin. He would have been the ideal signing for the Canaries, a central defender who could also play on the left side of defence. To their surprise, it was Watson who caught the eye, with both men subsequently reporting back to Ken Brown about his performance and potential rather than that of Irwin, claiming that Watson was the man the club should be looking to sign.[2] That was enough for Brown who knew and trusted Stringer enough to go on his recommendation alone.

The fact that such a respected ex-player and one time Liverpool man himself in Livermore also spoke highly about Watson merely strengthened Brown's hand when he approached the board to get their consent to open talks with Liverpool about making an offer for Watson. It was a footballing no brainer with no further debate to be had and no need for any more scouting trips, not even for Brown himself. The club had to sign Watson, and fast, especially if Norwich's interest started to pique that of their closest rivals. Watson had, in effect, whilst still at Liverpool, suddenly become the Canaries most important player – quite an ask of someone who had, up to that moment, only played twelve reserve games for the Reds. The deal eventually went through with Norwich playing an initial fee of just £50,000, an amount that would be due again if and when (though there never seemed any doubt of that happening) Watson made his twentieth appearance for the Canaries, with a further £100,000 due if he played for England whilst he was at Carrow Road. Clearly, it would seem, he had been more highly rated at Anfield than he might previously have thought.

Watson later admitted that he'd had just one doubt in his mind when the chance to sign for Norwich came about, the fact that Liverpool was so far away from where he would be restarting both his career and life. Luckily for him there was, just as there is to this day, a direct rail link from Liverpool through to Norwich.[3] Thus, after enjoying a first-class trip down on the train with his father with all expenses paid by the club (Watson later admitted his Dad had a bottle of brandy with him on the trip!), they were met at the station by Ken Brown. Brown was, if anything, Norwich's greatest ambassador as well as being the best choice of manager they could have had at the time, with his friendly manner and good humour appealing to Watson from the off, the player later admitting, 'First impressions of Ken Brown ... were "what a lovely fella!" and that was a big pull straight away to have someone greet you with a nice smile and a face like Ken. Them meeting us. Dougie Livermore ... Mel Machin, it just had the right feel about it.'[4]

The club took its time letting Watson settle in. The need to bed in a young, strong and long term central defender was great and the temptation to immediately throw him into first team action must have been overwhelming. However, this need was tempered by the fact the club also knew they couldn't take a risk in rushing Watson straight into the first team, something which could have been an act of monumental folly. Many clubs, then, as now, have rushed young players with big reputations into their first teams before they might be ready. Not necessarily, with regard to their talent and playing ability either, but before they are mentally and emotionally prepared for the pressure and expectation that comes with the job. One past example of this at Norwich had been that of Steve Govier. He'd made his debut for the Canaries when he was nineteen with big things were expected of him; a player seen as the natural replacement for either Forbes or Dave Stringer. Yet, despite making thirty appearances for Norwich, Govier never really settled into the role as well as had been expected and eventually left Norwich for Brighton. Maybe, if he had been nurtured a little more, given time and patience to grow into the position and responsibility, he would now have been there for Brown and the centre back shortage wouldn't have arisen in the first place. But that hadn't been the case. Watson had, very quickly, just as Govier was, been identified as a player with the potential to be a big star. And Liverpool already knew it.

Why, after all, had Liverpool insisted on a separate clause in the deal that would see them receive £100,000 if Watson played for England whilst he was at Norwich? It might have seemed daft at the time but Liverpool knew what they were doing, their coaching hierarchy knew full well he would, in time, become a class act. He just needed a top class club to join where that ability and potential could have been realised. Luckily for Watson, Norwich were just that, a club where he would be given all the time he needed yet, at the same time, one that he knew would start to give him regular first division football as soon as they knew he would be ready, something that Bob Paisley realised was unlikely to happen for him at all at Anfield.

Watson was finally deemed ready a month after he had signed, making his Norwich debut at, of all places, Ipswich Town at Portman Road on Boxing Day 1980, playing alongside the experienced Phil Hoadley. It wasn't the best of debuts for him, at least not as far as the game itself was concerned. Ipswich were near the top of the table and hadn't lost at home for well over a year. They also had, in attack, the formidable pairing of Paul Mariner and Alan Brazil. So it wasn't going to be easy for Watson. Not as easy, certainly, as it might have been had Ken Brown given him the nod a week earlier for the home game against Coventry City. But then again, maybe Brown was exercising a little psychology? No one expected Norwich to do well at Ipswich; in fact, it was seen as a home banker on the day. So Watson wasn't under as much pressure as he might have been in a game that the club was expected to win. And, even if Norwich did, as expected, lose to the old enemy over the border, he didn't disgrace himself and looked comfortable on and off the ball. But there was still no great rush for him to play. He was rested for the club's next game, a 2-2 draw at home to Tottenham before returning to the side for the FA Cup tie at home to Cambridge United on 3 January,[5] maintaining his place in the starting XI from then on until the end of the season.

Watson was already beginning to look as if he was the real deal. This was good for him and good for Norwich as it looked as if, finally, they had a man in place who just have been up to the herculean task of replacing Duncan Forbes, not only in the Norwich side but in the hearts of the club's supporter. The problem was, Forbes was just one of three yellow and green icons who were gone and greatly missed. Brown had excelled in replacing Forbes but could he count on being so lucky when it came to finding a player who would both inspire and lead from the Canaries midfield as well Martin Peters had done? This task was going to be a lot harder, not least because the type of player needed was going to be one who, like Peters, had seen it, done it and worn the T-shirt. Or at least the shirt of his home country. He needed to be experienced, able and, preferably, an international player, someone with proven class, experience and pedigree. Which meant that the club was going to have to go out and spend some money, something which, after the Muzinic affair, the board was somewhat reluctant to do.

Yet, against all the odds, Ken Brown drew another rabbit out of the Canary top hat. The story of Martin O'Neill's three spells, twice as a player and once as a manager, at Carrow Road is worthy of a book in itself. He joined Norwich in February 1981 for £250,000, no small amount for the Canaries at the time and the most they had ever paid for a British born player. The fact that he even considered coming to Norwich in the first place was a surprise, he was, after all, a player who had, with Nottingham Forest, won a League title, two League Cups and, most significantly of all, two European Cup winners' medals.[6] He would therefore have had, you would have thought, his pick of top English and European club sides to choose from when the time came for him to leave Nottingham Forest, unhappy at being instructed by Brian Clough to play on the left hand side of midfield rather than his preferred position in the middle. At just twenty-eight, he was in his prime, a top class player with a lot to offer. You almost sensed that Brown made the initial enquiry for him out of sheer devilment, convinced that Forest would not sell and, even if they would, O'Neill would hold out for a bigger club than Norwich to come along. At least, you would think that would be the case. But it wasn't. Norwich, seemingly, had the way clear as far as making a bid was concerned. They made it, Forest accepted it. And, with his reputation of dispensing with players he no longer wanted (Asa Hartford signed for them on 26 June 1979, leaving for Everton a little over two months and three games later) as swiftly and with as little fuss as possible, Clough wasn't going to stand in anyone's way.

So, much to most Norwich fans astonishment, the two time European Cup winner Martin O'Neill signed for the Canaries, making his debut two days later in a comfortable 3-1 win over Brighton on 28 February, the win a crucial one for Norwich as their opponents were, like themselves, struggling near the bottom of the table.

O'Neill's impact on the team was, as you would expect for a player of his class and experience, virtually instantaneous. Slotted into his favoured central midfield role and playing alongside Graham Paddon, the two of them made a formidable duo in centre of the Norwich midfield, a short lived one as it turns out and, for that, a much forgotten one that was, or could have been, one of the best in the club's history had circumstances not dictated otherwise. One of, sadly, a whole host of 'what ifs?' that cast a shadow over the club's history, players and partnerships, managers, transfers that should have happened as well as those that never happened, games won when they looked lost and lost when they looked won. The Canaries are awash with such possibilities and maybes, with O'Neill, on more than one occasion, being the focal point of all the speculation. The Canaries had eleven league games left when O'Neill signed; he played in them all and, thanks mainly to his presence and 'on-field' leadership qualities, Norwich only lost four of that eleven, a remarkable run of form given that, prior to his signing, they'd lost eighteen from twenty-two. Martin O'Neill's short time at the club helped them turn around a points per game average of 0.685 before he arrived to 1.18 per game in the eleven he played in. That average would, had it been maintained from the beginning of the season, equated to forty-nine points and a finishing place in the top ten of Division One.

If anyone ever tries to say to you that no one player can improve a team overnight, they are wrong. There are plenty of cases when they have, and, that winter, Martin O'Neill did exactly that at Norwich City.

O'Neill was happy to sign for Norwich. He'd still be playing at the highest level of the domestic game in England and in his favoured central midfield role. Then there was Ken Brown, someone who was already getting a reputation as someone who wanted to play the game in the 'proper' manner i.e. the short passing game he'd been used to at Forest. Plus he wouldn't need to relocate, at least immediately. His signing for Norwich still came as a surprise to a lot of people, including quite a few Norwich fans but also to those clubs who might have thought they would either have stood a good chance of signing him themselves – and, if they hadn't, then why not? Everton, Leeds, Wolves, Tottenham, Manchester United, the list of clubs where you might have thought there would have been interest in O'Neill was a long one and not exclusive to those clubs mentioned. All things considered it was a strange one, one that did, as the Norwich fans soon came to realise, come with an unfortunate caveat.

O'Neill had, upon signing for Norwich, insisted on one specific clause being added to his contract. It was to state that, if the Canaries ended the season as one of the relegated clubs then he would be allowed to leave. Norwich had, of course, no choice but to agree to the clause in question. But then there would have been little doubt, certainly as far as Ken Brown was concerned, that it would ever have to be activated by the player. It was more than fair to say that the Canaries were in a spot of bother when O'Neill signed. They were twentieth in the table on the day he made his debut but, with a good performance and win following in that 3-1 victory over Brighton and with winnable games (including Middlesbrough and Leicester City at home, as well as Wolves and Everton away) to come, most people were confident that the club would pull away from the relegation zone in time. This would ultimately mean that concerns about O'Neill leaving almost as soon as he had arrived in the first place would be allayed, a win-win situation for all concerned. And, with Norwich following up that win over Brighton with five more victories in their next eight games, it did look as if they would be safe, especially after winning at Carrow Road against Ipswich on 20 April. That had been the club's fourth league win in succession, one that took them to the relatively giddy heights of seventeenth position, their highest in the league since the previous November.

That impressive run of form had started with a welcome 2-0 win against Manchester City at Carrow Road, a game that had seen two more players signed by Bond also impress, nullifying their opponents potentially dangerous attack, one that included Steve MacKenzie, Tommy Hutchinson (a onetime Canary target for Bond) and, most significantly of all, Kevin Reeves, that impressive trio kept at bay by fine performances by Watson's new defensive partner as well as a new goalkeeper, Norwich's third that season alone.

Brown had never been convinced by either Roger Hansbury or Clive Baker.[7] Both were extremely capable goalkeepers. But there were, inevitably, always going to comparisons made between them and Kevin Keelan. Thus, if either of them made a mistake in a game, however slight, they'd immediately find themselves subjected to criticism, with, not surprisingly, snap judgements and unfavourable comparisons to Keelan being made. Was this fair? After all, Keelan wasn't flawless himself. He'd made errors in his time at Norwich but these would have largely been forgotten due to the fact that, time and time again, he would have put in a man of the match performance. He had a legacy at the club, one that had given him time to build up a history as well as his career and reputation. Neither Hansbury nor Baker had the same privilege, they were only ever going to be judged on their last game. Providing, that is, it had been a particularly bad one or if Norwich had lost. If the Canaries had won of course, they wouldn't have got a mention. Such is the fate of the goalkeeper. If you play well but an outfield player performs better then he gets all the praise. But if the whole team plays badly then, more often than not, it's going to be the last line of defence that gets criticised, especially, as was the case here, you were replacing a club legend. Not a good position for either keeper to be in. Nothing to win and everything, it seemed, to lose. Ken Brown must have had similar feelings and decided that, as much for, in particular, Hansbury's career as it was for the club, it might have been better if he was to play his football elsewhere, and, with Baker seemingly content to remain at the club as cover for the new man in the number one shirt, Brown set about looking to bring a new goalkeeper to the club, content that the new man would not, at least, have the responsibility of following on from Keelan weighing heavily on his shoulders.

The question was, who would it be? It was unlikely that Norwich, especially as they were struggling, would be able to attract anyone away from a Division One rival. Paddy Roche at Manchester United might have been an option, maybe he was fed up with his role as cover for Gary Bailey, the bright new hope in English goalkeeping? Then there was George Wood, once of Everton and currently with Arsenal, signed to replace Pat Jennings but now finding Jennings immovable and typically imperious in the Gunners goal still, even at thirty-five. Steve Ogrizovic at Liverpool might have been another option, as would up and coming Tony Coton at Birmingham City. Coton might even had ended up being discussed as a possibility. He was young (nineteen) and highly rated but was being kept out of the Birmingham side by Jeff Wealands. Yet he still had some experience of playing in the First Division, having made his debut for the Blues that December, saving a penalty in the first minute. That hadn't stopped Wealands retaining his place in the side, unsurprisingly so as he had been the club's Player of the Year the previous season. But would Coton, a local lad, want to leave Birmingham? And even if he did, and Birmingham agreed to sell him to Norwich, would the Canaries be able to afford him?[8] As it turned out, Brown was eventually successful in bringing a young and highly rated goalkeeper to Norwich, someone who, like Dave Watson, would end up playing for England whilst still a Norwich player. What an accomplishment by Brown. Two signings, both reserves with their clubs at the time, both signed within four months of each other and both going onto play for England.

John Bond may well have known the worth and importance of making sure his Norwich side was populated with a few wise old heads. But Brown was going in the opposite direction, signing two players who were 'young and hungry' before the phrase had even been invented, building, as he did, the backbone of a Norwich side that would grow along with those players, players who would, eventually, earn the club a great deal of much needed money as they eventually left for bigger and better things.

The goalkeeper who had caught Brown's eye was twenty-one-year-old Chris Woods who was then at QPR. Woods had shot to national prominence during Nottingham Forest's run to the final of the 1978 League Cup when, with the recently signed Peter Shilton, he impressed throughout, no more so than at Wembley as well as the subsequent replay of the game against Liverpool, keeping a clean sheet in both games. He had also performed well in Forest's earlier games in the tournament which had included a two legged semi-final success over Leeds

United, as well as victories over fellow Division One sides West Ham and Aston Villa, gaining himself a reputation as one of the most promising young goalkeepers in the country in the process. It wasn't long, therefore, before his and Forest's progress in the competition drew him received a lot of positive media attention, especially as Shilton, the man he was understudying, was already establishing himself as one of the best goalkeepers in the world. The situation with the two of them at the City Ground eventually became similar to that which Shilton had experienced himself when he was at Leicester City as understudy to one of the greatest of them all, Gordon Banks. Shilton, like Woods, had already shown his potential at Leicester, leaving the club with the daunting yet inevitable prospect to face that they couldn't play both of them so, as a consequence one would have to leave the club. Yet which one would they choose to sell? England's World Cup winning goalkeeper or the up and coming youngster? It sounds a no contest. Yet, the decision that Leicester City eventually took was to dispense with Banks, with their manager, Matt Gillies, saying to him, 'We think your best days are behind you and you should move on'. Banks was, at the time (1967) still only twenty-nine, yet, even taking that into consideration, they already felt that Shilton, still in his late teens, was the better long term bet, retaining his services and seeing Banks move onto Stoke City after mooted moves to Liverpool and West Ham fell through.

Now Shilton found himself in the same sort of situation that Banks had a decade earlier. Would Brian Clough have the same attitude as Gillies and cash in on his famous and established international keeper in favour of the young upstart or would he remain loyal to Shilton? Silly question. Clough had long championed Shilton and both his value as a player as well as his exceptional goalkeeping skills, saying that his mere presence in goal alone was worth several points a season. Woods would have no choice but to move on himself which he did, dropping a division in the process by joining QPR in the summer of 1979. Now, eighteen months later he was on the move again with QPR manager Terry Venables bizarrely opting for the experienced but nowhere near as capable John Burridge in favour of Woods. Norwich's subsequent interest saw Woods initially join the Canaries on loan, with him making his debut in a 3-0 defeat at Wolves on 14 March. A disappointing result but perhaps, given the circumstances, understandable. Woods and his back four had never played together whilst one member of that new look defence, Watson, had played less than ten games for the club and was still settling in. That was also the case with Martin O'Neill who was playing just his second game for the Canaries. Then, as if that wasn't enough as far as change is concerned, there was yet another new signing and debutant to take into consideration. The new player in question this time was Steve Walford, signed from Arsenal for £175,000 as the new central defensive partner for Watson. He and Watson would barely have had time to say hello to each other prior to the match, never mind get used to how their new partner played-let alone the rest of the team. So they had to start to learn the hard way – and against a club with both aggression and pace to spare. Little wonder, therefore, that Woods and Norwich found the going tough at Wolves. Yet at least the new man in the number one shirt acquitted himself well. He even saved a penalty from the normally reliable Wayne Clarke, his confidence and presence at the back, even in defeat, suggesting that he and his new teammates might yet all prove to be valuable signings. But, good players as they all were, had the new boys arrived too late to help prevent Norwich from the now very real threat of relegation?

As far as the Norwich board were concerned, relegation was neither a threat nor an option. They'd sanctioned Brown's new signings with a view to seeing them not only help secure the club's top flight status but to help improve on it year on year with the eventual aim of qualifying for Europe. Since the Canaries return to Division One in 1975, the likes of QPR, Ipswich, West Brom and Wolves had all finished in the top six. Were any of them bigger clubs than Norwich, better or more ambitious clubs? Not as far as the Norwich board were concerned. If they could reach such lofty heights, then so could Norwich. Make no mistake, the signings made during that season were brought in to play a big part in establishing Norwich as a club that regularly finished in the top six to eight clubs in the league not to help them avoid relegation. And Brown knew it. Relegation had never been an issue once John Bond had got Norwich back into the First Division, so it would not look good at all if the club then went down as soon as Bond had left. So Brown was under a lot of pressure, the sort of pressure that only a demanding and ambitious football club that's given you a lot of money can spend can put you under. And without saying a thing.

Yet the very fact that the club had sanctioned the signings and the considerable financial outlay that signing Watson, O'Neill, Woods and Walford had committed them to shows just how much faith Sir Arthur South and the Norwich board had in their new man. It wasn't just the players in question who were seen as long term investments as far as they were concerned – but their still relatively new manager as well. They were, as ever, reluctant to spend what little money the club did have on new players, preferring to rely on young players being brought through from schoolboy and youth level into the first team. Admirable of course. Yet the very harsh truth of that policy was that not enough were coming through, at least, not enough in terms of the sort of quality that both the club and the level of football they played at demanded. John Bond had worked miracles with the club's youth policy as soon as he'd arrived at Carrow Road, arranging for the team to play in the competitive and well-organised South East Counties league with regular opponents the likes of Arsenal, Chelsea and Tottenham, as well as the old rivals from across the border, Ipswich Town.

That in itself had proved to be a struggle for Bond and the club as the FA had initially refused Norwich permission to join that league, citing that Norwich was 'too far away' in terms of the distances that their fellow clubs would have to travel for matches. Bond had countered that argument by saying that the Canary youngsters would, in that case, play all of their matches in the league away from home. It did the trick and Norwich were in. It was a much better learning environment for the club's young players, previously used to trips to play non-league teams in the area like Gorleston, Great Yarmouth and Lowestoft, places where they'd more likely than not get the occasional kicking from some of the grizzled old has-beens that played at that level. More importantly though, it provided them and the club the chance to really bring their best young players through at a level where they would be playing their peers, an excellent grounding and education for the first team players of the future. It was working and players were making their way through the respective levels and into the first team. The problem was that not a lot of them were then going onto fully make the grade with the club, all too often making a handful of first team appearances before leaving Norwich and dropping down through the leagues or even packing up the game altogether. Steve Goodwin had been an example in Bond's first full season at Carrow Road. The young striker made a good early impression and made a name for himself in a 2-1 League Cup win over Sheffield United by scoring both goals, linking up well with Ted MacDougall in the process. Yet it never worked out for Goodwin at Carrow Road and he made only four senior appearances for the club before joining Southend in June 1975.

At least Bond had not been shy of giving the club's younger players the opportunity to make a name for themselves in the first team. But then he needed to be seen to be doing so, especially after he had done so much to drag the club's schoolboy and youth player policy, with no little opposition all round, into the club's thinking. Brown and Machin had inherited that same set up, one which, at the start of the 1980/81 season had been littered with the usual fair quantity of highly rated young hopefuls. In goal for example, there was Duncan Steward who'd played in the youth team throughout the 1979/80 season, eventually (and briefly) establishing himself as the club's third choice keeper behind Chris Woods and Clive Baker. But that was as far as it ever got for the Norwich born youngster who, after being released, signed for non-league Wroxham. Gorleston-born Adrian Harris was another player who, like Steward, was held in high regard by the club. He'd been good enough to be an integral member of the Canaries side that won the South East Counties League Cup in 1977. Yet, four seasons on from that success, his career had never developed in either the way he, or the club, would have wanted and like Steward, he ended up at Wroxham, that rich and undoubted early promise and potential never realised, just as it never was for others at the club during that time. Who remembers, for example, Gary Butcher or William Murphy? Another two members of the Canaries youth set up when Brown took over, another two players who moved on and away from the club without a first team appearance of any sort between them. Some, of course, did get a chance, however rare and fleeting. Andrew Hart made the bench for the league game at home to Newcastle United on 19 September1981, getting his chance when Mark Nightingale had to come off with an injury. Sadly, that seventeen minutes of first team action was all that Andrew ever saw at Norwich, he was with the club for another two years after that game but never came close to making the first team again. He, like so many of his onetime teammates, especially those who were locally born,[9] dropped down into non-league circles, joining Gorleston Town before ending his playing career with Norwich United in 1991.

The Canaries were not that adverse to taking a chance on bringing in young players from other clubs. One example was Londoner Peter Fishenden who was signed, with some accordant local publicity, from non-league Southgate Athletic. It proved to be a step up too much and too soon for the young midfielder, who, like so many other Canary fledglings at the time, left the club without having made any kind of impression on the first team. It's worth pointing out of course that such disappointment and unfulfilled hopes and potential are part and parcel of football. Even some of the most accomplished and well known youth team set ups in modern history have included team members who have failed to make a career for themselves in the game. Take, for example, the Manchester United youth team sides of 1992 and 1993, both FA Youth Cup finalists and sides that featured names like Gary and Phil Neville, David Beckham,[10] Paul Scholes, Nicky Butt and Ryan Giggs. No further introduction needed. Yet the opposite would be true of some of their teammates during those glory years of Old Trafford youth, the likes of Steven Riley, Richard Irving and Darren Whitmarsh. All deemed as the peers and equals of Beckham, Scholes and Giggs *et al* at the time, yet all also deemed wanting when it came to making it in the senior game. Success and pre-eminence at youth team level is, and always has been, no guarantee of the same at the highest levels and, as the Canaries were finding out, for every Justin Fashanu, there would be a Adrian Harris, Gary Butcher and Andrew Hart.

Yet Brown, like Bond before him, was determined to give youth its chance at Carrow Road, driven, no doubt, by a combination of the belief he had in some of those individuals, players he would have already known and worked with, as well as being aware that the club's permanent parlous financial state meant that going out and signing players for big money (or, indeed, any money at all) was not always an option and that the signings he had made were a rare exception rather than the common rule. He had been fortunate enough to 'inherit' some former youth team players who'd been given their chance by Bond and made the most of the opportunity. Justin Fashanu was, naturally enough, one of them but there was also players like Dave Bennett, a good friend of Fashanu's who'd been signed, at just eighteen, from Manchester City and Mark Barham, who'd signed at the club as an apprentice when he was just fifteen, swiftly making his mark on the youth team side by captaining them to the South East Counties league title in 1980. There was also King's Lynn-born Peter Mendham, another who'd impressed at schoolboy level, representing the West Norfolk as well as the Norfolk Schoolboys U15 and U19 sides at football as well as in cross country. He was swiftly noted by, of all people, Martin Peters who, after seeing Peter play for the youth side, commented, '... I noticed his red hair and he looked a real scallywag tearing up and down the pitch. He was very, very dedicated and I, for one, was certainly glad of his boundless energy when I was in the Norwich team.'

Brown therefore genuinely had that much beloved mix of predominantly youth with some experience to select from for his Norwich teams as the 1980/81 approached, fixtures wise, its final quarter. For the game at Leeds United on 31 January, he selected eight players who were twenty-three or under; three of whom, Mark Barham (eighteen), Justin Fashanu (nineteen) and Peter Mendham (twenty) had progressed through the club's schoolboy and youth team ranks whilst Dave Watson (nineteen) and Dave Bennett (twenty) had come from Liverpool and Manchester City respectively without having ever troubled their first team squads. In addition to that, his side for that game also featured Ross Jack, twenty-one, who'd signed from Everton a little over a year previously, plus the previous managers son, and Captain, Kevin Bond, still only twenty-three himself and goalkeeper Clive Baker who was twenty-one. That Norwich side, quite possibly one of the youngest, average age wise, that any Canaries manager has selected, acquitted itself extremely well against a dour and occasionally cynical Leeds side, one that featured a fair few seasoned old pros whose were able to extinguish the Canaries exuberance with sheer physicality, out muscling Norwich on their way to a undeserved 1-0 win at Elland Road. It was a performance and result that summed up Norwich's season thus far. Full of promise and of good things to come but lacking in proven top flight class. Clearly, the nous and experience of the club's most senior players, the ever admirable but overworked Graham Paddon and Joe Royle were simply not enough at that time for the club. With three more reverses to follow that one-against Southampton (1-2), West Brom (0-2) and Birmingham (0-4), it became clear that Ken Brown needed to bring in the class and experience that it was so badly missing, hence Brown being given the funds and budget to bring in those three afore mentioned high profile signings in Martin O'Neill, Chris Woods and Steve Walford. Good business unquestionably and players of the kind that Canaries fans were not that used to seeing wear the famous yellow and green. With a few exceptions, Norwich usually entered the transfer market to either bring in players approaching the end of their career who welcomed the opportunity to come to Norfolk in order to prolong professional life at the top level of the game; tried and tested players from clubs with similar expectations to themselves, or up and coming youngsters who might, or might not, make the grade. Three different player types with one thing in common, they didn't tend to cost very much in terms of money or long term risk, with always a chance that one might turn out to be a star in the making. O'Neill, Woods and Walford were the vanguard of a new player type that the Canaries sought to bring in, established names that would cost them a lot of money. It was a calculated risk but one which Brown felt gave the club the best chance of avoiding relegation at the end of what was turning out to be quite an eventful season, on and off the pitch.

The three new signings eventually cost the Canaries around £750,000, an absolute fortune at the time for all bar the top four to six clubs in the country. When that figure is added to the £300,000 the club had spent on Drazen Muzinic the previous Autumn, any accusations the club had ever had from its fans of being loathe to spend any money could be well and truly blown out of the water: those four players had cost the club in excess of £1 million. They had to deliver and, to a man, three of the four did just that with Muzinic the exception. It was an utterly wretched time for him on and off the pitch where he looked permanently ill at ease, remote and uninterested. It soon became very clear that the only thing that would motivate him would be the opportunity to return to Yugoslavia, one Brown was not keen to immediately fulfil on his behalf.

Unfortunately for Norwich, as good as Brown's quartet of signings were, they'd come a little too late to prevent what had looked an inevitability since the humiliating 6-1 reverse at Middlesbrough back in October. That game now seemed doubly significant. For a start, it was one which proved to be the watershed moment for John Bond, a match and performance that made him painfully aware that his time at Carrow Road was drawing to a close. In addition to that, it was also the game that, more than any other that campaign, illustrated the lack of quality and experience, playing wise, at the club. Middlesbrough were nothing special after all. The Teesiders had only won three games prior to the game against the Canaries that season and had already endured a heavy defeat themselves, a 5-2 thrashing by Crystal Palace. To be so comprehensively swept aside by one of the top clubs was one thing. Yes it was, and would always be unacceptable. But, if the likes of Arsenal, Liverpool or eventual Champions Aston Villa hit their stride in a game then you had to take the consequences and regard it as a lesson learnt. But Middlesbrough? They shouldn't have been able to put six past any other club in the table and for it to happen spoke more of their opponents failings rather than the qualities of Bobby Murdoch's side. For Norwich, the reason for that defeat and their ongoing problems that season were simple. Too many important players had left Carrow Road without being swiftly and adequately replaced and, despite Brown eventually bringing in that some much needed class and experience late on, it was action which was taken far too late to give the club a chance of turning things around and avoiding the drop, let alone pushing on and up the table as the board expected.

There had been a glimmer of hope in April when, with Woods, Watson, Walford and O'Neill now bedded in to the side, Norwich ran up four successive league wins which raised them to seventeenth in the table and seemingly out of danger. But it was not to be. A 1-0 defeat at Manchester United in their penultimate league game came on a day when two of the club's relegation rivals (Brighton and Coventry City) also won meaning that the Canaries had to win their last game of the season against Leicester City at Carrow Road as well as hope that some other results, notably in the matches involving Brighton, Wolves and Sunderland's all went their way. And, to be fair it wasn't a lost cause. Norwich were at home where they had lost only four league games all season (fewer than Leeds and Everton) against a side that were already down whilst Sunderland were at Liverpool. So there were grounds for optimism. After all, a Sunderland reverse at Anfield looked very likely and, with that comforting thought in mind, most of the Norwich fans who made up the attendance of 25,307 at Carrow Road on that final day were confident of a win-win double i.e. one for Norwich and one for Liverpool, one that would keep them up for another season and give Brown a Summer to fine tune his growing squad with a brighter future at the club seemingly now assured.

Did the Norwich players feed off all of that pre-match confidence? You'd like to think that, with all of the big game experience and nous in the side on the day that wouldn't have been the case. Yet, crazily, the Canaries found themselves 2-0 down to Leicester after barely twenty minutes of the game had been played; Jim Melrose scoring both of the goals. Would Norwich respond? They had to and did in the best possible way, Mick McGuire scoring within three minutes of Melrose's second. As the teams went off at half time, the Norwich fans learnt, to their collective horror, that Sunderland were 1-0 up at Liverpool so now were, as things stood, two points ahead of Norwich who were down. The unthinkable had, with just forty-five minutes of a long and eventful season left, suddenly become a very grim and dark reality for all at Carrow Road that afternoon.

The Canaries at least gave it a go in the second half of that game with Justin Fashanu scoring on the hour mark but, with Leicester playing with the sort of carefree abandon that comes when you know your fate is already sealed, there was always a chance that Norwich would concede another, fatal, goal. Which they did when Melrose completed his hat-trick with a little under ten minutes to go, that late winner ensuring that Norwich would be joining him and Leicester in Division Two for the following season.

Norwich's fate left many of their fans in a state of shock. They had not, no matter how well anyone tried to talk it up, had a good season. They'd started it well with that 5-1 win over Stoke City and Justin Fashanu's hat-trick, a game and performance that, under the warm blue skies of a sunny August afternoon and on that verdant swathe of green in Norwich NR1, it seemed to bode well for the season ahead. Yet the dawn had been a false one. Four consecutive defeats followed that game with an acrimonious managerial departure not long afterwards, the eventual additional departure of Bond junior being almost as unpleasant for all concerned as he joined his Dad at Manchester City shortly afterwards. Losing to Bond's new side in November had been bad enough, but losing to them to the tune of 6-1, as Norwich did in the FA Cup fourth round in January was worse. The hurt of that defeat was intensified all the more when Kevin Reeves, the onetime prodigal son who went astray, joyfully scored one of the goals in that rout, one that was played in front of a grinning Bond plus nearly 40,000 delirious Mancunians. King John had finally found the place where he belonged – and it wasn't Carrow Road after all.

Norwich were down and out. No one had expected the club to be relegated at the end of that season, least of all the club, the realisation that it might, after all, be something that needed to be considered coming, to some, as late as during half time in that last game of the season. Norwich were losing, Sunderland were winning and, all of a sudden, the Norwich fans, many of whom with half an ear to their transistor radios, were suddenly struck by what might be about to happen for the first time for the whole of that season. 'We could go down here.' We could. And we did. It was going to be a long and gloomy summer.

## CHAPTER THREE

# The Late, Late Show

*Norwich had huffed and puffed and generally looked out of sorts and uninspired at Brisbane Road and now, eight weeks later, it didn't look as if too much had changed.*

If Ken Brown hadn't quite treated Norwich's relegation from Division One with a flash of his trademark smile, it wouldn't have been very long before he was ready for the challenge that lay ahead of him that August, the not inconsiderable one of guiding Norwich City to a third promotion to the top division in a decade. Yet, even as he started to make his plans for the new season, he was immediately hamstrung by the departure of two of his best players. The first was inevitable. Martin O'Neill had signed for the club the previous February on the proviso that if the Canaries were relegated at the end of the season he would be free to negotiate a move to another top flight club. Clear cut and to the point. You could hardly blame him. He had won a League Championship with Nottingham Forest as well as a European Cup, those and plenty of other medals and plaudits and, still only twenty-nine, wanted to continue playing in the top flight of English football. Norwich had agreed to the condition – not that they had a choice. But doing so hadn't concerned them unduly as the club wasn't going to be relegated, a stance that held firm and true until the last hour or so of the season. Ken Brown and the Norwich board as well as, in all probability, a few of the Norwich players, tried to get O'Neill to change his mind but to no avail. Norwich had gone down so he was exercising his right to leave which he did as soon as he returned from his holidays, joining Manchester City for £275,000 that June.

Justin Fashanu's departure, on the other hand, wasn't seen as being quite as inevitable as O'Neill's had been and the club exercised strong hopes that he would stay, reaffirm his commitment to the club who had given him his big chance and stay to lead the attack in the club's quest to return to Division One at the first attempt-just as they had done in 1975. It seemed a reasonable hope. Fashanu, unlike O'Neill, had the very great majority of his career ahead of him still, he was nearly a decade younger than his now ex-teammate so had plenty of time to grow as a player and eventfully seal a move to one of the biggest clubs in the country. That this would ultimately happen was never in question at all. Fashanu was a superstar in waiting, a player of extraordinary ability and skill, one who, it seemed, could, and probably would achieve just about anything that he wanted to in the game. But that could perhaps wait for a season or two. Because as far as the club were concerned in the summer of 1981, Fashanu was staying put. Yes, they had just been relegated and yes, he was, by some considerable distance, their most valuable asset one who, like Reeves before him could realise a lot of money for the club. But if he was worth £500,000; £750,000, even £1 million now, what might he then be worth a year to eighteen months later having just helped Norwich regain their Division One status and, in doing so, got himself into Ron Greenwoods England squad? £2 million? Or more? The British record transfer fee in the Summer of 1981 was the £1,469,000 paid by Wolves to Aston Villa for striker Andy Gray just under two years earlier.[1] Gray was, and continued to be a strong, fast and brave striker who both made and scored goals, something which the Wolves board, cash rich with the £1,450,000 Manchester City had just paid them for midfielder Steve Daly fully appreciated. Then, just as now, strikers were prime real estate and you had to pay the price for getting a good one. In effect therefore, Gray 'only' cost them £19,000 of their own money, a bargain! But the message was clear. Top-class midfielders may well fetch a lot of money. But a good striker might fetch even more. It seems extremely probable that the Norwich board regarded Fashanu as someone who could break the record again and, feasibly, become British football's first £2 million player in the process. First of all they had to convince him to stay for another season, confident that his physical presence and goals would be the platform for an immediate return to the First Division.

Fashanu already had his admirers. Leeds United had supposedly been close to signing him during the previous October whilst he had been tipped for a reunion with John Bond at Manchester City almost as soon as Bond had been confirmed as manager at Maine Road. There were other possible takers as well. Everton, Arsenal and Tottenham were all aware of his qualities and would unquestionably have had him watched on more than one occasion. But no concrete bids were made and it looked as if Fashanu would be staying put, at least for the time being, until a late and somewhat unexpected expression of interest made their intentions known – or, rather, hinted at what might be to come. The person in question was Nottingham Forest manager Brian Clough who took time out one evening that Summer to make a telephone call to Norwich striker Joe Royle. After the initial pleasantries were done with, Clough cut to the chase, asking Royle for his honest opinion on Fashanu as a player. Royle was honest in his reply, stating that, in his opinion, Fashanu was one of the most exciting strikers he'd played alongside in his whole career – quite a recommendation. With that, Clough thanked Royle for his time and abruptly rang off.

Would Royle have mentioned the call to Ken Brown? Almost certainly. The Norwich manager would, doubtless, have greeted the news with a wry smile and shrug of the shoulders. He wanted to keep Fashanu at the club, his teammates wanted him to stay and so too, of course, did the fans. But the fact was that the club had not only recently been relegated but had, in the space of a year, spent out £1 million in transfer fees. They now needed to recoup some of that money – and Forest were offering much of it up front in order to seal the deal, not something that had been forthcoming from Manchester City where Kevin Reeves had been concerned. In any case, neither Brown nor his Chairman, Sir Arthur South, wanted to sell Fashanu to Manchester City. They'd poached the Norwich manager as well as two of the club's best players. If Fashanu had to leave then it was not going to be to go to Maine Road. With that decision made, Brown made Fashanu aware of Forest and Clough's interest. Unsurprisingly, the young striker wanted to meet the man who had expressed interest in him, to look into the possibility of playing for him and a team that had recently won two European Cup finals. With that, Brown and Fashanu set off to a Peterborough hotel to meet Clough where, upon their arrival, Clough asked Brown for some time alone with his young striker. Settling down for a long wait, Brown would hardly have time to pick up the day's paper before Clough and a beaming Fashanu came back to where he was waiting, the deal for him to sign for Forest agreed, done and dusted with Fashanu later going onto say he had no doubts at all about signing for Clough.

In hindsight of course, the talented and popular Fashanu had made a mistake although it was one that he could never have been foreseen at the time. Clough's exciting side and his unerring gift of making mediocre players good ones and good players great ones suggested that Fashanu's career could only go one way with his signing for Forest and Brian Clough: onwards and upwards. The fact that it didn't and his true potential, in life as well as in the game remained unfulfilled was, and remains, a tragedy. Fash's life post-Norwich is systematically and sensitively covered in Nick Baker's book about him *Forbidden Forward*,[2] and it is to that I would suggest anyone wanting to know more about the both man and the player should turn if they would like to learn more about Justin and a life and career that was tragically cut short.

The fee paid by Forest for Fashanu was reported to be slightly over the £1 million paid by Manchester City for Kevin Reeves, that slight increase a possible insistence of the Norwich board who, if they were going to cash in on their most saleable asset, at least wanted to offer the club's support the relative 'comfort' that they had obtained a new club record fee for his services. Exact transfer fees are rarely, if ever, made public, but it is fair to suggest as far as this one is concerned, if Norwich received £1 million for Reeves, then the amount they managed to squeeze out of Forest for Fashanu was perhaps £1,050 million or even £1,100 million. Enough, in other words, for Norwich to feel they had struck a hard bargain and got a record fee, but not so much more that it might have forced Forest to back out of the deal.

Forest had certainly made their intentions very clear from the beginning with, at one point, a story in the *Daily Express* suggesting that Clough was ready to consider any one of his players joining Norwich in part exchange for Fashanu apart from Peter Shilton and Trevor Francis. When you consider the playing riches available at the club at that time it sounds a potentially very attractive proposition if it was true with Norwich free to browse the club's squad at will with such playing talents as Kenny Burns, Frank Gray, John Robertson and Ian Wallace all seemingly available. Whether, of course, any of them or their teammates would have even considered dropping down a division is another point as is whether Norwich would even have been able to afford them. Maybe, in signing Martin

O'Neill earlier that year, Norwich had suggested to Clough that they were a club that could afford to pay big wages. On the other hand, maybe O'Neill joined Norwich at the first opportunity simply because he wanted to get away from Clough as soon as he possibly could. The important thing was that Norwich now had the cash in the bank and that Ken Brown would be able to strengthen his squad ready for the new season that was due to start on 29 August with a trip to play Rotherham United at Millmoor.

The prospect of the long trip up to South Yorkshire would have been the last thing on anyone's minds when, a week after that shattering home defeat to Leicester City which had confirmed their relegation, the Norwich players found themselves on yet another (following China in 1980 and Australia and New Zealand in 1979) end of season tour, this time one that took them to the USA. Such tours were considered essential by many English clubs at the time, taken not, as is the case today, a week or so after pre-season training has begun i.e. in or around the beginning of July but almost as soon as the domestic season has finished. Thus, only a few days after the Leicester match, the Norwich coaching staff, players and not a few wives and partners found themselves flying out to North America's east coast where, on 9 May, Norwich dispatched a side from the University of Florida 6-0. Two days later the Canaries lost 2-1 to the Atlanta Chiefs before, twenty four hours later, facing the Fort Lauderdale Strikers and, not surprisingly, considering it was their third game in four days, losing 4-0.

With that, a season that had started the previous July with a 4-0 win over Cambridge United was, finally, over. Nine and a half months of virtual non-stop football, a total of, friendlies included, sixty-one matches played. And it was all set to start again in just over twelve weeks with a game against Glentoran, one of two the club were scheduled to make in their rather more modest pre-season tour of Northern Ireland with the club due to fly out on 5 August. And, whilst the players might have welcomed the opportunity for a break with family and friends before pre-season training commenced, there was little to no time for Ken Brown and Mel Machin to indulge in such luxuries. Their preparation for the new season had to begin as soon as the previous one was over, their job to not only prepare and motivate their players for a campaign from which promotion back to Division One would not only be expected by Sir Arthur South and the Norwich board – but demanded. With, in all probability, their jobs at the club depending on it.

Two big money transfers or not in recent years, the Canaries went into the 1981/82 season on the back of worrying financial reports that stated that the club had suffered an annual loss of £327,000 in the previous financial year, a colossal amount at the time and one that, intriguingly, was not much more than the amount (£300,000) paid for Drazen Muzinic the previous summer. Comparisons couldn't help but be made and, all of a sudden, the hapless Yugoslav became as much a symbol of the Canaries woes off the pitch as he had been on it. His signing, a first for the club in so many ways had turned out to be, one year on, an unmitigated disaster with no redeeming features or positives to be drawn at all. Yet Brown felt obliged to give him another chance. Muzinic's last appearance for the first team the previous season had been in the instantly forgettable 4-0 drubbing the Canaries had received at the hands of Birmingham City when he had been hauled off to be replaced by Ross Jack.

For many in attendance day the combination of the result and risible performance of Muzinic on the day suggested he'd never play for Norwich again with the club's ultimate relegation only serving to strengthen that belief. Muzinic, surely, would now want out of the club? He had, after all, played in World Cups and European Championships, he wouldn't want a season of being kicked from one end of the pitch to another at places like Shrewsbury, Grimsby and Oldham. He'd been signed to dominate the game from one end of the pitch to the other at places like Anfield, Highbury and Old Trafford. Which he hadn't been able to do. But then again he hadn't dominated anywhere or anyone throughout the whole season, least of all in and around the club and training ground where it had been hoped his undoubted pedigree as a player would have had the same impact as that which Martin Peters had upon arrival. Had Muzinic been the success the club had hoped he would have been then at least they might have expected interest from other clubs post-relegation, in England as well as Europe. But he was now well and truly off the radar of anyone and everyone who mattered. The Canaries therefore had two choices. He could either spend his time in the reserves or Brown could try, again, to integrate him into the squad and team. Bearing in mind he was probably still the club's highest-paid player there was only one option. Muzinic had to play.

As far as who Muzinic would be playing alongside come August remained to be seen. Most pre-seasons for clubs that have recently been relegated are characterised by a high turnover of playing staff. Most of the departing players will be keen to return to the higher level of play whilst others will, because of their high wages will be moved on more at the behest of their clubs rather than of their own choice. There will also be a number of fringe and youth team players heading out of the exit door as well, either because their contracts will have expired and the club can neither afford, or even want to renew them; or, quite simply, because they are released, footballs kind way of telling a player he has been sacked. For the Canaries however, the internal 'churn' during the summer of 1981 was fairly low key. Of the twenty-six players who had made at least one competitive league appearance for the club during the 1980/81 season, nine of them had since moved on or stayed within the club itself to a new role. The players in question were Kevin Bond (joined Seattle Sounders in February 1981 from whence he joined Manchester City in September 1981); Justin Fashanu (joined Nottingham Forest in August 1981); Duncan Forbes (retired); Steve Goble (Gronigen, August 1981);[3] Roger Hansbury (Eastern Athletic, April 1981);[4] John McDowell (appointed Reserve Team Coach, August 1981); Martin O'Neill (Manchester City, June 1981); Tony Powell (San Jose Earthquakes, March 1981) and Keith Robson (Leicester City, September 1981).[5] So much for those that were moving on. But what about the new faces? It was obvious that Ken Brown was going to have to rebuild his squad to a certain extent, given those players who had, or who were, in the process of moving on. Much of his work had been done towards the end of the previous season. Dave Watson, Martin O'Neill, Chris Woods and Steve Walford had all been brought in, at considerable expense, with half an eye on the 1981/82 season, even if that campaign had always been regarded as one that would take place in Division One. O'Neill had since moved on again but no such conditions or clauses had been requested or implemented by the remainder of that quartet who remained committed to the Canary cause of promotion at the first time of asking. Its perhaps true to say that, if that had not been achieved, then all three of them may have joined O'Neill in wanting away from the club, but, for now, they were fit, motivated and ready to go. And it's reasonable to say that, potentially at least, they formed a central defensive spine that was as good as any other in the division as the big kick-off got ever closer.

Ken Brown also intended to make use of the Canaries youth players throughout the new season. It had, as we have previously discussed, seen players come through and into the first team in recent years with the obvious stand out success being Justin Fashanu. There had also been disappointments, players who had worked their way through all the playing levels at the club before, at the last moment, been found wanting in some way or another. Brown, like Bond before him, reckoned that the only way you could tell if someone was going to be good enough to make it was to give the best of them their chance in the side. From then on it was mostly up to them if they went onto be a success or not. But they had, at least, to be given an opportunity, a refreshing attitude compared to that of many Coaches in the modern game who seem to think there is never a good reason to give one of their club's up and coming youngsters a first debut. Brown, fortunately, did not share that opinion, and, by the end of the 1981/82 season, four of the club's young players had been awarded their competitive Norwich City debuts – with one of them going onto play for England.

A player who had made his competitive debut for the Canaries in a long forgotten FA Cup tie in January 1980 was also given a chance by Brown to impress in the club's opening league fixture at Rotherham. Nineteen year old Greig Shepherd had joined Norwich in March 1979 following unsuccessful trials in Scotland with Hibernian and Hearts, having already impressed as a schoolboy with Rangers where he had won three Scottish youth caps. Bond had given him his debut for an injury-ravaged Norwich squad in their 1-1 draw to Wolves at Molineux in an FA Cup fourth round match, Shepherd coming on for Justin Fashanu – the player whose leap to prominence had, ironically, overshadowed his own early career with the club. He did enough on the day to convince Bond to give him another chance which he got in the club's penultimate league game of that season, a 2-0 away defeat to Nottingham Forest, again replacing Fashanu who'd been fined and dropped from the side after head butting Bristol City's David Rodgers in the club's previous game. Shepherd was energetic and worked hard but not hard enough, it seemed, to convince Bond to retain him in the side for the last game of the season when he recalled Fashanu for the 4-2 win over Derby. Now, over a season late, Shepherd was, finally, getting another chance, playing alongside Keith Bertschin, the only new signing the club had made over the summer at a cost of £200,000 from Birmingham City.

Whilst Shepherd was still young and inexperienced, Bertschin was anything but. He'd made his competitive league debut back in April 1976, scoring in his club's 2-1 win over Arsenal before following that up with another against West Ham two days later-an impressive start to life in English footballs by any standards. He'd done that with the Canaries nearest rivals, Ipswich Town, going onto score eight goals in total for them from thirty-two appearances. Unfortunately for Bertschin, he had made his debut at a time when Ipswich were one of the leading club sides in the country, a position and reputation they'd won for themselves through having some superb attacking options at that time. Norfolk-born Trevor Whymark was one, David Johnson, later to join Liverpool was another whilst, in September that same year, the club signed Paul Mariner from Plymouth Argyle for £200,000. It was clear that Bertschin was only ever going to be regarded as a squad player, something which must have made his decision to join Birmingham in July 1977 an easy one. Now, 143 appearances and forty-one goals later, he'd moved to Norwich, his Suffolk origins forgotten, if not quite forgiven, by most of a yellow and green hue. His brief at Carrow Road was short and to the point. He'd never been a prolific goal scorer but was, despite all of that, the type of player who effortlessly and unselfishly brought others into play with his bravery and willingness to put himself about in opposing teams' penalty areas; taking the kicks and winning the knockdowns. Brown knew if he could find a goal poacher to play alongside Bertschin, there was every chance that, if the two of them developed a quick understanding, then they might be able to complement one another and contribute between them 20–25 goals per season, a good foundation for any promotion attempt, especially if the rest of the team pitched in with their fair share of goals as well. His main hope at the start of the campaign was that, with another £200,000 spent on Bertschin, he might yet be able to curtail the spending a little by finding a goal scoring partner for Bertschin from within his own ranks.[6] Which is why, ultimately, he made Shepherd his initial choice to fulfil the role.

The Canaries line-up for the game at Millmoor saw Steve Walford and Dave Watson line up in the centre of the Norwich defence, a partnership they would maintain for all but five of the club's forty-eight competitive games that season with Walford an ever present. With Graham Paddon and Mick McGuire adding guile and bite respectively to the centre of the midfield whilst the width was provided by Peter Mendham and Dave Bennett, the Canaries looked to have a strong side, one that would provide plenty of options and support for Bertschin and Shepherd in attack. If there was one question that might have been raised at the time, it would have been with regard to the full backs, with Mark Barham and Drazen Muzinic operating as right and left backs on the day. Neither were naturals in the role and, although Barham was an effective and swift player to have on the right side of the pitch, he was more used to playing in an offensive role rather than a defensive one. The fact that both players were not used to the roles they were being asked to play and therefore would be vulnerable is something that would not have escaped the attention of former Liverpool and England Captain Emlyn Hughes, the Rotherham manager. He'd briefed his tricky right winger Tony Towner to run at Muzinic at every possible opportunity, a responsibility which Towner revelled in outsmarting Norwich's record signing again and again. It mattered not that Shepherd put Norwich ahead after just seven minutes for, less than a minute later and with Towner already a rampant thorn in Muzinic's side, he crafted an equalising goal for Rodney Fern. Towner continued to wreak havoc for the remainder of the match, one that ended up 4-1 in Rotherham's favour. Fortunately for Muzinic, by the time referee Vic Callow drew proceedings to an end, he had long departed the scene to be replaced by Mark Nightingale, who, like Muzinic was essentially a midfielder. He did at least look a little more comfortable in the role and, unlike the Yugoslav, never let his head drop or looked to shy away from the action, qualities that led Brown, embattled after just one game, to keep him in the side for the club's second match of the season the following Wednesday which was against Crystal Palace, another recently relegated club.

Hughes had, after the Rotherham match chosen not to gloat or espouse his teams qualities, preferring to devote some time to saying how, despite the result, he felt that Norwich were a team full of quality and one that would, come the end of the season, be challenging for promotion. It was an unusually understated comment from a man who was, for much of his career, more familiar with hyperbole. Was he downplaying his own team's chances with those carefully chosen words, or was he, as some might have suspected, talking himself up for the manager's job at Norwich should Brown's time at Carrow Road prove to be short and swift? Genuinely expressed or not, they were of little comfort to the returning Norwich fans who, just over a year after seeing a Fashanu inspired Norwich crush Stoke City 5-1 in their opening game had now seen their team, less Fashanu, nearly suffer the same fate themselves at Rotherham. Brown would have to turn things around and fast if he was to win the faith of the Norwich fans, most of whom were expecting nothing more than a swift return to the top flight by the end of that campaign. Results like the one they had just witnessed could only suggest that such dreams were forged in hope rather than expectation.

Brown had to make changes for the Palace game at Carrow Road and he did. Nightingale retained his place in defence whilst there was a first appearance of the season for the popular Greg Downs at left back in place of Muzinic, summarily and, predictably, dropped after just one game. Downs was no left back himself, at least, he had not been originally, starting his career in the game as a striker before being converted to a left back early on in his Norwich career. He had accepted the switch with some aplomb, becoming, in the process, the sort of left back so beloved of the game today; one who has boundless energy and is as happy running down the line with the ball at his feet in an attacking role as he is covering an opposing right winger doing exactly the same thing. In attack, Greig Shepherd deservedly kept his place whist there was a starting place for ex-Everton man Ross Jack at the expense of Peter Mendham who was on the bench. Mark Barham also kept his place, albeit in a more advanced role as a right sided midfielder with the brief to play as a winger, the short and somewhat flawed experiment of playing him at the back now thankfully, and permanently, disregarded.

Fittingly, it was Barham, playing in the more advanced role for Norwich, one that his excellence at would later win him England recognition, who was the architect of the game's only goal, the sort of fortuitous one that teams like Norwich needed if their luck was going to change. The Rotherham defeat might have seemed only the one game but, if it was added as part of the run of results that the Canaries had experienced at the end of the previous season, it was their third defeat in a row, one that had cost them eight goals conceded for only two scored. So it was good to see the balance readdressed a little, even if the only goal, one that saw Jim Cannon deflect Barham's teasing cross pass his own goalkeeper, was down to an opposition error rather than an opportunistic strike by the home side. But it was a win nonetheless, the first for the Canaries that earned them three, rather than two points, and a chance for Brown and his squad, many of whom were still new to the club, to put a run of good results together.

Norwich then went on a run of six league and one cup game that saw a return of four wins, two losses and two defeats, the one cup game being a League Cup 2nd round, first leg tie at home to Charlton that saw a 1-0 victory. Average form and disappointing results, a sequence that, by the beginning of October and a hugely disappointing 2-1 defeat at home to Oldham Athletic saw the Canaries drop to ninth in the Division Two table, five points shy of early leaders Luton

Town. What was more significant about those seven games was the fact that one Norwich player managed to score in every single one of them. Seven games played, seven games scored in, seven goals scored – a remarkable record. The player in question was Inverness born Ross Jack, known to some as the 'Jack in the box' who'd signed from Everton for just £20,000 in December 1979. Jack had certainly been under no illusions of what was expected of him at Norwich with Mel Machin describing him as the club's answer to Ipswich's John Wark.

Quite a brave comparison to make and one which must have seemed daunting to Jack the moment he heard it. Wark had already won FA and UEFA Cup winners medals with Ipswich, was a full Scotland international and had, in 1981, won both the PFA and the Young European Player of the Year Awards. No pressure then! In addition to all of that was the fact that Norwich had signed Jack as a striker but intended, over time, to convert him into an attacking midfielder, something which seemed a little short sighted after those seven goals scored in seven games. They'd all come in games that had seen Jack played as a striker, new signing Bertschin missing four of them due to injury. Jack ended the 1981/82 season as the Canaries top scorer with a total of fourteen goals from forty-one League and Cup games, twelve of which had come from the bench.

Despite Jack's form and prowess in front of goal, Brown knew that his defence still needed some strengthening. Watson and Walford were proving to be an admirable combination in its centre but the side still lacked quality and depth in both of the full back positions with, more often than not, opposing sides copying Rotherham's ploy with Tony Towner on the opening day and running at both of the full backs playing, confident of getting the majority of their crosses over and into the danger area, something reflected in the fact that City had only managed a clean sheet once in their first seven league games, with three different players (Muzinic, Downs and Richard Symonds) played in the left back role alone. Brown had hoped to sign Manchester City's Tony Henry who, as well as being able to play in either full back position was also comfortable in any midfield role, that sort of versatility making him an ideal player for Norwich, someone who, more often than not, find himself in the team every week. It looked as if Henry was set to sign as well until, at the last moment, he accepted an offer from Bolton Wanderers who secured his signature for £120,000 – an amount which, if both Brown and the club were honest, was perhaps a little more than they'd hoped to pay. What did pay was Brown's swiftly improving relationship with his predecessor at Carrow Road, Manchester City manager John Bond who would have been able to advise Brown that former Maine Road favourite Willie Donachie, who'd been playing in the USA for Portland Timbers was looking to move back to England.

Donachie's signing was a bit of a coup for the Canaries. Not in the Martin Peters league of course but, nonetheless, one they'd been able to seal from under the noses of some of the bigger and more high profile clubs that might have been interested in him. He ended up costing Norwich £200,000 which was almost certainly a lot, lot more than the club had been initially willing to spend, but, as Brown would have unquestionably argued, look at the player and the experience that they were getting for the money. He was a full Scotland international and a member of the Scotland squad that had taken part in the 1978 World Cup finals in Argentina as well as a relative 'veteran' (and still only twenty-nine when he signed for Norwich) of 351 League games played for Manchester City, all of them in the First Division.

Top flight club and international experience and expertise – plus all of the know how that went with it and for just £200,000? Brown had got a bargain.

Donachie made his Canaries debut in the 1-2 home defeat to Oldham on 3 October 1981 – the Canaries third loss in just eight league games that season. They lost again a week later, this time on the controversial plastic pitch at Loftus Road, home of Queens Park Rangers for whom John Gregory and Simon Stainrod scored. Four defeats in their opening nine games for Norwich who'd only lost one of their first nine the last time they played in this league back in 1974. It hadn't been a disastrous start. But it had seen them slip down to 13th position in the league, their lowest league placing since September 1970. It wasn't enough, yet, to provoke questions and doubts about Brown's position at the club and whether or not he'd be able to get Norwich back into the top division at the first time of asking. Not publicly at least. But there would have been a few with unexpressed doubts at this time. Fortunately, that didn't extend to the club's boardroom so much so that, when another sequence of disappointing league results from 24 November to 30 December (five played, no wins, two draws, three losses) drew speculation that Brown's job was now indeed on the line and that the club was considering the likes of Martin Peters, Geoff Hurst and Mike England as potential replacements, Canaries Chairman Sir Arthur South felt compelled to give Brown the dreaded vote of confidence, imploring for everyone at the club, supporters included, to 'pull together'. That statement had come about as the result of a hastily convened board meeting that followed the 1-3 defeat to leaders Luton Town on 28 December, a game that had seen Luton score their three goals in under a quarter of an hour from kick-off, much to the horror of the club's biggest home attendance of the season, 19,348. It could have been worse. Luton had struck the bar twice, said bar quite possibly saving Brown his job for it is unlikely that, for all of South's support, he could have let the manager stay on after a 1-5 humiliation on home soil-and three days after Christmas.

It was around this time that the club had announced the previously mentioned annual loss of £327,000, one that forced them to lay off several members of their backroom staff. The fact that the club had found itself in financial difficulties again, even after selling two players for fees of around £1 million, both angered and puzzled the Canaries support – the club had made a lot of money through the sales of Reeves and Fashanu, how come they'd still made such a massive loss? The answers lay partially in the financial woes afflicting another First Division club, namely Manchester City. They'd agreed to sign Reeves for £1 million but as to how much of the fee Norwich had yet received was questionable with, as it turns out, the vagaries of the whole transfer system something that would eventually come to light later on with regard to a future deal that involved the club. Right now the Canaries were skint – with Brown adding to the £950,000 already committed to the signings of Watson, Walford, O'Neill, Woods and Bertschin with the £200,000 Donachie had cost plus another £175,000 for John Deehan. When you added all of those figures together, it mattered little that Norwich had got £1 million for either Reeves or Fashanu as they'd already spent over £1 million (£1,325,000) on seven new players of their own. Easy come, easy go-with the Canaries not quite as cash rich as was initially thought.

Deehan had been seen as the perfect partner for Keith Bertschin in attack, the proverbial wily (but not so old) goal poacher who would be only too glad to feed off the knock downs, flicks, deflections and half chances that would come his way as a result of the presence of Bertschin in opposing teams penalty areas. He'd immediately impressed as well, scoring four times on his debut for Norwich in a friendly against Ipswich Town in Great Yarmouth just three days before Christmas. Friendly nor not, it was a much needed run out for the Canaries who hadn't played a game for nearly three weeks due to the icy snap that had set in over much of the country causing numerous postponements. It served its purpose as far as Ken Brown was concerned. Deehan looked sharp, motivated and, crucially, able to seize upon the smallest half chance and turn it into a goal – that goal poaching cum goal hanging quality that the Canaries hadn't had to call upon in their attack since the days of Ted MacDougall. One big difference between Supermac and Deehan was that the latter had arrived with substantial top flight experience to his name as well as the reputation to go with it. Prior to upping and moving to Norfolk, Deehan had spent his playing career in the Midlands, turning professional with Aston Villa in 1975 and going onto make 110 appearances for them, scoring forty goals; form and ability that saw him being called up by the full national side for a game against Brazil in 1978 although he ended up sitting that one out on the bench. The following year he signed for West Bromwich Albion for £500,000 but didn't make the same sort of impression at the Hawthorns that he had at Villa Park, getting just five goals in eighty-seven appearances for the Baggies, four of which were against the Canaries in the 1979/80 and 1980/81 seasons, games which saw him line up alongside an array of talented and attack minded teammates in Ron Atkinson's entertaining side, names such as Bryan Robson, Gary Owen, Peter Barnes and Cyrille Regis. You would have been excused for believing that, amidst such illustrious company, Deehan could only thrive, yet the opposite was true and the move to Norwich ended up being one that suited all parties, not least Deehan himself, who, after that impressive debut against Ipswich, scored again on his official league debut for the club in that otherwise more than forgettable capitulation against Luton Town at Carrow Road.

That defeat was followed by an almost as uninspiring 0-0 draw at Charlton, one that, in fairness, Norwich could have lost with the normally deadly Paul Walsh hitting the bar for Charlton before Martin Robinson somehow managed to miss when it would, as the saying goes, have been easier to score. Maybe the Canaries luck was changing, maybe that barely deserved point would see a change in their fortunes? The evidence for that was certainly there in the club's next game, a comfortable 2-0 win over Rotherham at Carrow Road on 16 January. The ease with which the Canaries dispatched their northern visitors that afternoon made a mockery of the manner in which they had surrendered to them on the opening day of the season. Yet it also gave some credence to Emlyn Hughes' comments after that match about Norwich still being one of the quality sides in the division. It wasn't, by any stretch of the imagination, an entertaining game, yet it did serve notice of things to come, one of them being, providing Ken Brown was able to continue to strengthen the squad, the evolution of a side that would be more than capable of putting together a promotion campaign the following season. No one expected it to happen at the end of this one now, not even after Deehan and Keith Bertschin had confirmed their potential as a decent strike force in the making with a goal each, Bertschin's chested-down half volley in front of the River End ending up as a candidate for one of the club's goals of the season.

Ken Brown had, by now, given full league debuts to three players who had come through the schoolboy and youth team ranks at Carrow Road, namely Andrew Hart, John Fashanu and Paul Haylock. Of these three, Paul Haylock was the one who made the very most of the opportunity, the Lowestoft-born full back going onto make nearly 200 league appearances for the club before the arrival of Ian Culverhouse from Tottenham saw him lose his place in the side. But, surprising as Haylock's rise to first team prominence might have been, it was, for many, overshadowed that season by the lack of impact made at the club by John Fashanu, Justin's younger brother who was held in similar high regard by the club. His first-team debut had arrived from the bench in the 2-1 win over Shrewsbury on 17 October and, if the game and circumstances were a little more low profile than Justin's debut in a game featured on *Match of the Day*, it was no less lively with John putting himself about in a similarly bold and confident manner.

Yet things never took off for John in the same way at Norwich as they had done for his brother. Perhaps the fact that he was following in his brother's footsteps counted against him from the start? Justin had exploded onto the senior footballing scene in spectacular fashion, his physical presence and prowess on the pitch nicely juxtaposing his quiet and immensely likeable character off it. Norwich fans had fallen in love with Justin from the start and he had reciprocated, feeling able to relax and perform in an environment where he felt cherished and protected from some of the pressured and expectations that came with the game. Now he had gone, people were, not unreasonably, expecting him to have a similar sort of impact on the football club. Expecting it, willing it, demanding it. This was all too much for John who, rather than being given the time and indulgences that Justin had been granted, was expected to hit the ground running. He ended up making just five first team appearances during the 1981/82 season, scoring one goal in the process which came in the 4-1 win over Derby County at Carrow Road.

It would be interesting to know quite what Ken Brown and the Norwich Coaching staff were expecting of John when he eventually broke through into the Canaries first-term squad. Most of the fans were hopeful he'd have the same sort of impact that Justin had, but was that unreasonable? John was, as things turned out, not a bad player at all, ending his senior career with eight years of top flight football with Wimbledon and Aston Villa, an FA Cup winner's medal and two full England caps. It was both a career and life in the game that ended up totally eclipsing that of his brothers, even if, for many more reasons, Justin is the brother who people more easily and fondly recall to this day-even if, with myriad television shows to his name as part of the wide ranging media career that John forged for himself, post football, ended up making John the bigger name but with Justin the abiding memory.

The fourth and final young player to be given a chance by Brown that season was Peter Mountford who made his debut as a second half replacement for Greig Shepherd in the 2-1 win against Chelsea at Carrow Road on 20 February. He, unlike Justin and John Fashanu had made quiet and relatively unheralded progress through the ranks at the club, so much so that, for some fans, his name was a completely unfamiliar one. Sadly for Peter, he wasn't able to seize both the opportunity and faith that had been placed in him and Paul Haylock by both Brown and Mel Machin and he eventually drifted away from the club and into non-league football after just four appearances for the Canaries. He wasn't able, unlike John Fashanu, to prove both the club and any doubters wrong either after he had left, going onto have a modest career in the game for much of the rest of the decade, one that included spells in London with Orient and Charlton Athletic.

Mountford's other appearance for the Canaries that season had come, again from the bench, in a 1-0 defeat to QPR at Carrow Road,[7] one that had seen Norwich remain in twelfth place in Division Two, nine places and nine points adrift of Oldham Athletic in third place – and with just sixteen league games remaining. Aspirations of promotion had long been forgotten but, despite that, the club announced that they were owed a considerable amount of money by Manchester

City for Kevin Reeves – even after the surprise (but welcome) return to the club by Martin O'Neill had seen the Canaries lower the amount outstanding for the Reeves deal by taking off the fee agreed for O'Neill from that total – assuming that Manchester City had even paid a fee for O'Neill in the first place. The whole affair brought footballing finances sharply into focus, making many fans aware, perhaps for the first time that, when two clubs agree a fee for a player, the amount initially paid is very small indeed with the balance due, as was the case with Reeves, due to be paid over a number of years. Folly perhaps on the part of Manchester City, committing themselves to a large transfer fee for Reeves that they clearly couldn't afford, yet perhaps the greater folly was made by Norwich for seeming to agree to a deal that was so clearly not in their favour. That is, of course, unless Manchester City defaulted on some of the payments, something which the return to Norwich for O'Neill suggests may well have been the case.

O'Neill had left Norwich in the first place because he had absolutely no desire at all to play his football in the Second Division, yet, barely eight months after he had left Norwich to join Bond and Reeves at Maine Road, here he was, back at Norwich, ready and prepared, it would seem to play twenty league games at just that level for a team that was, even then, didn't look as if it would be making an immediate return to the level O'Neill saw himself playing at. Maybe Manchester City had defaulted on the fee agreed for O'Neill and, in much the same way any business will respond if new goods are not paid for, Norwich had responded, not unnaturally, by insisting upon their return. On the face of it, his second coming was as surprising as the first. O'Neill remained an exceptional player, one who would, had his availability been more widely known, have courted much interest from several clubs in the First Division. Surely Manchester City could have sold him to one of them for a higher price than they had paid Norwich for and merely paid Norwich whatever was owed out of that fee? Failing that, they might also have tried to keep their yellow and green creditor at bay by offering Norwich a fringe player in lieu of the money owed rather than someone who would have been regarded as a key member of the squad. Then there was Martin O'Neill himself. Did he have any say in the deal that saw him ending up back at the club which he had, the previous spring, announced himself as being desperate to leave? He'd done so in what many had considered a mercenary manner as well – leaving because the club couldn't give him what he wanted even though he'd been an integral part of the team that had failed to sustain First Division football the previous season. The abrupt manner of his departure would hardly have endeared him to either the football club management or the Canary fans – even though it had been negotiated into his contract when he originally signed. But then no one at Carrow Road thought the club was going down at that point.

He certainly announced his renewed presence in the Canary ranks in some style, scoring a tremendous long range goal in his second debut against Sheffield Wednesday at Carrow Road on 3 February, a game Norwich lost despite being 2-1 up with only a quarter of an hour to go. It was the club's fifth league defeat in eight games and, even at that early stage, it appeared that the club was now playing for nothing more than mid-table respectability with all chances of promotion gone. The problem with that was that many of the club's up-and-coming players might not have been too willing for another campaign in Division Two, especially as some of them would already have admirers from clubs playing at a higher level; the likes of Chris Woods, Dave Watson and John Deehan, as well as O'Neill, all players who it might reasonably be expected would be off if the Canaries didn't go up.

Which would mean that, having built one new team, Ken Brown would probably have it all to do again the following summer. And with no guarantee that any of the funds that would be raised by the expected departures of some of the club's more high profile players would be made available for him to spend. But, more to the point, just how attractive a proposition would the club end up looking to those sort of players it might have still hoped to have a chance of signing? A recent relegation, the failed attempt to get promoted at the first (and best) opportunity and well known financial problems that had led to the departure of some of the club's best players. It was something that had a taste of a club going nowhere and a club that had little ambition. Not an attractive proposition for anyone, least of all those who were currently at the club. It was hardly a crisis, not by Norwich City standards at least. But, with the Canaries entering March in mid-table anonymity, Brown had a considerable task on his hands if he was to motivate his players enough for them to at least make something of the remaining two and a half months of the season and, in doing so, give the club's support at least some hope for the following campaign as well as boosting his chances of holding onto his job. There had already been talk of his possibly being replaced earlier in the season, rumours that would, undoubtedly, resurface as the club played out its remaining fixtures, especially if results and performances continued to be unsatisfactory.

Following the defeat to QPR, the club didn't have another league game for a fortnight when the visitors were Watford. The Hornets were having the sort of season that Norwich had expected for themselves – at kick-off they were second in the league and had experienced just five league defeats all season. The Canaries, on the other hand, had suffered five league defeats since just after Christmas and, when John Barnes put Watford ahead at Carrow Road after just five minutes, heads would have dropped on and off the field. There had been a glimmer of hope when O'Neill had equalised with a fine shot from Mick McGuire's pass, yet, just three minutes later, Les Taylor put Watford 2-1 up, a lead that they managed to hold onto until half time.

You get the feeling that Ken Brown knew it was now or never for both him and his team at the interval. A second successive home defeat would have led to some very searching questions being asked about him, the team and his continued position as manager of the club. And he wasn't prepared to let that happen. His reaction, much to the surprise of his players, was to let them have it. Both barrels, full hair drier treatment, no holds barred. Said players were, not surprisingly, shocked at his outburst. They were used to being hammered verbally by Mel Machin, but that was Mel's role, he was the bad cop to Ken's good one. For Brown to take on that mantle himself would have shown everyone in that dressing room, Machin included, just how frustrated and angry he was. He had a good team, he knew it, and the players knew it. Money had been provided and the evidence of the board's recent largesse was collectively sat in front of him in the shape of Chris Woods, Dave Watson, Martin O'Neill, John Deehan and nine others, with three of the clubs starting XI on the day not subject to a transfer fee when they had joined the club. In Woods, Watson and O'Neill the club had, quite possibly, the best goalkeeper, central defender and midfielder in the division. Yet neither they nor the club were, and had been, performing as well as he, the fans and, critically, the board of directors thought they were capable of. It was beyond frustrating and, for once, Brown had ran out of sympathies, patience and his trademark good humour with stories swiftly emanating from the club that he had told the players he was 'ashamed' of them, adding that they had played 'like fairies'. Good old fashioned abuse but the sort of abuse that professional footballers, then and now, don't like to see levelled at them. They offered little in response, at least verbally. But the light that had come on in their eyes in retaliation at Brown's tirade told him all he wanted to know. And that was that he was going to get the reaction he'd hoped his uncharacteristic outburst would result in.

The second half of that game was the turning point for the Canaries, not just for that season but Brown's tenure as manager of the club. Prior to then he had been regarded with respect and no little admiration, yet he had, for some, always been seen as the safe hand at the tiller, a quiet and uncontroversial figure perfectly suited to lead the club in the wake of John Bond's departure. Yet he was much, much more than that. Brown, like his predecessor, had been steeped in the rich footballing traditions of West Ham United, the club where he had spent fifteen years as a player, winning an FA Cup winners medal as well as one in the European Cup Winners Cup. He'd played at the highest level and had the medals to prove it. He'd even played for England on one occasion, no mean feat when you consider the calibre of player he was up against at the time to even merit a place in the squad, never mind the team itself. There was little doubt in his mind that he could achieve as much in the game as a manager as he could a player, but if he was to do that, then his expensively gathered team had to deliver which is exactly what he told them during the half time break in that game against Watford. And they delivered. Fifteen minutes into the second half, the bleeding and battered figure of Dave Watson soared above the massed ranks of the Watford defence to head the equaliser. Five minutes later, Norwich were ahead after John Deehan scored from a penalty. There was even time for a fourth goal for the Canaries when Keith Bertschin scored in the seventy-fourth minute. Norwich were now 4-2 up and in complete control, seeing the game out without giving their opponents, especially the dangerous Barnes a second to dwell on the ball, squeezing the life out of their opponents, snapping into their tackles and pressing high up the pitch. It was, without a doubt, their most impressive display of the season, one that showed just what they might be capable of and what might have been if this realisation had come about earlier. The Canaries were now in thirteenth place, eleven points shy of Blackburn in third place.

More to the point, Leicester City, the team directly above them in the league by one point also had the luxury of three games in hand over Norwich, grim facts that soon cast a cloud over the post-match celebrations that had, albeit briefly, sparked talk of a late surge for a place in the top three (leaders Luton were now eighteen, and, potentially, twenty-four points ahead of Norwich with their own two games in hand) and an unlikely promotion, hope rather than expectation that was immediately dimmed three days later when Norwich travelled to East London to face Orient, twenty-first in the table and fresh from two heavy defeats that had seen them concede eight goals. If there was to be a footballing renaissance at Norwich, a comeback from the mid-table dead that would have shamed Lazarus himself then the Canaries had to prove it by winning games like this one.

Which they didn't.

It was an appalling game of football played in front of just 2,933 mostly cynical souls at Brisbane Road. Billy Jennings, an FA Cup winner with West Ham in 1975, had put Orient ahead after just ten minutes and, with Mervyn Day, one of his Wembley teammates on that Saturday afternoon having one of those trademark 'worldie' performances that opposing keepers always seem to have against Norwich in crucial matches, things looked bleak for Norwich for a while, especially after Day miraculously kept out a Deehan effort, only for the ever alert and hugely underrated Ross Jack to follow up by nodding the resultant loose ball into an empty net, a goal that should, just as it had done a few days earlier, sparked a yellow and green surge of attacking play and goals. Watford, after all, hadn't been able to contend with a Norwich side in full flow, so should Orient? Seemingly yes, they could and, with their recently beleaguered defence now collectively having the game of their lives, the Os held on for the draw. The only real spark of life on the pitch in the second half being the stretchering off of Orient midfielder John Margerrison, who'd come out second best after a challenge from the ever lively Bertschin, a forwards tackle born out of frustration that, yet again, after seemingly taking a step forward, Norwich were taking two back again. It was frustrating, it was annoying, and it was painful. It was Norwich City.

Which is why the run of form the Canaries suddenly found themselves in after their visit to the Orient was so mystifying. That and all manner of good things, yes, of course it was. But that didn't alter the fact that, suddenly and completely unexpectedly, the club won ten of its remaining twelve league fixtures, a sequence that between 17 April and 8 May 1982, saw six consecutive wins, the eighteen points won in that time lifting Norwich from mid-table to, on the dawn of their penultimate league game of the season, to a potential promotion winning place in third place. And what a run it was. Amongst the sides swept aside were Charlton Athletic (5-0), Derby County (2-0) and, in one of their finest league performances of the entire decade, never mind that season, fellow promotion hopefuls Leicester City, Gary Lineker (so that's why he doesn't like us?) and all who were crushed 4-1 at Filbert Street with Norman Leet's own goal adding to the Foxes woes after John Deehan, Mark Barham and Keith Bertschin had made the game safe. A tense but ultimately well-deserved 2-1 win against Grimsby Town at Carrow Road followed four days later which meant that, on the morning of Saturday 5 May, the Canaries were preparing to meet Orient in a game which, if they won, would almost certainly mean that if they followed that up with a win against Sheffield Wednesday at Hillsborough in their last game of the season, a very unlikely promotion would be confirmed, one that had looked dim, distant and thoroughly out of reach after the scrappy point won against Orient themselves just a few weeks earlier. Not surprisingly, it was a nervous and jittery Norwich that took to the pitch against their already relegated opponents who must have wondered what all the fuss had been about. Norwich had huffed and puffed and generally looked out of sorts and uninspired at Brisbane Road and now, eight weeks later, it didn't look as if too much had changed. Was this really a team that had won nine out of their ten league games? If it was, then, on the evidence of their first half display at Carrow Road, they most certainly weren't about to make it ten out of eleven. And Norwich probably wouldn't have done if it hadn't been for Ken Brown. It had been Brown who'd given them the out of character bollocking at half time in the game against Watford that had inspired them to a vital win, one that had been the springboard of their remarkable late season run.

Now he found himself in the same position in this rather more important match with players looking to him for inspiration and a reason to believe they could overcome their nerves and get the win they desperately needed. And Brown delivered. But not with angry words, gestures, accusations or flying teacups. Not this time. He would have been passionate yet very calm; gently cajoling his players to give one more big performance, reminding them that they were all better players than their opponents and that the win was within their grasp, a win that could lead to bigger and better things that August. How much did they want to win, how many of them would prefer games at Anfield, Old Trafford and Highbury next season over trips to the Abbey Stadium, Boundary Park or Gay Meadow? 35,000 at Manchester United or down at Orient again in front of a couple of thousand? What do you want more? He spoke, his players listened. And they delivered. No more than three minutes of the second half had gone when O's defender Nigel Gray upended John Deehan in the penalty area, the resultant penalty seeing Bertschin score with consummate ease. Carrow Road erupted in joy and relief, just as it did again near the end when Dave Bennett sumptuously shot past Day to make the score 2-0 and six consecutive league wins for the Canaries, a sequence that now had them on the edge of promotion, something which would have been regarded as completely and utterly unthinkable only a month earlier.

Promotion was attainable. But it was going to make for a nervy last day for anyone and everyone connected with the club. Prior to the last Saturday of the league season, the top of the Division Two table looked like this:

|  | Played | Points |
|---|---|---|
| 1 Luton Town | 40 | 84 |
| 2. Watford | 41 | 80 |
| 3. Norwich City | 41 | 71 |
| 4. Rotherham | 41 | 67 |
| 5. Sheffield Weds | 41 | 67 |
| 6. QPR | 41 | 66 |
| 7. Barnsley | 41 | 66 |
| 8. Leicester City | 40 | 65 |

It looked clear-cut. And, for the most part, it was. Luton were going up as champions with Watford in second place with the Canaries set to join them as the third promoted team, that nervous win over Orient meaning that none of Rotherham, Sheffield Wednesday, QPR or Barnsley could now catch them.

Except of course, Leicester City, seemingly down and out in 8th place could – and their last two games were at home to Shrewsbury Town, who were in the bottom six and the long ago doomed Orient – whilst Norwich's last game was at Sheffield Wednesday who were fifth and, if out of the promotion race, a team that would have more than enough about them to give Norwich a game at Hillsborough. If Norwich lost that game whilst Leicester won both of theirs – both very plausible scenarios – then it was possible that Leicester might yet beat Norwich to that third promotion place on goal difference. So things were going to be very tense indeed up at Sheffield on a sunny spring afternoon. Yet, with nearly 10,000 Norwich fans making the trip north, everything was in place for a promotion party. Even a draw would be enough for Norwich, surely that wasn't beyond them? And yet, just as it had done against Orient, the Canaries found themselves affected by nerves on the day. That wasn't surprising. Hillsborough was a mighty stage, the reward for success even mightier. But the fans were united at Wednesday with Brown, barracked mercilessly earlier in the season, and eleven goal Bertschin now the subjects of adulation rather than criticism.

Norwich's 10,000-strong travelling army of support had endured a tense first half that had seen a few near misses and scares. But they survived to the break with the point they needed in hand as the two teams went in with the scores at 0-0. Then news filtered through of Leicester's game at home to Shrewsbury, one everyone expected them to win. That was also 0-0. Things were looking good.

They weren't looking quite so good at around 4.15pm however. With radio reports informing anyone who wanted (or didn't want) to know that Leicester were putting increased pressure on the Shrewsbury defence and looking likely to score, Sheffield Wednesday did just that themselves when Andy McCulloch met a Terry Curran corner to put the Owls 1-0 up. Pandemonium and panic ensued in the massed ranks of yellow and green when it was revealed that Leicester had finally scored and were now 1-0 up and looking to comfortably secure the win that everyone had expected they would get. Desperation set in amongst the Norwich fans which turned to sudden, unadulterated delight when Keith Bertschin met a cross from Dave Bennett to equalise. Now promotion was suddenly there for the taking for Norwich, all they had to do was hold onto the precious point Bertschin's strike would gain them and they'd be promoted, regardless of what Leicester did in their game.

Yet, as the swaying, dancing and jumping Norwich fans took their collective eyes off the game to focus on the party, there was another twist to the tale when Gary Bannister stole into the Norwich penalty area to head a Mel Sterland pass past Chris Woods to put the Owls 2-1 up only a few seconds later. Despair that had become delight became despair again, all the more so as Wednesday held on for their win, one that saw them finish it just one point behind the Canaries, and agonisingly close to promotion themselves. But not as half as agonising as what the Norwich fans were going through. The season, for them, had ended. Norwich remained in third place in the table with 71 points and a goal difference of +14 whilst Leicester, by virtue of their 1-0 win over Shrewsbury were up to sixth place with a goal difference of +12 meaning that a three goal winning margin for them in their final game at Orient would see them go up instead of the Canaries. And, at that time, as the final whistle went at Hillsborough that Saturday afternoon, there would have been more than a few Norwich fans who would have thought them more than capable of doing that against a team that had already conceded ninety-eight league goals that season.

And yet things weren't quite as they had initially seemed. Because Leicester

City had not won their game against Shrewsbury, or even scored the goal that had set the cat in amongst the 10,000 Canaries. In an age where instant digital communication of any kind still strictly in the realms of science fiction at best, the rumour about the Leicester goal had been made, spoken, spread and believed. No one had bothered to check because there was no way of doing so, short of pressing a despairing ear to *Sport on Two* on the radio. Yet there it was, in the still and quiet of the post-match wake it transpired that their game had ended in a 0-0 draw and that Norwich City were promoted.

It had been a close thing. Had, for example, the new system of three points for a win not been introduced at the beginning of the 1981/82 season then, under the previous one of two points for a win, it would have been Sheffield Wednesday, not Norwich who would have been going up in third place. It also brought into focus just how important Norwich's 4-1 win at Leicester had been, because had Leicester won that one, as expected then yes, it would have been them finishing the season in third place and not Norwich. But then if Norwich had not put together that remarkable end of season run, one that saw those eleven wins from a very lucky thirteen games prior to the Sheffield trip, then they would have ended that campaign nearer to the bottom three in the division than the top three.

Ken Brown would, very likely, have found himself out of a job. Yet he was now a hero, a man who had repeated the much lauded achievements of Ron Saunders and John Bond in getting the Canaries promoted to the top flight of English football, securing, in the process, his long term prospects in the job, a remarkable achievement for a man who, less than six months earlier was being seen as an imminent managerial casualty, something which Bond became himself the following February when he was sacked as Manchester City manager. It's highly unlikely that Ken Brown took any pleasure in his onetime colleague's demise at Maine Road – yet, at the same time, he might also have been excused for being glad that he'd ended up staying where he was and enjoying First Division football again with it whilst Bond remained out of work until he accepted an offer to manage Burnley, then in Division Three four months later. The two men, teammates and colleagues for such a long time at West Ham, Torquay, Bournemouth and Norwich would not come up against each other in a match ever again.

The footballing Summer of 1982 was dominated by the World Cup, held in Spain and won by Italy. For Norwich fans, there was the thrill of watching one of their own play in the tournament as Martin O'Neill skippered Northern Ireland to some notable triumphs, not least their 1-0 win against the home nation. The Canaries almost had a second representative in the finals in Wynton Rufer. He was in Spain as the youngest member, at just nineteen, of the New Zealand national team, appearing at their first ever World Cup. Rufer was still a relative newcomer to the squad but had more than distinguished himself by scoring the winning goal in the Kiwis 2-1 win over China, that victory being the one that secured their place in the finals. He'd already been voted the New Zealand Young Player of the Year in 1981 and 1982, more than enough to have attracted the attention of Ken Brown who invited Wynton plus Shane, his old brother, to Norwich for a trial, the younger Rufer impressing enough to be offered a professional contract which he signed in October 1981. His signing caused quite a stir locally with lots of attention focused on the Canaries first Kiwi by the local media as well as, an ultimate accolade, a place for Rufer in one of *Shoot!* magazine's legendary 'Focus On' features which included a photograph of Rufer in his Norwich shirt.

Despite the signing, Norwich fans never got the opportunity to see Rufer feature in a competitive first team game as,[8] almost from the minute he signed, the Home Office made things as difficult as they could for him to get the work permit needed in order for Rufer to play for his new club. The more effort and advice that the Canaries took in order to get the necessary paperwork signed off, the more difficult it seemed to become for them, the decision of the Home Office not to grant it bordering on the ridiculous, considering Rufer's standing and reputation in the game already as well as the fact that he was all set to play in a World Cup. And all of this in addition to the fact he was from a nation that was part of the Commonwealth where, it was thought, the eventual granting of the relevant permit would be nothing more than a formality. Yet, despite all that, the Home Office's decision was final and irrecoverable and, just over six months after he had signed for Norwich, the Canaries had no choice but to release him from his contract so that he could pursue his career with FC Zurich in Switzerland. He had considerable success there as well as, later on in his career, with Werder Bremen in Germany's Bundesliga for whom, in 1992, he scored their second goal in the club's 2-0 win over AS Monaco in that seasons European Cup Winners Cup final. Even to this day, the decision taken by the Home Office seems a puzzling one. Clubs were not, as is the case today, filling their squads with players from all over the world, yet there was still a fairly generous number of continental players in the English game, many of whom had no problems whatsoever getting a work permit. This was even if they were, as was the case, for example, of Drazen Muzinic and other Yugoslav's e.g. Dzemal Hadziandic who'd signed for Swansea from FK Velež Mostar.[9] Rufer's eventual success and longevity at the highest level of the game[10] make an absolute mockery of the Home Offices refusal to grant him the work permit he needed to play in the game in England with Norwich not the only club to have had their squad building plans thwarted by that departments inconsistency, one which happily marries politics with sport and, all too often, despite a positive decision clearly being in everyone's best interests, is only too happy to let the former sully the latter.

Thus Norwich fans sat and watched O'Neill have an outstanding World Cup for Northern Ireland, thinking, as they did, of what was to come. Plus what might have been as Rufer did more than enough to show that both the Canaries and English football had a potential star in their hands-one, that is, who was now set to display his talents in Switzerland. Some might have thought that it was a pity that the Home Office hadn't been so officious with their ruling when the Canaries had signed Drazen Muzinic. His struggles to adapt to life in and around the club since his arrival from Hadjuk Split two years previously had been pitiful – not least, it should be added, because of Muzinic's desire to come for the money first, second and third – with the football a lot further down the line. He hadn't integrated at all and his insistence of using a translator, employed by the club, only added to the overall farce that his signing, a Norwich record, had been. Fortunately, mercifully and not a second too soon, Ken Brown had, by the end of the Canaries unexpected promotion season known to cut his losses, releasing Muzinic from his contract with the club a year in advance. With, unsurprisingly, no new offers forthcoming from any clubs in England, Muzinic swiftly returned to Yugoslavia and out of the game altogether, becoming a restaurateur on the Adriatic island of Brac. One not quite and one never was then as far as the playing ranks at Carrow Road were concerned in the build up to the 1982/83 season. But then it wasn't as if Ken Brown needed to completely revamp his squad in time for their latest assault on Division One football. He had, remember, brought in a number of quality players during the club's relegation season before adding some more during the club's promotion season. Indeed, both his and the club's intentions seemed more focused upon lowering the club's wage bill by shipping out some of the Canaries fringe players. In addition to Muzinic therefore, the summer of 1982 also saw the departures of Andrew Hart, Mark Nightingale and Grieg Shepherd. With those four being added to the five players who had, for one reason or another, left the club during the 1981/82 season (Willie Donachie, Phil Hoadley, Graham Paddon, Joe Royle and Clive Woods) it meant that Brown would be starting the new season minus nine of the players who had commenced the previous one with him back in the Second Divison. From that list the player who would perhaps be missed the most, as far as the fans were concerned, was Graham Paddon. His role and prominence in the team during the 1981/82 campaign had been, admittedly, peripheral (he made just 8 league appearances all season) but he was still very much a fans favourite. He'd started the season in the number 10 shirt but lost his place in the team after being substituted in the 2-1 home defeat to Oldham on 3 October, his last, as it turned out, game for the club. He went onto join Millwall on loan before ending his professional career in the USA with the Tampa Bay Rowdies, a flamboyant stage and club for one of the games true entertainers as well as a genuinely nice man, one who was lost to the game when he died at the tragically young age of fifty-seven in November 2007.

The experience and nous of Joe Royle would also be missed by the Canaries. He'd been forced to retire from playing in April 1982 having made forty-seven league appearances and scoring ten goals – a more than respectable return for the man who was, lest we forget, the first ever player to score a goal in a Norwich City game played in the top flight of English football – albeit with Everton, Royle scoring the opener in the 1-1 draw at Carrow Road on 12 August 1972. It was, therefore, sadly fitting that he should end his playing career at the club where he was the first player to make his mark at the highest level a decade earlier. Not that he was finished with the game. Royle was appointed manager of Oldham Athletic in July 1982, returning to Carrow Road as their manager for the first time in January 1992 where goals from Andy Holden and Paul Bernard earned his side an unexpected victory at his previous footballing home.

The Canaries first match back in Division One was, fittingly perhaps, against Manchester City at Carrow Road on 28 August 1982, an early chance for Ken Brown to get the proverbial one over his former colleague and friend John Bond. The match-up between the two sides – or, rather, the two men – generated a lot of local headlines which, not surprisingly, Anglia TV attempted to turn into a television event reminiscent of the meeting between Don Revie and his successor at Leeds United, Brian Clough in the summer of 1974 which was instigated by Yorkshire TV. Brown and Bond both turned down the request of Anglia's Gerry Harrison to get together for a pre-match studio meeting, choosing to focus on the game. It is, of course, more than conceivable that the two of them had both moved on by then anyway and that any conflict or bad blood between them was all in the mind of those that wanted to talk up the supposed fall out of a few years earlier. As it was, the two publicly got together at the end of the game anyway, in their own time and at their own behest, that simple little act making it quite clear that there hadn't been, and wasn't, an issue between the two of them. And, as a Norwich fan, it was good to see. For, in one way or another, John Bond has never really gone away from Carrow Road, much as Ron Saunders (who, ironically, also quit the Canaries for Manchester City) had also been prominent in the club's immediate history after he left, albeit with Aston Villa. Bond would, on the day, have been the happier of the two men, Manchester City winning the game 2-1 with, and here's another ex-Canary connection,[11] former Norwich striker David Cross opening the scoring for the Sky Blues after just three minutes with Paul Power scoring a second right on half time. Norwich played well and deserved their goal, scored by John Deehan, yet ultimately found the Manchester City defence, one that was superbly marshalled by Tommy Caton too strong to breach a second time.

An opening day defeat then but no disaster. Two years previously the Canaries had beaten Stoke City 5-1, a game and result that caused a lot of excitement only for the season to end in relegation whilst, twelve months earlier, they'd crashed 4-1 at Rotherham only to end the season as one of three promoted teams. A narrow defeat therefore neither suggested either forthcoming calamity or goals and table topping glory. But it did suggest progress and a team that, slowly but very surely and confidently, was looking like it might be one of the finest the club had put out for many a season, one that might even go onto eclipse Bonds 1975/76 team that had finished that season 10th in Division One. Time would tell but the signs were encouraging, particularly if Brown could add a little more depth to his squad which was rich in talent yet one that would, given the inevitable injuries and suspensions that came throughout a season, would have to rely rather too much on a host of young and, for the main part, inexperienced players, a possibility that was made reality when Brown ended up giving four more of the Canaries youth team players their competitive league debuts by Christmas.[12]

Three days later the Canaries made the trip down to Highbury to play an Arsenal side looking to get their season up and running after losing their opening game 2-1 at Stoke City. With Greg Downs missing, Ken Brown took the opportunity to give a Norwich debut to Colin Smith, signed after his release from Nottingham Forest earlier in the year. Brown's signing of Smith was a punt, something that might, or might not, have come off. He was twenty-four and had been with Forest for six years without making a first team appearance but had, at least, progressed to Captain of Brian Clough's impressive reserve team, his own access to first team football blocked by the form and consistency of the Forest defence, one that boasted names like Viv Anderson, Frank Gray, John McGovern, Larry Lloyd, Kenny Burns and David Needham. No easy task. He could, therefore, have been another Dave Watson in waiting and it was undoubtedly with that in mind that Brown made him his first signing of that season.

Smith did well enough at Highbury, where Norwich secured a creditable 1-1 draw to keep his place in the Norwich defence for the following game at Swansea. The Swans had enjoyed a fantastic start to the previous campaign, winning seven out of their opening ten fixtures to lead the table by mid-October and had stayed the course throughout, ending the season in sixth place. They had been tipped to struggle this time around but had started the season with one loss and one win, going onto make it two wins from three by giving the Canaries the sort of hammering that would have reminded too many fans of their struggles in the top league last time around, Bob Latchford's hat trick doing the majority of the damage in their emphatic 4-0 win. Three games played, one point and just two goals to show for it and, if Ken Brown wasn't yet worried at his teams start to the season, he would have been keen to get a first win as soon as possible. That game in the Canaries next game where they scored, rather than conceded, four goals – and by half time, eventually seeing off a woeful Birmingham City 5-1, a win made all the more satisfying as the man in charge at St Andrew's was none other than former Canaries manager Ron Saunders. The highlight of the game was an outstanding performance by Martin O'Neill who also contributed two goals, the enigmatic midfielder now fully settled back into things at Carrow Road and revelling in the central midfield position that had been given to him by Brown. Yet O'Neill needed grafters alongside him in the Norwich midfield in order to dominate the game in the way he could, players who could win the ball, read and place a pass and generally supplement him as well as he did them. O'Neill was therefore fortunate to be playing alongside Mick McGuire and Peter Mendham, the latter, in particular, blossoming into a fine player, one who would almost certainly be capable of taking on the O'Neill role in the side himself when the day came, as most people thought it would, for the Northern Ireland Captain to announce he was on his travels again. There remains a feeling that he was back at the club through no real choice of his own, that it was a decision and move foisted onto him through Manchester City's growing financial crisis-plus the fact they owed Norwich a lot of money, money they simply did not have. If that was the case, O'Neill was supremely professional about it in both his attitude to the club and the forty-three League and Cup appearances he made that season. He did, of course, leave the club – and, for the second time, before anyone at Norwich wanted him to go, returning to Nottingham to sign for Notts County the following August.

He returned to Norwich for the third time in 1995 to become the Canaries new manager, but, again, his stay at Carrow Road was shorter than hoped as he left prematurely for the third time, this time to take over as manager of Leicester City less than six months after replacing Gary Megson at Norwich. He has since admitted that, on that third occasion, his error was not leaving Carrow Road after such a short time but taking the job in the first place, telling *The Journal* in 2012 that '... my dear old friend Mel Machin was a coach at Norwich and he told me, "Don't go, because you won't get on with Mr Chase" – and of course, I did not take his advice. He was right.'

Despite O'Neill's presence as a player in those opening weeks of the 1982/83 season, Norwich struggled, that win over Birmingham being their only victory in their opening ten league games. By the time Tottenham had won themselves a point at Carrow Road with a 0-0 draw on 16 October, the Canaries were just one off the bottom of Division One, their poor run of form now including defeats at home to West Brom (1-3) and at Sunderland (4-1). In a desperate attempt to pep up his side, Ken Brown had now given Canary debuts to three more new faces, namely left back Dennis van Wijk on a free from Ajax; Phil Alexander, a £2,000 purchase from Wokingham Town and Mike Walsh, a proverbial no-nonsense centre half who had been signed on loan from Everton to replace Everton fan and defensive lynchpin Dave Watson who was out with injury. In the five game run of matches he missed, the Canaries won just one game, conceding nine goals in the first three of them.

Watson was already proving himself to be one of the club's most important and valuable players, so important in fact, that Ken Brown went onto describe him as the club's 'crown jewel'. Watson was certainly enjoying himself and his role in the side as the season progressed – although, as he later admitted, some of the coach rides back to Norwich after an away game could be a little bit trying, describing each day away as '... a three-day camel ride ... I remember Keith Bertschin when he first came to the club, just sitting, looking out of the window on the bus back to Norwich and him saying, "If I see another, I'm going to crack!" because that's all you could see for miles and miles – all these bleeding cabbages.'[13] The big skies and vast agricultural plains of East Anglia might have been proving a difficult nut for Watson to crack. But he was having no such problem adapting to First Division football week in and week out, so much so that he made his England U21 debut in September 1983, lining up alongside teammate Chris Woods in a 4-1 win over Denmark. The fact that the game was played at Carrow Road and his, plus Woods (playing his first game at that level since April 1980) appearance might have had something to do with the FA wanting a big crowd (it was just 7,836) on the night might have been one consideration but it wasn't a one off as he went onto make another six appearances at that level, scoring in a 6-1 rout of France in a Euro U21 quarter final tie the following February. It was clear that the Canaries had a future star on their hands – but how long would they be able to keep him at Carrow Road? As far as the Canaries League form was concerned, things didn't improve much at all from that disappointing start and, by the end of March, City slipped back into twenty-first place and one off the bottom after a 1-1 draw at home to West Ham. Things were looking bleak. With little to no money to spend, Brown had blooded youngsters Mark Metcalf, Mark Crowe and Louie Donowa into the first team. Of that youthful trio, big things were expected of Mark Crowe in particular with his former teammate in the Canaries Youth side at the time and future Norwich legend Jeremy Goss having no doubt at the time that Southwold born Crowe, a striker, was going to make it at first team level, Goss recalling in his 2014 autobiography that, 'Mark Crowe was, perhaps, of all the players in our squad that season, the one who was most fancied to go on and have a big career in the game. He was named the Youth Team Player of the Season at the end of that [1982/83] campaign, that in a team, remember, that did the League and Cup double – so some achievement. He made his first team debut as a sub in the game at Brighton that December when he was still seventeen and was our Captain and an England Youth International. Everyone talked about him. Mark Crowe, next big thing to come out of Carrow Road.'[14] Except, sadly for Norwich and for Crowe, he was not. Despite his stellar performances for the Youth team and all the goals he scored, his one and only senior game for the Canaries was that debut game as he came off the bench to replace Steve Walford at Brighton, one that City lost 3-0, that game also turning out to be Peter Mountford's fourth and final game for the club. The Canaries bright young things all seemed, with one exception, to be failing to deliver as expected. Brown needed to get a wise old head aboard, and fast, if the season was not going to end with another relegation and with it, almost certainly, the sack.

The answer came in the shape of a twenty-four-year-old who had otherwise been seeing time and his football career, at least, at Bristol Rovers, then in Division Three, the man in question turning up at Eastville after a brief spell playing in Australia as well as just four appearances for Newcastle United. Hardly inspiring stuff – that is, at least, until you considered the earlier part of his playing career. It included forty-six appearances for England during which time he scored twenty-one goals as well as securing an FA Cup winners medal. He was, of course, the irrepressible Mike Channon. The ever-popular Channon now confesses he feels that he was fortunate to have even been given a chance by Norwich in the first place. In an interview he gave to the Norwich City club programme in March 2015, Channon looked back at the circumstances that led to Norwich signing him, saying, 'I was a lucky lad then because I was in the twilight of my career – perhaps I should say I was just at my peak! – and I was lucky that Ken Brown picked me up to give me another chance at Norwich.' Exactly who was the luckiest is questionable. Channon may well have thought he was fortunate but then so were the Canaries, who got one of the most experienced and respected players of the age in their team-and for nothing. It was a signing that John Bond, who had, of course brought Martin Peters to the club as well as being unsuccessful in trying to add Bobby Moore and Alan Ball to his Norwich side, would have been proud to call his own. Yet, when it came to bringing ageing maestros to Carrow Road was concerned, Brown wasn't finished yet. Channon made his Norwich debut in the thrilling and wholly unexpected 3-2 win over Ipswich Town at Portman Road on 27 December. Their opponents had enjoyed (or endured) a bit of a roller coaster season up until that game, dropping to bottom place in Division One after a 3-2 home defeat to Stoke City on 18 September before rallying and winning seven of their next twelve games to lift themselves up into 7th place. Two more defeats followed so, by the time Norwich came calling, Bobby Ferguson's team were determined to put things right and get back on a winning run again-and who better to do it against than the old enemy, one who had been struggling for form and results themselves. The excitement that the game generated was enough to not only nearly fill Portman Road but, unusually, see a game there played in something resembling a good atmosphere as both the home fans and the massed ranks of yellow and green attending looked to out sing, chant and generally abuse one another. For those that focused on the pitch rather than one another, a classic game was promptly served up with Norwich taking a shock lead after twenty-four minutes when Peter Mendham headed past Paul Cooper. Pandemonium followed as the shocked Ipswich fans demanded an instant reply, something which they got, albeit not straight away, when Russell Osman buried a header of his own to make it 1-1 at the break.

In amidst the carnage, rough and tumble was Channon, enjoying every second of his shock return to the big time, making, despite his advancing years, those little runs and dashes for space that characterised him as a player, desperate for even a half chance so he could celebrate a pell-mell debut with a goal. A second goal did come but not for Channon, as the ever busy Mendham crashed a second in via the crossbar. Again a Norwich lead against the odds, again the demands from the home fans for an instant equaliser. This time they got it for, only three minutes later, Paul Mariner converted a cross from Eric Gates. 2-2 and twenty minutes left, time for a hero. But who would answer the call? For the home side there was a wide array of suspects, of proven danger men in a side that was ladled with quality. Mariner, Gates, Thijssen, John Wark or Alan Brazil. Or, for the visitors, Keith Bertschin, as keen as you would expect to score against one of his former clubs, Mark Barham or the increasingly influential Martin O'Neill. In the end it was O'Neill who broke the deadlock, his marvellous curling shot from distance with two minutes left coming at exactly the right time for Norwich, giving the Canaries only a short time to hold on to their lead which they managed to do, securing, in the process, their most impressive and certainly their most important win of the season so far. In terms of league placings, it hadn't done much – a short step from twenty-first to twentieth place in the table, still, admittedly, in one of the relegation places but, as both the first away win for Brown's side that season as well as the first away league fixture since early October that saw the Canaries even score a goal, it was a priceless boost to the teams morale especially with a winnable home game to come against Luton just twenty-four hours later.

Yes, two games in two days, a quirk of the fixture list in the 1980s that would have today's players united in protest. But not then. Footballers just wanted to play and Ken Brown had no qualms whatsoever in selecting an unchanged side for the game against the Hatters, similarly buoyed themselves after a derby game win themselves the previous day, a 1-0 success over Watford. But Norwich were not to be denied this rich opportunity to seal back to back league wins in the top flight for first time that season with Channon rolling back the years after just over ten minutes to score his first goal for Norwich in their 1-0 win in what was an otherwise unremarkable match, characterised by tetchiness on both sides, something highlighted by Luton manager David Pleat officially reporting Norwich coach Mel Machin to the Football League post match for attempting to delay his team in their efforts to take a throw in. Pleat's actions were perhaps not too surprising-he was now beginning to find himself under the same sort of pressure as Brown had been earlier in the season. That pressure was now, at least, a little less intense as far as the Norwich boss was concerned but, with four crucial league games to come for Norwich in January, two of which were against Manchester City and Everton, Brown knew it was time for his club to start a good run if they were to avoid the 'too little, too late' manner of their relegation two years earlier when a run of four consecutive wins in their last six league games had been – well, too little and too late. The recovery had to start now and it had to start at Stoke City on New Year's Day.

Stoke though, had something to prove themselves and were as desperate for a result as the Canaries were. They'd lost 4-0 at Notts County on the same day as Norwich had seen off Luton, a result which had seen them slip down to fifteenth place in Division One. A win for Norwich would see them move up to just one point behind Stoke meaning that the Potters would then be tangled up in the relegation fight themselves, along with the Canaries and half a dozen or so other teams. It was no surprise then, in a match that saw two sides whose first priority was not to lose, that the game turned into an attritional slog with few chances and even less football played. For Norwich, John Deehan slotted into an unfamiliar left back position in order for Brown to continue to play Channon and Bertschin in attack, a thankless task for them as it turned out with a very physical Stoke City side, one that contained more than its fair share of tough, uncompromising players,[15] keeping them both quiet with Norwich's best chance falling to Deehan, marauding upfield like a prototype Gareth Bale in his left back position having a shot cleared off the line. In the end, Sammy McIllroy's first half goal won the game for Stoke, the former Manchester United player capitalising on a slip from Deehan to score.

Two games in five days followed for the Canaries, both against Swansea City. Most fans would have willingly forfeited the FA Cup third round game on 8 January in return for a league win five days previously and, when Mike Channon stole in to give Norwich the lead, a goal that saw the Canaries dominate the game from then on in, most would have been happy to have the three points in exchange for a characteristic early exit from the FA Cup that weekend. It was certainly not a tie that grasped the imagination of the Norfolk and Norwich public. An attendance of 16,296 had turned up at Carrow Road for the league game yet only 13,222 bothered with the FA Cup follow up. Where had the 3,000 missing fans gone? They missed an entertaining game, one that Norwich won 2-1 thanks to two goals from Keith Bertschin who also missed a penalty. That win constituted a Cup run for the Canaries whose recent record in the FA Cup, just six appearances in the 5th round in the last twenty years, was, to say the least, abysmal for a club that had once reached the semi-final as a Division Three side – and that was about it. There was now some hope that Ken Brown would take steps to put that right and set the club on a decent run in the competition. This was, after all, a time when the competition still held its old fashioned allure, a trophy everyone wanted to win, maybe even more than the League itself. The fact that Ken Brown made just one change to the side which had played the Swans in that important league game (Dennis van Wijk in for Channon) is testament to that, a competition which was still, at the time, treated with a great deal of respect.

Three consecutive league defeats followed the league win against Swansea, a seasonal nadir made worse by the fact that in those three games Norwich only managed to score one goal – but conceded eight in reply. The 1-0 reverse at home to Everton had been bad enough. City had huffed and puffed throughout but offered little to nothing in attack, the loudest cheer of the day coming when fans favourite Bertschin came on as a substitute in place of Dennis Van Wijk. But the cheers swiftly turned to jeers by the end of the game, a whole chorus of them accompanying the team's departure from the pitch, Kevin Ratcliffe the scorer of the Everton goal. That game had been preceded by a 4-1 defeat at Manchester City,[16] a result that did little to save John Bond from the sack at Maine Road with his dismissal being confirmed a little over three weeks later after a run of just three wins in twelve league games for the Sky Blues.

Much later on in his career, John Bond admitted that he'd regretted leaving Norwich. He had, after all, a job for life at Carrow Road, having been offered the security of a ten year contract by Chairman Sir Arthur South, unheard of then as it would be now. Yet, for all the job satisfaction and intense professional and personal happiness that he had at Norwich, Bond had yearned for the opportunity of working for a big club. A big club with big money to spend and big ambitions to match, something which he was never going to have at Norwich. Maybe he saw the opportunity at Manchester City as his one and only opportunity to fulfil that ambition? He'd been able to spend some of their money certainly with Trevor Francis, signed from Nottingham Forest for £1.2 million evidence of that. Yet for all the satisfaction that bringing an England international and European Cup winner to Maine Road would have brought him, the deal still got him into trouble with his Chairman Peter Swales, a man as easily agitated as Sir Arthur South had been avuncular. Swales had, even as the negotiations for the deal were ongoing, warned Bond that the club couldn't afford the price that Forest were expecting of their star player. To that, Bond gave Swales an ultimatum. If we don't sign Francis then you can find yourselves another manager. It seems now an extraordinarily uncharacteristic reaction by a man who, if and when chided by South for looking to spend what the latter might have thought was too much of the Canaries hard earned money, would have simply asked what he could spend and cut the yellow and green cloth accordingly. From a purely personal point of view, I do wonder if Bond regretted the move to Manchester not that long after he had made it. The manner of his departure from Norwich had not been without some rancour and he had, of course, allegedly fallen out with Ken Brown over his decision not to ask him to accompany him to Maine Road. He did, at least, halt the decline that had set in and around Maine Road, leading his new club to the 1981 FA Cup final as well as a respectable twelfth place finish in the league that year. A year on from then they'd finished tenth and, at one point during the 1982/83 season, he had them as high as second in Division One, a 1-0 win over Southampton on 6 November lifting them to those relatively giddy heights. They'd even topped it at one point the previous campaign so, all in all, it did look as if he was the right man for the job, despite any misgivings he may have had along the way, misgivings and the occasional longing for the rather more calm and unpressurised surroundings in and around Carrow Road perhaps?

Characteristically, some of the signings he made during his time in Manchester were classic Bond signings, deals and players you can't help wonder might have happened at Norwich had he stayed. Thirty-three-year-old Tommy Hutchinson, a player Norwich had once been linked with, had been his first signing there, arriving from Coventry City for just £47,000 and ending up playing, and scoring for both teams, in an FA Cup final. Bobby McDonald was another signing from Coventry; he, like Hutchinson, had played (and scored) in the Sky Blues 5-4 win over the Canaries on 27 December 1977 – and Bond never forgot a face or a good performance. Maybe he tried to bring them both to Carrow Road at one point, maybe he didn't. If he had they would, without question, have been fine additions to the Canaries squad, just as they had been for him at Maine Road.

Bond's exit from Maine Road may well have caused some Canary fans to inwardly chuckle in a 'grass is not always greener on the other side' manner. But it would only have been in passing. Yes, football fans have, by and large, mastered the act of schadenfreude. Yet, when there is a danger that others might soon be enjoying your own misfortune, you tend not to exhibit it too much. So, following two FA Cup ties against Coventry City, the Canaries winning the replay at Carrow Road 2-1 after the first game ended in a 1-1 draw, a team buoyed by a good performance in that game set off for the south coast to play Southampton at The Dell, a game that had all the signs of being the proverbial six pointer with, on the day, the Saints just four points and three places ahead of the Canaries in seventeenth. The Canaries had been here before of course. The game at Stoke had been a similar encounter, two teams near the foot of the table struggling for wins and points, three points that the Saints happily helped themselves to with a resounding 4-0 win, the Canaries cause not helped in the first half when Dave Watson had to go off with a head injury.

With just one win in their next five games – and that a resounding 3-0 victory over second placed Watford at Carrow Road, the Canaries found themselves just one place off the foot of the table after a depressing 1-1 draw at home to West Ham on 26 March. Ken Brown was, by now, under a lot of pressure again with idle speculation beginning to spread about his future with the club and who, if he did leave, he might be replaced by. The name of John Bond was inevitably raised as an unlikely but tantalising possibility as would, for a second time, Martin Peters, whilst there might also have been support for Bobby Campbell, then cutting a fierce swathe through Division Two with Portsmouth. Yet Sir Arthur South stood by his manager. He knew the importance of calm and stability, that and having someone in charge at the club who, at a time when there is some pressure and an expectation to deliver despite that. So Brown's job was safe – for now with relegation likely to mean he'd be politely asked to step aside. But only in that eventuality. It was the same up in Manchester where, with Bond gone, Peter Swales had appointed Bond's one time assistant John Benson as their new manager. Benson, like Brown, knew the club, the players, its culture. They were both the best, and only, bets to get their respective clubs out of the perilous state they now found themselves in.

South's faith in Brown suddenly paid off when, with the season gradually coming to a conclusion, Norwich, in a similar manner to how they had suddenly performed two years earlier, put together a mini-run of four successive wins in the league, these being over Birmingham City (4-0); Sunderland (2-0); Arsenal (3-1) and Liverpool (2-0).

A fantastic run of form and results. Four games, four wins, eleven goals scored and only one conceded. Norwich fans had been more used to their side of being on the sort of run that had seen the opposite of what they had just achieved. Yet here they were on one which, after the win at Liverpool, had seen them rise, Phoenix- rather than Canary-like, to thirteenth in the table. It was the best result of the Canaries still brief top flight history and, without question, the shock of the season bar none. Liverpool were, after all well, Liverpool. They'd been spending the season doing what they did best-winning games and scoring goals. They'd beaten Southampton 5-0; Everton 5-0; Aston Villa 4-2; Manchester City 5-2 and 4-0 and Stoke City 5-1, free scoring their way to eighty-five goals in 37 games. With five still to play, pundits were suggesting they might end the season with 100-plus goals to their name, adding that it helped that Norwich were next up at Anfield as, in their previous three home games against the Canaries, the Reds had helped themselves to thirteen goals with only one being scored against them in reply. It was, if ever there was one, the home banker to beat all home bankers with 37,022 attending on the day to witness the ritual slaughter.

Yet, amidst all of the expectation, there was a tiny detail missing. And that was the fact that, back in December when Liverpool had met Norwich at Carrow Road, the Canaries had won 1-0 thanks to a goal from John Deehan. That setback

*Above:* Norwich City team line-up prior to the 1981/82 season.
Back row, L-R: Ken Brown (Manager), Ross Jack, Joe Royle, Steve Walford, Chris Woods, Dave Watson, Keith Bertschin, Dave Bennett, Tim Sheppard (Physio), Mel Machin (First Team Coach).
Front Row, L-R: Mark Barham, Drazen Muzinic, Mick McGuire, Richard Symonds, Peter Mendham, Clive Baker, Greig Shepherd, Mark Nightingale, Phil Hoadley, Graham Paddon, Greg Downs. (*Photo Courtesy of Norwich City Football Club*)

*Right:* Chris Woods, winner of a League Cup winners medal at Nottingham Forest without ever making a league appearance for them; he went onto win another with Norwich in 1985. (*Photo Courtesy of Norwich City Football Club*)

Greig Shepherd opens the scoring for Norwich against Rotherham on 29 August 1981. Four Rotherham goals would come in response. (*Photo Courtesy of Norwich City Football Club*)

Drazen Muzinic on the ball. The one-time Yugoslavia international came for a big fee and with a massive reputation but was ultimately a major disappointment. (*Photo Courtesy of Norwich City Football Club*)

Joe Royle who joined the Canaries in the twilight years of his playing career. He scored, during his time at Everton, the first ever goal in Division One football at Carrow Road. (*Photo Courtesy of Norwich City Football Club*)

Martin O'Neill. Once, twice, three times a Canary. (*Photo Courtesy of Norwich City Football Club*)

Captain Dave Watson with the Division Two Championship trophy, presented after the 4-0 win against Leeds on 3 May 1986. Also, left to right, David Williams, Steve Bruce and Chris Woods. Note Chris Woods' shirt does not show the club sponsor. Fosters Lager took the place of Poll Withey from the start of the 1986/87 season. (*Photo Courtesy of Norwich City Football Club*)

*Right:* Steve Walford, a £175,000 signing from Arsenal. He first met and played alongside Martin O'Neill at Norwich, the two of them going onto form part of a managerial team under O'Neill that has worked together at several different clubs. (*Photo Courtesy of Norwich City Football Club*)

*Below:* Greg Downs. The popular full back made 206 League and Cup appearances for Norwich, winning the club's Player of the Year award at the end of the 1981/82 season. (*Photo Courtesy of Norwich City Football Club*)

*Above:* The aftermath of the fire at Carrow Road which completely destroyed the main stand in 1984. (*Photo Courtesy of Norwich City Football Club*)

*Left:* Ken Brown with the Milk Cup (as the League Cup was then known) with two accompanying bottles of champagne. (*Photo Courtesy of Norwich City Football Club*)

*Right:* Dennis Van Wijk. The Dutch defender joined Norwich from Ajax in 1982, going on to play in a variety of positions with the club, wearing almost every shirt number from 1 to 11. (*Photo Courtesy of Norwich City Football Club*)

*Below:* Mel Machin and Ken Brown celebrate after Norwich's win over Sunderland at Wembley. (*Photo Courtesy of Norwich City Football Club*)

*Above:* Louie Donowa and Asa Hartford on the lap of honour at Wembley. Number 5 is a very happy Peter Mendham. (*Photo Courtesy of Norwich City Football Club*)

*Left:* Mick Channon who thoroughly enjoyed his time at his 'village green' club. We enjoyed you as well, Mick. (*Photo Courtesy of Norwich City Football Club*)

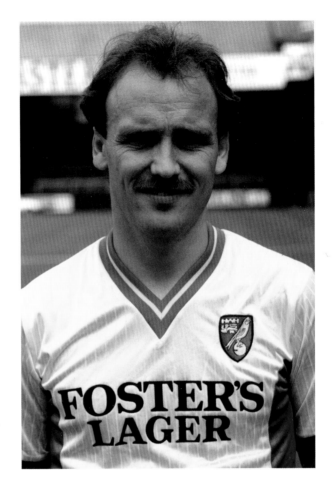

Mike Phelan. His display and spectacular winner for Norwich against Manchester United at Old Trafford in March 1988 clearly impressed Alex Ferguson. (*Photo Courtesy of Norwich City Football Club*)

John Deehan, a man whom Sunderland's David Corner will never forget. (*Photo Courtesy of Norwich City Football Club*)

Peter Mendham, Norfolk born and bred and with green and yellow blood in his veins. (*Photo Courtesy of Norwich City Football Club*)

Steve Bruce. Went on to do rather well in the game after scoring an own goal in the opening minutes of his Norwich debut. (*Photo Courtesy of Norwich City Football Club*)

David Williams, cultured midfielder and a hugely respected coach. (*Photo Courtesy of Norwich City Football Club*)

Dale Gordon, winner of the Barry Butler Player of the Year award at Norwich in 1989. (*Photo Courtesy of Norwich City Football Club*)

Ian Culverhouse, as bargains go, for just £50,000 from Tottenham, he is right up there as one of the biggest as well as one our best players ever. (*Photo Courtesy of Norwich City Football Club*)

Wayne Biggins, from King's Lynn to Celtic via Carrow Road. (*Photo Courtesy of Norwich City Football Club*)

Kevin Drinkell, signed from Grimsby Town and scorer of 54 goals in 138 League and Cup matches for the Canaries before joining Rangers. (*Photo Courtesy of Norwich City Football Club*)

Ruel Fox. Made his Canary debut in 1986 in a 2-1 win over Oxford United at Carrow Road. (*Photo Courtesy of Norwich City Football Club*)

Dave Stringer who guided the Norwich City Youth Team to a League and Cup double in 1983 before taking the senior side to an FA Cup semi-final and 4th place in Division One in 1989. (*Photo Courtesy of Norwich City Football Club*)

turned out to be Liverpool's only league defeat in a run of twenty-seven games, one that had seen nineteen wins and seven draws. It was, however you looked at it, a devastating run of form that formed the backbone of an eventual league title win which they secured eleven points clear of Watford in second place. They'd pretty much had things their own relentless way all season. But had tripped up at Carrow Road. No one expected it to happen again at Anfield, of all places.

No one that is, apart from Ken Brown.

Brown's tactic was to do exactly the opposite to what he suspected everyone, including the Liverpool management and players, would expect them to do in the game. Norwich would, surely, as a team still desperate for points, look for the point, playing it tight and defensively, looking to catch their illustrious opponents on the break – much as they had done so, for the main part, at Carrow Road – and, after all, it had worked then, so surely it could, and would, again? But not this time. He knew that Liverpool would anticipate, just as they did for all visiting teams at Anfield, Norwich to come into the game with a mixture of fear and respect for what they were about to face. Because as far as playing 'mind games' was concerned, all Liverpool needed to do was be Liverpool. The ground, the players, the history, the Kop, the communal singing of 'You'll Never Walk Alone' before games and, of course, the sign over the tunnel that boasted 'This Is Anfield'. Teams crumbled mentally before they even got onto the pitch, it was all too much for them. And Liverpool FC had done nothing other than to extend the friendly hand, to give anyone and everyone connected with the visiting team nothing but the warmest of welcomes and generous of hospitalities. A glove of silk that contained a steel fist, a hand of welcome that Brown would shake in his usual friendly manner. The respect would be all his. But he didn't expect his team to show Liverpool any once the game had started. And they didn't. Right from the kick-off, the Canaries were in their illustrious opponents' faces, pressing high up the pitch and pressing whoever in a red shirt was in possession. It was something Liverpool weren't used to and certainly not at their own ground where teams would stand off them, invite them to attack and hope but hope to resist the red tidal wave. But not today. The only surprise about the half-time score of 0-0 was not that Liverpool had failed to score – but that the Canaries were not yet on the score sheet. And they kept pushing right from the start of the second half with suitable reward for their entertaining play coming when Mark Barham broke free on the Norwich right, his low, hard cross into the Liverpool penalty area intended for Keith Bertschin but met instead by the outstretched boot of the despairing Mark Lawrenson who put the ball past Bruce Grobbelaar for the Canaries opener. A surprise but deserved lead for Norwich which, rather than sit back on, they tried to increase with John Deehan seeing a shot go just wide whilst former Liverpool man Dave Watson went close with a header from a corner. A second goal seemed due and it came on 73 minutes when Keith Bertschin found Martin O'Neill who, after a languid stride or two into the space given him by the Liverpool defence, hit a shot from nearly 30 yards out past Grobbelaar to the accompaniment of joy from his fellow players and the Norwich fans as well as sporting applause from the Liverpool support. A good day then for the Canaries, including the evergreen Mike Channon who, according to Anglia TV's Gerry Harrison had done very well that weekend, as he had not only picked two winners from the Friday race meeting at Sandown Park but had also enjoyed a winning flutter on the Canaries in this game, putting some money on them to win at odds of 13/2. In an interview he gave immediately after the game, Channon was asked if Norwich had travelled up to Anfield with any specific plan tactical plan in mind. 'No, we've been playing well. In our last eight games we've had good results, we just set ourselves up to come and have a go, and we had nothing to lose. It's like a Cup Final for us in lots of ways, we just set ourselves up and thought, let's go and have a crack.' Typical Mike Channon, as laid back and relaxed about things as ever. It was left to Ken Brown to give a fuller explanation about the club's unexpected win and run of good form when he spoke to Martin Tyler after the game.

'I think we've been tightened down in midfield a little more and, to put it basically, we've been consistent in our play. We were very disappointed when we played at Brighton to be dumped out of the Cup there and I thought our hardest job then was to go to Notts County and play.[17] I was dreading it, all that week I was dreading the game actually because we could easily have fallen flat as anything – and it didn't work that way, it went the opposite way, the lads responded and we should have won six or eight there ... but we got a draw in the end [and] it's been going ever since then.'

The refusal to give Liverpool too much respect on the day was best summed up by Dave Watson who, when asked about his opposition to Norwich forming a guard of honour for the Liverpool players as they came onto the pitch for the start of the game, told Tyler, 'It's a big day for them and I'm a great fan of theirs, they're my number one team. But to come out and clap them, I think that's a load of rubbish. We've come here to get our minds on our job ... you can't come and clap teams, we've come to do a job. And it's a serious one.' Watson's attitude was a refreshing one. Ultra-professional, steely-eyed, determined. With the focus on his and his teammates game, not the opposition. They had, as he said, a job to do – and it was a 'serious' one. The new Norwich that Brown was building was, in many ways, similar to the one that John Bond had left behind. Attractive to the eye, a club that fashioned its play on a short and swift passing game, one practised and mastered by a team that had the traditional and well-tested mix of grizzled old professionals and impetuous youth. Yet here, with that display and win at Liverpool, was something else, something that had been fashioned by Brown and put into practice by his team, young and old alike. The Canaries now had, to borrow a phrase from a popular film that was released that year, a darker side, one that was dedicated to winning matches and having a winning mentality. The very fact that the win at Anfield had been Norwich's fourth straight victory, part of an unbeaten run of nine games underlined that, a run that became ten without defeat when, a week later, Manchester United, one time hopefuls for the title themselves had come to Carrow Road and been held to a 1-1 draw, Norwich fully deserving of their point which they got courtesy of Mark Barham's 59th minute reply to Norman Whiteside's opener. It was, arguably, the Canaries finest home performance of the season and one that they had deserved to win.

Three remaining league games followed,[18] a disappointing 1-0 defeat at West Bromwich Albion and a game that, for all of the Canaries growing prominence as the season wore to close, was played in front of a miserly attendance of just 9,221. It was also a case of the club falling prey to the fabled manager of the Month curse as, pre-match, Brown had been named the recipient of that award for April, the Canaries league record for that month reading as an impressive played seven, won five, drawn two, lost nil with thirteen goals scored and just two conceded with an average of 2.42 points per game. Had they maintained that over the course of the season, the Canaries would have been champions with 101 points! Ridiculous of course and wholly unrealistic. But what that league run, the points won and deserved accolade for Brown that came as a result of it did show was what the club was capable of, what it might achieve if it really wanted to. It was a tantalising thought. Norwich had a settled squad and a respected manager. What might the club achieve if it was able to build on these achievements, to add to the squad it already had? All of a sudden, even with two games of the present season to go, Canary fans found themselves looking forward to the 1983/84 season more in expectation than hope.

It was a strange feeling. But a good one.

CHAPTER FOUR

# Treating Those Two Imposters
# Just the Same

*He promptly took ownership of the ball and prepared to go through the motions, the red and white devotees gazing at him in adoration as they also prepared, this time for ecstasy. But this is the cunning ecstasy, its darker brother that becomes despair.*

Following the Canaries' last game of the 1982/83 season, most Norwich fans would have considered the season that had just ended a relatively successful one. It had, admittedly, had some low spots, not least the 4-0 defeat to Southampton on 5 February, one which had seen the Canaries slip down to twenty-first place in Division One and look, in doing so, certainties for a quick return to Division Two. Yet it wasn't just the defeat that had been the cause for great concern, but the manner in which it came about. Watson had, in the first half, gone off with a head injury. Uncertain as to whether he would be replaced or not, the Canaries coaching and medical staff prevaricated near the touchline whilst the match continued, Steve Williams making the most of the gap in the Norwich defence to put the Saints a goal up.

A man down, a goal down – and thoroughly disorganised. The decision was eventually made to bring Watson off. But the damage had been done. Greg Downs had come on to replace him, yet, at just 5 foot 9 inches, he conceded over two inches to Watson in terms of height – and a lot more in sheer physical presence. Thus a game that Norwich might reasonably have expected to get a positive result from became a rout as the Saints breached their fragile back line twice more in six second-half minutes before Steve Moran put the seal on their win a little over a quarter of an hour from the end.

It hadn't been a good day. Yet, somehow and against all of the odds, the Canaries had pulled themselves together and, within a month, commenced a good run of games and form that saw them lose just two of their remaining fifteen games, said run including the impressive 2-0 win at Liverpool that features in the previous chapter. Thus it wasn't, come 14 May, the once expected post mortem of looking back and wondering where it had all gone wrong but at who had contributed the most to it all, in the end, coming right. Because for all the misery that had accompanied that defeat at The Dell, that and all the other low spots of the season, there had been, without doubt, some incredible highs.

And they were the games and the moments that you tended to remember, the memories that stuck around and provided the foundations of belief for the season yet to come.

A league double over Liverpool was one thing. There had also been the two wins against Ipswich; one in the FA Cup and one at Portman Road in the League, the latter coming courtesy of two goals from rising star Peter Mendham, a relative 'veteran' of 115 senior games for the club now and someone whose ability and presence in the Canaries' midfield was getting him some rave reviews as well as notes in dispatches from seasoned observers at other clubs. To cap all of that, the likeable Mendham was a Norfolk lad, one of the club and counties own. Born in King's Lynn and a former pupil of the town's Gaywood Park High School, Ken Brown had famously described him as someone who, '... if you cut him open, his blood would flow yellow and green'.

All clubs needed a player like Peter Mendham. The great bonus that his presence at the club and within the side was that it went beyond sentiment. All too often clubs would parade, push and promote their 'local lads', primarily because they wanted their fans to see that they hadn't lost touch or contact with their roots but also to show that their recruitment policy and investment in promising young players from the local area was working. Norwich had been no different in this regard. Ron Saunders, John Bond and Ken Brown had all given local lads their chance to impress, to stake a claim and make a first team place their own in recent seasons. Saunders had done so with Steve Govier and Glenn Self; Bond with Paul Wilson and Phil Lythgoe whilst Brown had given debuts to Andrew Hart and Mark Crowe, Norfolk lads all and as proud to wear the Canary shirt as the club's fans were to see them out on the pitch representing them and the club.

Yet with regard to all of those names, there was a big and significant difference between them and Peter Mendham. And that was the fact that Peter Mendham had made it as a player and was in the team on one consideration and one alone: he was a very good footballer indeed, the exception to the rule which seemed to state that most Norfolk-born lads didn't quite have what it takes to be an established player at Norwich City Football Club.[1]

If Mendham was the bright, young (and established) hope at Norwich as the club prepared for the 1983/84 season then, at the opposite end of the age and experience bracket you had, of course, the one-off that was Mike Channon. Signing him had been a gamble of Brown's, a massive one that could quite easily have not only been one that didn't come off-but which could also have been his epitaph. When Brown first approached Channon about coming to Norwich, the ex-Southampton and Manchester City striker was thirty-four and, certainly as far as he was concerned at the time, seeing out his career under the management of Bobby Gould (who was only two years his senior) at Bristol Rovers, a club that Channon had made nine league appearances for without scoring a goal. Prior to joining up with Gould at Eastville, Channon had signed for Newcastle United where he teamed up again with his old Southampton and England teammate Kevin Keegan. He even scored on his debut against Middlesbrough, clearly relishing not only his return to the big time, but the opportunity to play alongside Keegan again. Yet, within a month, he was gone again, bombed out by the Magpies as quickly as they had signed him in the first place, a telling final comment he made suggesting that things had possibly not been right between him and certain individuals at the club from the start, with Channon confessing that, '... the results are not why I'm leaving'.

And that could have been that. Prior to his joining Newcastle, he'd spent some time playing in Australia and now, with his move to Bristol seeming to have not worked out as well, no one would have been surprised if he had decided that enough was enough and given up one game in order to more fully focus on the great love of his life, then and now, horse racing. Except that Ken Brown didn't think so and thought that Channon just might have enough playing nous and character to act as an inspiration to the younger players at Carrow Road. And a character he certainly was. Jeremy Goss, then a member of the Canaries youth team was given the onerous task of being Channon's apprentice when he joined the club and recalls his time in the role with the somewhat mixed feelings you'd expect of a raw teenager given the job of looking after one of the game's superstars – and one, for that, who wasn't adverse to making life hell for whoever was looking after him.

> ... when Mick turned up at Trowse for the first time ... I ended up being his apprentice and let me say, for all the lovely, cuddly, friendly image he cultivates, he made my life as an apprentice hell. He'd leave his kit all over the place else throw a pair of socks or shorts up into a tree and expect me to climb up and get them. Then he'd want them all cleaned and back again, boots included before I even had a chance to get started.

Channon wouldn't have expected any special treatment when he signed for Norwich. He would, however, have anticipated, given his achievements and experience in the game, the club 'indulging' him in his approach to training and playing, something that, perhaps, hadn't gone down so well at Newcastle as it did at Norwich. Jeremy Goss again:

> Mick pretty much had the run of the place when he was at the club. He'd stroll into the dressing room after placing his bets and taking a race in, look Ken in the eye and say, 'Sorry, just putting a bet on.' Nothing would be said. Mick did as he pleased. He'd do that, go out and play, invariably perform brilliantly, come back, clear off and do his own thing. One of a kind.[2]

Channon's knowledge and footballing nous, along with Peter Mendham's verve, energy and determination to do his very best for a club he clearly loved were just two of the reasons why Canary fans were feeling optimistic at the end of the 1982/83 season. And there were plenty of others. Dave Watson for example. He was now one of the mainstays of both the team and the club as a whole, a fiercely ambitious footballer and born leader, someone who only, as his comments post-Liverpool had shown, wanted to win. The same could be said for Chris Woods, now very firmly established as the Canaries' first-choice goalkeeper. Then there was Mark Barham, another young English player who the club had signed as an apprentice and whose pace and skill on the wing were beginning to make him as invaluable as Woods and Watson already were. All three would, in time, earn full international honours with England, and all would make their England debuts whilst they were still at Norwich. Such recognition was testament to Brown's ability to spot and nurture a player, he had certainly done that with Barham who'd actually made his debut for the Canaries whilst he was still just seventeen, under the management of John Bond. Bond knew a good young player when he saw one, and Brown knew how to make him an even better one, turning Barham, in the process, into the full England international that he became in the summer of 1983.

No wonder there was quite a lot of optimism in and around the club over the summer of 1983. It had been a tough season, an exceptionally tough one in fact. Not that anyone had expected otherwise. The Canaries had stole into the last promotion place eighteen months previously on the back of a good run at the end of that season, their first consistent set of good results that campaign. Yes, they had come when it had mattered and promotion was often a case of a team timing its run up the table at just the right time. Yet that team had still lost fifteen of their forty-two league games that season – only five fewer than Wrexham who had been relegated. So they were very much a work in progress, a team that might even have benefitted from another season at that level before taking the step up again. Yet, just as they had during that 1981/82 promotion season, Norwich had defied the odds as well as the expectations the following campaign, their win over Liverpool a crowning glory in that end of season run and form that was now formed the foundation of a generally held belief that the 1983/84 season could turn out to be a special one for the club.

As in previous years, the club chose to spend a portion of the summer on a foreign tour, an opportunity for the players to begin preparing for a new season in different surroundings as well as one for the staff of the club to treat as a bit of a holiday cum perk. Not that any of these tours were considered or treated as 'jolly's' and the players weren't the only ones expecting to put a tough shift in whilst the club was away. It was also a chance for the club to engage in PR duties overseas, to spread the Norwich City word and make their hosts aware of the club and City in general. Previous trips had seen the Canaries fly out to Jamaica (1982); the USA (1981); China (1980) and Australia and New Zealand (1979) and, after an immediate end-of-season wind-down visit to Norway (the club flew out immediately after the their last game against Brighton and proceeded to play four games in five days),[3] the players were given two months at home before setting off for a tour of Kenya where they were due to play the first of four friendlies there before popping over to Norway for a second visit at the beginning of August ,meaning, with a few domestic pre-season friendlies into account, the total of games the club played during pre-season 1983/84 totalled fourteen – a third of the total of league games they'd play during a normal domestic campaign. The club had toured Kenya before, back in the summer of 1975 when, amidst their five-game trip, accusations of witchcraft had been directed at some of their opponents, a method employed in the belief that it might help them get a more favourable result in their game against the Canaries. No stories of that nature emerged this time however, and, as both an opportunity for the players to get up to fitness and as a PR exercise for the club, the tour passed off without incident. As far as the games the club played were concerned, that hadn't been quite as planned results wise with Norwich losing their first two games to AFC Leopards Nairobi (0-1) and Gor Mahia Nairobi (2-4) before beating Cargo FC Mombasa 3-0 with a 2-2 draw against Kenya Breweries Mombasa bringing the tour to an end.

The fourteenth and final game of the club's busy pre-season was held in the somewhat more prosaic surroundings of the Abbey Stadium in Cambridge as Norwich drew 1-1 with the home side before losing the opportunity to lift the Cambridge Professional Cup, eventually going down on penalties. That had been on Sunday 20 August, less than a week before the start of the league season, one which that previously held optimism had faded a little, not least because of the departure of two of the club's most important players.

Martin O'Neill had looked like, again, someone who was only passing through the club on his way to somewhere else. His original arrival as a player in February 1981 had seen an immediate improvement in the club's form but had come, alas, too late to save the club from relegation, something which, as far as his contract was concerned, was unacceptable. His subsequent departure to Manchester City had not worked out – at least, not for the buying club, who, finding themselves in the position of not only owing the Canaries a lot of money and defaulting on payments due, had no choice but to redress the balance by offering Norwich one of their existing players, taking off that players transfer value from the total Norwich were owed. Whether or not O'Neill wanted to return to Norwich is a moot point. I have previously suggested that his return to Carrow Road was a lot more to do with Norwich taking back sold goods by default after the buying party failed to make their payments in time, much in the same way a car showroom will repossess a car if payments are not regularly made on that. But, regardless of whatever circumstances had led to O'Neill's unexpected return, he had faced up to his new role and responsibility with relish, so much so that, for ten games during the 1982/83 season, Ken Brown had made him Captain in the absence of Dave Watson. However, with the Canaries top flight status assured, O'Neill now wanted to move on again and to a club nearer his Midlands home. He did just that, signing for Notts County the day before the new season was set to start for just £40,000, a ridiculously low fee for a player who was still one of the best midfielders in the country and who had skippered Northern Ireland at the 1982 World Cup finals in Spain the previous summer. In fairness to the Canaries, that low fee hadn't been what they had asked. Notts County had, presumably safe in the knowledge that O'Neill was intent upon joining them and them alone, initially offered Norwich just £15,000 for O'Neill whilst Norwich had asked for the slightly more realistic (but still under-priced) £100,000. The matter eventually went to a transfer tribunal which settled upon the £40,000 fee that the Magpies ended up paying, a criminally low sum for such a talented, influential and important player, one who would now end up playing against the Canaries at some point during the pending season.

The other major departure from the Canaries' playing ranks was the somewhat more unexpected one of Steve Walford. His impact on the side had been immediate from the moment Ken Brown had signed him from Arsenal nearly two and a half years earlier as a defensive partner for Dave Watson. He'd gone on to prove himself to be as reliable fitness wise as he was in terms of performance, missing just two games from the total of 100 that the Canaries played in the League and Cup during the 1981/82 and 1982/83 seasons. His departure, to West Ham for £160,000 (less than the amount paid for him by the Canaries which is puzzling, given he was now very much an experienced top flight player)[4] citing, at the time, that the opportunity to return to London to play was one he couldn't afford to turn down, Walford having been born in Highgate. It's interesting, in hindsight, to consider the reasons given by both players for their moves away from Norwich, that seemingly unquenchable 'urge' in footballers to live and work in familiar surroundings near to childhood homes and family. O'Neill, admittedly, had been born in Kilrea, but had moved to Nottingham when he was just nineteen, spending a decade living and working in the City and county before his move to Norwich, so he clearly had an affinity to the area, just as Walford clearly had for London.

Yet Norwich, for all of the reputation it had then, as it does now, was hardly a one horse town at the end of the road to nowhere – even if some of the club's longer coach trips to away games might have occasionally suggested it – and you can't help but imagine if the motives for both moves weren't rather more focused on what they would be earning at their new clubs, rather than some romantic notion about wanting to go home. Certainly as far as Walford was concerned, he was still at an age where ambitious young, whatever their backgrounds and professions, usually had the urge to stretch their proverbial wings and fly away, getting as far away from home as they possibly could in the process. As far as Martin O'Neill and Steve Walford were concerned of course, the fact that they both left Norwich to go their separate footballing ways at around the same time didn't mean they would never work together again with their subsequent teaming up again during O'Neill's career as a manager, Walford proceeding to work with him in a coaching capacity in a partnership that has endured since 1990, seeing them work together at Wycombe Wanderers, Leicester City, Celtic, Aston Villa, Sunderland and the Republic of Ireland – as well as, of course, O'Neill's third spell at Norwich, his ill-fated time spent back at the club as Canaries manager in 1995. Five other players who had started the previous season at the club had also since moved on, amongst them was former captain and influential midfielder Mick McGuire who'd joined Barnsley that March and Colin Smith who'd taken up an offer to play in Hong Kong. Another, surprising, departure had been that of Richard Symonds, a player of whom big things had once been expected, so much so that, at one point very early in his Norwich career he was the subject of a £50,000 bid from Bobby Robson at Ipswich Town. He'd been all set to accept an offer from Grimsby Town only for the move to break down at the last moment with Symonds feeling that the terms offered him by the Mariners were less than acceptable. He went onto surprise many people by opting to join non-league Poringland instead, going onto successfully feature in local non-league football for several years afterwards. Ross Jack had also moved on, joining Lincoln for £15,000 whilst John Fashanu signalled the beginning of the end of his Norwich career that August as well by joining Crystal Palace on loan. Seven out then. But how many in? Norwich still had, in Woods, Watson, Mendham and Deehan as a strong central spine, the potential to once again over achieve in Division One and look to push on from their fourteenth place finish at the end of the previous campaign, but it was achingly obvious that reinforcements had been needed, even before the departures of O'Neill, Walford and those lesser lights from the first team squad of the previous season. The club had expressed a very serious interest in signing ex-Ipswich and England defender Kevin Beattie as a replacement for Watson. Beattie had been forced to retire from the game due to injury in December 1981 but had since made a playing comeback of sorts, firstly with Colchester United, followed by a four game spell at Middlesbrough, a bid that fell through due to ongoing complications with Beattie's insurance pay out after he had initially quit the game and claims that, if he signed for the Canaries, Norwich would have had to repay it. It all made for a good story in the end but something that was probably never going to happen, especially given Beattie's past with the Suffolk club as well as his ongoing and very obvious allegiance to them. That nonsense eventually died down and, in the end, Ken Brown opted for another experienced centre back to fill the void left after Walford's departure by signing former Tottenham and Arsenal centre half Willie Young from Nottingham Forest. It looked an astute signing. Young, who was thirty-one, had played in nearly 300 league games at the highest level for his previous clubs and arrived with a reputation for being a tough and somewhat uncompromising defender, someone who, in short, would be a perfect partner for Watson, someone who was still learning and growing into the game as both a player and a man at the time, even though his presence and importance at the club had already been recognised by Ken Brown who had, following the departures of McGuire and O'Neill made Watson captain. Quite how the wily and somewhat grizzled old pro Young would make of being expected to toe the defensive line as dictated by the much younger man, someone who had still been at school whilst Young was playing in an FA Cup Final for Arsenal, was questionable but Brown, doubtless though the different challenges that situation would present for both players made it a more than worthwhile one to offer up.

On the same day as Young joined the Canaries, Brown also clinched the signing of another defender, namely John Devine from Arsenal. Devine came, as you would expect of a young Gunner, with a very good pedigree; he'd played in both domestic and European club finals whilst he was still only twenty-one as well as having represented the Republic Of Ireland at youth, U21, and full international levels. His capture was yet another coup for both the club and Brown. Devine was a very highly rated defender indeed, one who'd progressed through the youth team ranks at Highbury alongside contemporaries Liam Brady, David O'Leary and Frank Stapleton. He had seemed, set like them, for a long and successful career with the Gunners only for injury to keep him out of the side for long enough to enable John Hollins to take his place. Unable to immediately reclaim his place as a regular starter for Arsenal, John opted to move on and, whilst it was a surprise that Arsenal agreed to sell him and, if anything, an even bigger one that Norwich had been the club to buy him, Ken Brown knew he had, as with Steve Walford, signed another gem from the North Londoners.

Young and Devine both made their debuts in the Canaries' opening league fixture, a 1-1 draw against Sunderland at Roker Park, a game that the Canaries might have won had Young not slipped in attempting to challenge Sunderland's Colin West, that error enabling the Sunderland striker to score just five minutes after Keith Bertschin had put Norwich ahead. Norwich followed up that game with a home game against Liverpool four days later and were unlucky to lose 1-0 with Bertschin and Young both having efforts cleared off the line whilst, late on, Mike Channon did score, only for the goal to be adjudged offside. Two games, one point and one goal scored – but encouraging performances in both games with, as had been hoped, the Canaries' form 'clicking' in their next game, a 3-0 win over Wolves at Carrow Road on 4 September, one which had seen two goals for John Deehan plus one for his strike partner Bertschin. One low point from that game had been the attendance – just 13,713. The visit of Liverpool just four days earlier had seen an attendance of 23,859 and whilst it is true that the appeal of visiting players John Humphrey, Geoff Palmer and Mel Eves et al might not have had the same appeal as the likes of Kenny Dalglish, Ian Rush and Graeme Souness, the great disparity in crowd numbers for the two games (over 10,000 fewer people attended the Wolves game) very clearly and evidently suggested that a large proportion of Norwich fans were picking and choosing their games depending on the calibre and reputation of the opposition and the visiting players rather than a desire to see their own team play and hopefully win.

This was disappointing. And frustrating. In those days where club income largely depended on home attendances rather than TV and sponsorship money, Norwich needed good crowds to merely survive at the top level, never mind prosper. Devine and Young had been the only close season signings and, as far as new faces at the club were concerned, they remained the only ones brought to Carrow Road where transfer fees were concerned. Yes, there were a further six first team debutants that season to follow in the footsteps of Young and Devine, but five of those were players that had been promoted to the first team from the club's youth side, one that was, at least, proving to be more than successful under its coach Dave Stringer, having done the 'double' the previous campaign in winning both the South East Counties League Championship and FA Youth Cup, the latter being the first time that the club had won this most prestigious trophy for the nation's youth team sides. Their success and the elevation of so many of their players to the first team, for varying degrees of success, had been a triumph for Stringer who had taken to coaching like a natural, inspiring and leading his squad of young players to the sort of heights the club would scarcely have thought possible even less than a decade earlier-and certainly when the perceived cream of its schoolboy and youth were being kicked, elbowed and pummelled into submission by the older, grimmer and occasionally bitter men that frequented Norfolk's non-league scene. Stringer had used a total of twelve players in his sides three games against Everton in the 1983 FA Youth Cup Final, eight of whom made at least one appearances for the Canaries in a first team, with the most successful of that quartet being Jeremy Goss (188 appearances), Tony Spearing (eighty-two) and Louie Donowa (eighty).⁵

Thus those financial shortcomings, ones made evident by the club's often disappointing home-attendance figures meant that most of the new faces that Norwich fans saw for the entirety of the 1983/84 season post-Young and Devine were players from the youth team. Debuts were therefore awarded to Daryl Godbold, Paul Clayton, Jon Rigby and Jeremy Goss, the last of the eight to do so with the remaining four having already done so. The Canaries had also signed Mark Farrington who had played in that final for Everton against Norwich with the Canaries swiftly stepping in to bring him to Carrow Road after he was being released by the Toffees. Farrington went onto make his Canaries' bow in the same game as Goss did his; a 2-1 defeat at Coventry City in Norwich's penultimate game of the league season. Despite having to subsist, at least players wise, on a footballing equivalent of 'make do and mend', Norwich enjoyed a good first half to the 1983/84 season, one that peaked after the 1-0 win at Birmingham City on 10 December, a victory that saw them climb to seventh in the Division One table before they moved up another place to sixth without even playing, following Tottenham's defeat to Manchester United the following Friday. It was an admirable achievement for a club that was not only strapped for cash, but, it seemed, still strapped for fans as another disappointing attendance, this time 16,646, turned up the day after the Canaries moved to the top six for the home game against Coventry City, a game that, had City won, could feasibly see them climb to fourth place. That game ended up as a 0-0 draw, an entertaining one as they go with the Sky Blues also enjoying a good run of form, one that, at kick-off, had seen them two points and two places above Norwich in the table. That game was the first of a winless run of five for the Canaries before a dominant display against Sunderland at Carrow Road on 14 January ended in a 3-0 win for City, thanks to first half goals from Greg Downs, Keith Bertschin and Norwegian international Åge Hareide, an impressive win with a virtuoso performance by Mike Channon a particular highlight, all played out to another meagre attendance, this time just 13,204 – nearly half of the total that had packed out the ground in the 0-0 draw against Ipswich (25,679) a little under three weeks earlier.

With the Canaries now attracting near sell-out attendances for all of their league fixtures (the average attendance for the Canaries whilst they were in League One during the 2009/10 season was 24,755 with a seasonal best that campaign of 25,506 for the visit of Hartlepool United) it now borders on the unbelievable that a Norwich team that was playing top flight football and, in the process, flirting with the top ten in the league, could repeatedly get such low gates. Even the club's short-lived season back in Division Two just under a decade earlier had seen regular attendances of over 20,000 at Carrow Road with 23,252 in attendance for the game against Oxford United that campaign whilst 29,512 were in attendance for the match against Fulham on Easter Monday 1975. The capacity at Carrow Road for the 1983/84 season was 29,000 which meant that the ground was often half empty, something which must have been demoralising for the players who were giving it their all to ensure that the Canaries didn't just survive in Division One that season, but looked to progress and do all they could to establish themselves at that level in what was only the tenth campaign they had competed in at that level in their history, one that would, by the end of that season, be entering its eighty-second year.

Not that there was anything the club could do about it other than keep playing well, keep winning games and hope that, eventually, the missing thousands would come back and that occasional spectators, such as those who came along for home games against Liverpool and Ipswich would find the same attraction in games when the likes of Luton and Notts County were the visitors. This was a time, after all, when owning a season ticket was the exception at Carrow Road rather than the rule and, because of that, fans had become accustomed to picking and choosing their games, their choices often determined by the quality of opposition, the weather, other commitments on the day-anything and everything infact, with, more often than not, that 'anything and everything' taking precedence. Fortunately for the Canaries, they did have that loyal hard-core base of supporters who would turn up regardless, a solid base of around 10–12,000 and is thanks to their efforts that takings at the gate were at least enough to help keep the club going financially although there was no spare money available for Ken Brown to spend on any new players for whole of that season.

Not that there wasn't a total embargo on new player recruitment during the 1983/84 season. The club signed Michael Pickering on loan from Sheffield Wednesday at the end of September in order to increase their options on the left hand side of midfield. He'd made just over 100 appearances for Sheffield Wednesday, however, the fact he had done that over a period of six years suggests that he was never much than a squad player during his time at Hillsborough – but, nonetheless, one good enough to have been valued and picked by Jack Charlton, his manager for much of his time spent with the Owls. Pickering was named as substitute for the visit of Manchester United at Carrow Road on 1 October and, if ever a player had to sign on and off again for Norwich with just one game for his troubles but to do so in style, then it was Pickering. Norwich, with teenage striker Louie Donowa replacing the injured John Deehan in attack were three down after just under an hour with Norman Whiteside (two) and Frank Stapleton the scorers for a dominant Manchester United side, who, after scoring the third goal, let their guard down. This was all City needed to find a way back into the match which they did when Dave Bennett seized on some hesitation in their defence to loop a header over the stranded Gary Bailey after sixty-four minutes. Mike Channon made it 2-3 after heading Peter Mendham's precise free kick past Bailey and now, all of a sudden, with around ten minutes to go, it was the Red Devils with their backs to the wall as Norwich pushed forward, launching attack after attack, the sight of the players in yellow and green, teeth gritted, fists clenched and blood stirred, putting their perceived illustrious opponents and players who had, in their desperation not to concede a third goal, resorted to time wasting, feigning of injury and any and all excuses to moan, complain or simply sound off at referee Ray Lewis a surreal one – surely it was meant to be the other way around? Surely United were meant to be the strutting, preening, über-confident cocks of the walk and Norwich the meek and kow-towing opponents? Not here and not now. It did look, for a time, as if they would hang on for their victory but they continued to underestimate the resilience of their opponents and Norwich got their reward when, with barely a minute remaining, Louie Donowa, making his full debut for the Canaries, ran onto an astute chip played by Peter Mendham into the Manchester United penalty area to slide the ball past Bailey, the resulting celebrations, both on and off the pitch, something those who were there would not forget for a very long time. For Pickering, who had replaced Watson just after Channon had scored the Canaries second goal, it must have been a case of '… is it like this here every week?' His eleven minutes of action had, of course, seen him amongst the melee of Norwich players celebrating Donowa's last minute equaliser but that was as far as his career in a Norwich shirt went. He didn't make the match day squad for the rest of his short stay at Carrow Road, becoming, with that short but sweet appearance off the bench in that game, the Norwich City player who, to date, has had the shortest lived senior career at the club as regards first team playing time – and, even if he has not, he will certainly be amongst the top three and a name that people will forever remember, not because of who he was but that one famous game he was involved in.

The one remaining new face to Norwich City supporters that season was, in terms of experience in the game and age, a polar opposite to Pickering. He'd already been a professional footballer for five years when he arrived at Norwich, a comparative veteran of over 250 senior appearances for Barnsley, Southampton and Sheffield Wednesday. Robert Rosario, on the other hand, was combining taking his A-levels whilst playing for non-league Hillingdon Borough where he had made quite an impact, scoring five goals in nine Southern League games for the Southern League club, more than enough for someone to tip the proverbial wink to Canaries Assistant manager Mel Machin about him. Machin and Norwich saw enough in the seventeen year old striker to offer him a deal with Rosario promptly continuing his goal scoring exploits as soon as he joined the club, scoring nineteen goals in assorted youth and reserve team football for the Canaries.

This was more than enough to give him a chance at first team level and Ken Brown gave him his debut in the home game against Watford on 7 April, mindful, perhaps, of the fact that the Hornets had an FA Cup semi-final to play the following weekend and, with their league status already secure for another season, might not have their minds totally on proceedings at Carrow Road; an ideal opportunity, therefore, for Rosario to come in (replacing the injured Dave Bennett) to the side for his first team debut.[6]

It was another high scoring game to remember. And, regardless of whether the Watford players focus was on their pending FA Cup semi-final or not, it certainly wasn't at this game with Norwich winning 6-1. As luck would have it, ITV's cameras were at the game, along with commentator Brian Moore who featured Rosario as the teams warmed up before kick-off, pointing out that he had been at school during the week and had needed to get permission to miss his lessons on the previous day in order to train with his teammates. John Deehan opened the scoring for Norwich after just eight minutes, a goal that was the very definition of route one football as he met a long kick from Chris Woods to head the ball over Steve Sherwood. It was the first of four for Deehan in the game, two of which were penalties, with Greg Downs and John Devine the other scorers, the fabled resilience and strength of the Watford team non-existent on the day. So was, fortunately for the Norwich defence, the presence and danger that could have been posed by their two highly rated wingers, Nigel Callaghan (a player who England manager Bobby Robson, present at the game alongside a former England manager in Sir Alf Ramsey, would have been observing on the day) and John Barnes, both of whom had uncharacteristically quiet games. Yet that is to take nothing away from Norwich and their performance on the day which was full of attacking intent, purposeful and thoroughly professional, something which was particularly well illustrated by the fact that, with the game well won, Norwich still pressed for more goals right to the end of the match with their last two coming in the 83rd and 87th minutes.

The Canaries also had fairly decent runs in both domestic Cups during the 1983/84 season, reaching the fifth round of the FA Cup and quarter finals of the League Cup, the competition they had won in 1962 as well as reaching the finals of in 1973 and 1975 with a losing semi-final punctuating those two Wembley years. Their run in the tournament this season took them past Cardiff City, Sunderland and, in front of a disbelieving and distraught home side, Ipswich Town in the fourth round, Mike Channon celebrating his thirty-fifth birthday with the only goal of the game. The club would meet Sunderland and Ipswich in consecutive League Cup rounds again the following season, albeit in rather more celebratory circumstances. But, for this year at least, the run came to an end in the quarter finals when Aston Villa won 2-0 at Carrow Road. That had been the Canaries third game against Villa in just eleven days as the two sides had also been drawn against each other in the FA Cup third round with Norwich winning the replay at Carrow Road 3-0 after a 1-1 draw at Villa Park, Mike Channon, Peter Mendham and Keith Bertschin the scorers. The Canaries bear Tottenham in the 4th round, again in a replay, winning that one 2-1 at Carrow Road, Dennis Van Wijk and Channon the scorers against a Tottenham team that featured two future members of the Canaries managerial team, Chris Hughton, who was Norwich manager from 2012 to 2014 and Tony Parkes, who had a short spell as the club's goalkeeping coach from 2014 to 2015.

The club's fifty-third and final game of the season was at Anfield, scene of that memorable 2-0 victory the previous season. Liverpool had, by then, already retained their Division One title and Anfield was, once again, in a celebratory mood and ready to party. Unfortunately for those legions of Reds fans, the Canaries were in the mood to be spoil the occasion once again and took the lead after twenty-four minutes when John Devine, who had enjoyed an excellent first season at the club, scored with a superb shot from some way out. Liverpool were not, however, to be denied on this occasion, equalising through Ian Rush just six minutes later. That goal seemed to act as a signal to both sides to play out the game happy with a point each which they proceeded to do, the only negative point as far as Norwich were concerned was the fact that Tony Spearing broke his ankle, a bitter blow for the young left back who was just beginning to mount a very real challenge to both Greg Downs and Dennis Van Wijk for the Number 3 shirt in the Norwich side.

Had the Canaries made the progress expected of them back in the summer? They'd finished in fourteenth place, an identical placing to their final position in the 1982/83 season but had, in the process, gained fifty-one points as compared to the fifty-four won that previous campaign. They'd also scored fewer goals (fifty-two in 1982/83; forty-eight in 1983/84) but had conceded fewer (forty-nine as compared to fifty-eight) – so their end of season goal difference of -1 was, at least, superior to the -6 they'd finished the previous season on, a very minor and fairly irrelevant detail. Irrelevant because, even if the statistics 'proved' that Norwich had failed to make progress during the 1983/84 season, the truth was they had done exactly that. Ken Brown had been hamstrung from the summer onwards, able to recruit only two players on a permanent deal from other clubs, having to resort, throughout the season, to giving debuts to four of the club's players from the side that had won the FA Youth Cup as well as relying on a further three who had already been blooded in the first team, primarily because, as was the case this season, a shortage of numbers in the first team squads made their selections necessary. Whether or not this early elevation to the first team came too soon and adversely affected the careers of players like Paul Clayton and Daryl Godbold is open to question. After all, it would be extremely unlikely, bordering on the extraordinary for all eleven members of any FA Youth Cup winning side to make a career for themselves – and that's a career, not a few appearances before drifting into non-league or even out of the game – in the senior game. But there is also an argument that young players can be given that promotion to first team duties before they are either mentally or physically ready to take that step, particularly the former. Brown had no choice but to select some of them and it is a tribute to both him and Dave Stringer that three did make a career for themselves in the game in later years, particularly Jeremy Goss, who played such a prominent part in the club's UEFA Cup run a decade later.

Following the final game at Anfield, the FA announced the names of the players who would be joining up with the England squad for their summer tour of South America, with two of the names selected being Chris Woods and Dave Watson. Woods had enjoyed an excellent season, he'd appeared in every one of the club's fifty-three League and Cup games,[7] ending the campaign as the winner of the club's Player of the Season Award, deserved recognition, especially given the quality of some of his teammates who would also have been contenders for the award that season – Watson certainly, but also Mike Channon (who'd started in forty-eight games himself), John Deehan (top scorer with seventeen goals) and the ever-improving and mightily impressive Peter Mendham. There was, however, a feeling in and around the club that, if they were to have any chance of making further progress in the 1984/85 season, they would have to invest in new players. Channon wouldn't, after all, last forever whilst the England recognition afforded to Woods and Watson meant that it wouldn't be long before bigger clubs were enquiring as to their availability, possibly that very summer. It came as no surprise then when Chairman Sir Arthur South concurred with popular opinion and publicly stated that he would do everything in his power to ensure funds would be available for Ken Brown to strengthen his squad that summer – even if he might have done so with one eye on the big money offers that might have been coming in for Woods and Watson – even though, deep down, you suspect he would have been only too happy to turn them down. For the time being anyway.

For now the Canaries had other things on their mind. Immediately after the Liverpool game, the squad, minus Watson and Woods, flew to Norway for a mini tour that involved them playing three games in just three days – no rest for the tired and weary then. Tired or not, the Canaries managed to stay unbeaten for those three games, beating Tromso (1-0) and Sortlands, the previous year's whipping boys (7-2), those two games coming either side of a 0-0 draw against Bardufoss & Omegn.

With that game against Sortlands played on 19 May, the 1983/84 season, one that had started for the Canaries in Kenya the previous July finally came to an end after a total of seventy-one games in all, of which eighteen had been friendlies of one type or another. Players and staff alike now had a little over two months to rest up before preparations for the 1984/85 season began – with yet another tour of Norway – the club's third trip there in just over a year. Clearly, with previous trips to Kenya, China, Australia and New Zealand and the USA having highlighted Canary summers in recent years, the club's financial situation was not only affecting its ability to actively seek out and sign new players, it had also put an end to those ambitious foreign trips as well.

The times at Carrow Road were most definitely a 'changin'.

As things turned out, the Canaries ended up touring Norway and Sweden, playing five games in the lands of the fjords and Northern Lights before playing a further five in Sweden; ten games in fifteen games proving, once again, that when it came to pre-season, the Canaries did gruelling with a capital G. Yet the trips had their benefits. The Canaries were able to establish cordial and familiar relationships with clubs and coaches from all over Scandinavia, this policy of promoting both the profile of the club as well as its culture one that would be rewarded in the coming years, it also put the Canaries in pole position should any promising players in either country be available for transfer as well as giving Norwich the opportunity to send players of their own over for a loan period at one of these clubs as they did with Jeremy Goss at Swedish club IFK Lulea over a couple of summers. So yes, the tours were hard work and intense, but they served a purpose in more than a PR sense in helping new players to bond into the squad as well as providing plentiful opportunities for match fitness.

As far as helping new arrivals fit into the squad in time for the start of the 1984/85 season, one significant new face who arrived in plenty of time to be part of the squad that left for Norway in late July was twenty-three-year-old centre half Steve Bruce who'd signed from Gillingham at the beginning of that month. Bruce's arrival, for what turned out to be a bargain price of just £135,000 was the club's second attempt at acquiring a new central defensive partner for Dave Watson. The Canaries had, a year previously, managed to secure the signing of Scottish defender Willie Young from Nottingham Forest but soon became clear that Young and the club were simply not cut out for each other with Young, at one point, complaining to Mel Machin about the amount of running the Norwich players were doing during pre-season, pointing out that he never used to do any running with Arsenal. Machin's reply, as you can guess, would have been brief, to the point and said with the intention of letting Young know exactly who was in charge. He certainly made Young work all the harder in response to his comment with one story told by an ex-teammate of Youngs at the time describing how Young had been so exhausted after one particularly gruelling session he had been physically sick – all over Machin's shoes. It was a marriage that was clearly never going to last and, after making just six appearances for Norwich, he and the club agreed to cancel his contract and Young eventually joined Brighton. His unexpected early exit meant that the Number 5 shirt was now available for any Norwich player that fancied making a name for himself as Watson's defensive partner and, by the end of the season, four different players (John Devine, Greg Downs, Dennis Van Wijk and Åge Hareide) had all worn the number five shirt although only Norwegian international Hareide was anything like a natural in the position – and he was already hinting that he might be ready to leave the club in order to return to Norway before the end of the season. Bruce would therefore need to settle into the side quickly in order for the Canaries to have both defensive stability and consistency as quickly as they could in the opening weeks of the new season, much to ask, of course, of a player who had only ever played his football in Division Three and who was now set to make his Division One debut against League Champions Liverpool at Carrow Road. But then again, Dave Watson had never played first team football at any level before he'd joined Norwich and he'd taken to it like the natural he was. With the one time student of the game Watson now acting as the teacher to new recruit Bruce, Brown paired them together for the first time for that Liverpool match and waited to see how quickly the two of them would develop an understanding. You could coach players as much as you wanted, you could sit them down in front of a tactics board else talk to them until you had nothing more to say. But nothing taught you, the coach, or them, the player, as much as playing in games, more so, games that mattered. And Liverpool, at Carrow Road, on the opening day of a new season mattered like nothing else on planet football to anyone and everyone at the club at that time. The two teams had, of course, met on the last day of the previous season when they had played out an entertaining, yet, nonetheless, amicable 1-1 draw. Liverpool were already confirmed as League champions, Norwich were comfortably off in mid-table. What was there not to like about that? This game would be different. And with good reason. Liverpool would want to start the season as they meant to go on, laying down their usual marker for other teams to follow. Or fear. They didn't always start league seasons as they meant to go on. Their record for their opening league fixture in the ten seasons prior to this one had been five wins, three draws and two defeats. Did this make them vulnerable especially early in the season? Perhaps. They'd lost their Charity Shield game against Everton a week earlier at Wembley which had stung, especially given the manner of their defeat, an own goal attributed to eccentric goalkeeper Bruce Grobbelaar. So, vulnerable or not, they'd want make up for that setback, one that felt all the worse as it was against Everton, as well as make a statement about those intentions early on. Plus they were playing Norwich, the team that had done the league double over them two seasons back. So they had every reason to want to win and to win well.

Norwich showed three changes from the team that had drawn at Anfield back in May. Tony Spearing was still missing, thanks to the broken ankle he had sustained in that game; Dennis Van Wijk slotting in to his place from the midfield role he'd had at Anfield whilst Watson, who'd missed that game, and Bruce came into the side at the expense of Greg Downs and Louie Donowa. There was also a debut for seventeen-year-old winger Dale Gordon, Great Yarmouth-born but an Ipswich fan who had, quite unfeasibly, either been overlooked or completely missed by the Suffolk club's scouting team. Their considerable loss and Norwich's gain, both on the field, and, ultimately, financially. Gordon took his place on the right hand side of a Norwich side that was very rich in attacking potential with Keith Bertschin, John Deehan and Mike Channon all starting, a clear sign that, yet again, Ken Brown was intent upon taking the game to his opponents rather than choosing to sit back and give them the sort of onfield respect that, for so many teams, usually met with defeat.

Unsurprisingly, therefore, it was a tremendously exciting game, one that debutant Bruce, in particular, would not forget in a hurry after, with just two minutes gone, his attempt at a clearing defensive header from fellow debutant Jan Molby's cross went straight past Chris Woods and into his own net. Did, you wonder, as he heard the mixed cries and yells of over 22,000 spectators in response ringing in his ears, wonder, even for only a split second, if, right then, right now, he'd prefer to be back with Gillingham and a home game, in surrounding he knew and amongst people he liked and trusted, against Newport County? Of course not. He got up and got on with things and, from that moment, a Canary legend was born. It might even be said that the own goal that came his way two minutes into his Norwich debut was the making of Steve Bruce, both as a Norwich player and a professional footballer in general, for it gave him the desire to raise his game and his efforts to new heights, qualities that never once deserted him from that moment onwards for the rest of his playing career. Lesser players than Bruce might, at that point, have chosen to hide. But he didn't, and neither did his teammates, even when, after just under half an hour, Kenny Dalglish put Liverpool 2-0 ahead. By now Norwich had already gone close with Peter Mendham's shot hitting the bar, and now, even with Liverpool's lead doubled, there was still belief, amongst both the players and the supporters that the Canaries could get back into the game. And they did. Gordon sent in a high, looping cross that Grobbelaar could only flap at, the ball rebounded into space and there was Peter Mendham, right place and right time, to make it 2-1 which was the scores at half time, John Deehan having missed the opportunity to make it 2-2 by putting his penalty well over Grobbelaar's crossbar. It was a disappointing moment and it meant that Liverpool still had the lead – but the game and the ascendancy was with Norwich which is how it continued into the second half when, despite having four Liverpool defenders around him (including Alan Hansen, some 'shocking defending' there Alan), Keith Bertschin wriggled through to make the score 2-2.

More goals looked certain but none came until the sixty-eighth minute when, after Paul Haylock wafted into the personal space of Paul Walsh in the Norwich penalty area, referee Ray Lewis gratefully took the opportunity to award Liverpool the penalty which they took and converted via Phil Neal. As the game neared completion, Lewis seemed to take pity on Norwich, awarding the Canaries a penalty of their own when Mike Channon tumbled, much like an exhausted horse at Becher's Brook, over the legs of Mark Lawrenson before picking himself up and stroking the resultant penalty away to make the final score 3-3. It was a deserved point for Norwich in an epic encounter which served notice of more to come from a team that was not only rich in attacking talent but which, in Bruce and Watson, along with strong options at full back in Paul Haylock, Dennis Van Wijk and Greg Downs, looked to have the foundations of as strong a back line as it had for many seasons.

Bruce was, unsurprisingly, the main point of interest after the game. Upon being asked about his own goal he replied in a typically candid manner, 'I couldn't seem to get me head to it, I stretched out and it was one of those should I leave it, or should I head it. I decided to head it and it went in the far corner past Woodsy.'

It was disappointing therefore when, after such an encouraging and exciting start, the Canaries, just as they had during the previous two seasons, started to misfire results wise. A 0-0 draw at Coventry followed in midweek before a run of eight league games that saw just two wins, those coming against West Brom (2-1) at Carrow Road and another high scoring home encounter against Watford that saw John Deehan hit his second consecutive hat-trick against the Hornets in a 3-2 victory. That game was noteworthy in one respect in that it saw the last of Chris Woods' remarkable run of 171 consecutive matches for Norwich, with Ken Brown opting for experience rather than youth as cover for Woods by drafting in former Manchester City and England goalkeeper Joe Corrigan from Brighton on loan. Corrigan played in three games for Norwich before Woods was declared fit to return to the first team, none of which were wins, indeed, it was to be over a month after that Watford game before City won again, the much needed three points coming in a 2-0 win over Queens Park Rangers at Carrow Road, Mike Channon and John Deehan the scorers.

There had been some doubt as to whether the game would even go ahead in the first place as, only two days previously, the club's main stand had been completely destroyed by a fire that was suspected to have started overnight due to an electrical fault. The fire was first reported at just before 3.30 a.m. but, despite the attentions of nearly forty firefighters and various appliances, little could be done to prevent the timber framed stand, which was part of the original stadium that had been built in just eighty-two days in 1935, from being comprehensively and irreparably damaged. The club bore the loss with fortitude. Any damage or destruction caused to a structure by fire has an impact and can be both upsetting and, logistically, sometimes overwhelming to deal with. No one had lost their lives in the fire, indeed, there were no injuries at all with the only real hurt being to the club's morale with the loss of some valuable archive material, including some of its historic and valuable trophies. Fittingly, the Canaries were fully insured by Norwich Union (now Aviva) and a pledge was made for a new and improved main stand to be built as soon as possible. Clearing up began immediately and, once permission was given for the match against Queens Park Rangers to go ahead, the club began to work out where season ticket holders might be temporarily relocated and, of course, given the dressing rooms were lost to the fire, where the players might change and prepare for home games. For this match at least, the QPR players prepared and changed in The Nest, a pub which, at the time, was part of the River End part of the ground before, post-defeat, taking a sweaty and reflective trip to the club's training ground at Trowse to shower and change again before heading back to London.

One Canary had at least tried to lighten the mood around the club after the fire with John Deehan arriving for training on the Friday morning afterwards clad in a fireman's uniform and wielding a watering can. It was typical Deehan, a classy and lethal striker on his day, one who was unlucky not to get international recognition during his time at Norwich. Yet, for all of his skills and ability on the pitch, he was also a renowned character and comedian off it, that and a student of the game as his coaching record and reputation he had as a coach in the years he has spent in the game following his playing career easily testify. The win over QPR was the start of a decent run of league form for Norwich that saw them win five games from seven, a sequence that included a 3-0 victory over Luton at Carrow Road and an impressive result and performance to go with it in a 4-2 win over league leaders Everton who, prior to their trip to Norfolk had kept five consecutive clean sheets. A fortnight later Norwich won again at Carrow Road, Mark Farrington scoring the decisive goal in a 1-0 win over West Ham that took the Canaries up into 10th position in the table. The club had, by now, reached the quarter finals of the League Cup with wins over Preston, Aldershot and Notts County. The two-legged tie against Preston had finished with an unlikely aggregate scoreline of 9-4 in favour for City with new signing Asa Hartford scoring two of the goals in Norwich's 6-1 home win. Hartford was, much like Channon, a player in the twilight of his top class career – but what a player he had been. He'd commenced his playing career with West Bromwich Albion in 1967, eventually making headlines during his time with the Baggies when a proposed transfer to Leeds United fell through after a medical found he had a suspected hole in the heart condition. Leeds immediately cancelled the deal and Hartford eventually joined Manchester City (twice) before spells at Nottingham Forest (just three games for Brian Clough) and Everton. He'd been playing in the US for Fort Lauderdale Sun when he joined Norwich, and, much in the same way as questions were asked when the club had brought in Mike Channon from Bristol Rovers, so they were again when Hartford joined him in Norwich.

Doubters then and doubters this time. Yet they should have remembered at just how good a judge of a player Ken Brown was and how age, in particular, was no barrier to him or the team he was building at Carrow Road. Several youth team players had been given their chance in the first team. Dale Gordon, at seventeen, had been given a debut in that opening league fixture against Liverpool – and had thrived – he was going to make, as it turned out, twenty-seven first team appearances for Norwich by the end of that season. And then there was Channon. The post-fire win against QPR had been his 850th senior game of football. And he'd played the whole match as well as scored – a month short of his thirty-sixth birthday, he was old enough to be Gordon's Father. Yet they both played and fitted in the same team, the veritable old warhorse who had put himself out to pasture with Bristol Rovers and the young player not long out of school who was not yet old enough to have a drink in the bar. Brown's mantra was simple. If you were a good player, you'd get into his team, no matter what your age or background. Hartford was a good player, and that was all anyone needed to know and would have been the one and only line of reasoning for defence Brown would have offered any of those doubters. Hartford's debut might have been against Preston. But he had treated the game and opposition as if he was playing Liverpool or Manchester United, else representing Scotland in a World Cup game. Professional in everything he did and a superb example for the younger Norwich players to look up to, learn from and engage with in all matters football. Yes, it might 'only' have been Preston in a League Cup game on a Wednesday night. But it mattered to Hartford, it mattered to Mike Channon too and he, inevitably, scored as well. How could they not be a positive influence in and around the club? It was another transfer masterstroke from Brown who had acquired the player for so many more reasons than his efforts on the pitch alone – although if he continued to play as well as he on the night for the rest of the season, then so much the better.

Having had two moderately good runs in both domestic cups the previous season, the onus was now on the Canaries to try and improve on that progress and see if they could reach the final in one of those competitions and, in the process, earn a third appearance at Wembley in thirteen years. Lucky thirteen? Maybe. As far as the League Cup had been concerned, the draw had been kind to Norwich. They'd reached the quarter finals via those ties against Preston, Aldershot and Notts County, who they beat 3-0 in the fourth round, Channon's goal on the night the 300th in his career. Those five games had seen Norwich score sixteen goals with only four conceded, reasons for optimism ahead of a potentially tricky tie against Grimsby Town on a frigid night in Cleethorpes which saw the players needing to worry as much about staying on their feet in the icy conditions as try to play a good game of football, those conditions leaving the Grimsby faithful confident that their Division One opponents wouldn't be to the task and that they would more than likely win the game as a consequence of the Canaries reluctance or inability to get 'stuck in'. But this was a different Norwich City, a team that was not going to roll over for anyone.

Much to the surprise therefore of those who had, given the conditions and the perceived fragility of Brown's team, tipped a Grimsby win, Norwich dominated the match without really scoring the number of goals that their dominance deserved. With two penalty appeals ignored by referee Joe Worrall as well as two clear chances missed by Mark Barham and a seemingly goal-bound effort from Steve Bruce hitting the crossbar, it might have been thought that the Canaries were going to have one of those nights teams have when, no matter what they do, they cannot get the ball into the back of the net. Luckily, after twenty-eight minutes, they did and that was enough as Barham's perfect cross was met and headed past Nigel Batch by the ever dangerous Deehan, enough for Norwich to win and set up the delicious prospect of a two legged semi-final against Ipswich Town with the trip to Wembley that awaited the winner not quite as great a prize as the bragging rights and pride that the supporters of the winning team would almost certainly feel for many years to come – and at least until the two sides met again in a cup semi-final.

Three days after the win against Grimsby, Norwich travelled up to Anfield, the scene of some notable performances and results for the Canaries in recent years. Not on this occasion though, with Liverpool making light work of their possibly fatigued opponents, winning 4-0. At this point, although the result was, naturally, a disappointing one, no one at Norwich was too concerned about a defeat in a week that had seen the club get to a major cup semi-final. Norwich had been handily placed in tenth position prior to the game at Anfield and remained there afterwards, five points shy of Manchester United in third place and, crucially, fourteen ahead of Ipswich who, at that time, occupied the first of the three relegation places. The league season had, so far, been a more than satisfactory one for the club and, even though a winless run of two draws and two defeats in their next four matches were less than satisfactory for all concerned, a 2-1 win over Coventry City on 30 March saw Norwich handily placed in thirteenth place with games in hand on all of their nearest rivals including three over Aston Villa, who were five points ahead of them in tenth, the position which was, for that season, the benchmark most people seemed to think the club should be aiming for. For those who were at Carrow Road for that Coventry game, one of their abiding memories of it will have been the performance of Mark Barham on the day. He was outstanding, the best player on the pitch by some considerable margin and, as far as Norwich's hapless, if not quite hopeless opponents were concerned, almost unplayable. Mike Channon scored the two Norwich goals in front of yet another paltry attendance, this time just 14,067 which, given the circumstances leading up to the game seems as disappointing today as it most definitely would have been to everyone at the club at the time. And with good reason. For, just six days earlier, the Canaries had finally had their day in the sun at Wembley, beating Sunderland 1-0 in a League Cup final which might have been dull for the neutral, but was anything but for the vast hoards of Norwich fans who'd made their way to Wembley early on that Sunday morning. And it was a day that started, as so many do for those legions, in the dark. A dank, cold dawn, too early for some. Yet not as early as that which the supporters of Sunderland would have had to endure to make Wembley in time. And, if Norwich had every right to cock a snook at Ipswich, the mad, bad and occasionally sad semi-final victims who'd been turfed out by Steve Bruce's thumping winning header at Carrow Road in the second leg of the semi-final, then so did they. Norwich had eliminated their deadliest rivals whilst Sunderland had seen off, in Chelsea, the proverbial London fancy dans, all West London swank and vulgarity, even then. Sunderland, fans and club alike were, like Norwich, a side fashioned from hard work and dedication, one followed by devoted, vocal supporters. Most pundits and football aficionados had predicted a Chelsea versus

Ipswich final from the beginning. The sides that hadn't been tipped for such potential glories were only too glad to disappoint them, now both wanting more after the taste of success they'd had in their respective semi-finals. Norwich's win over Ipswich in that two-legged game is now the stuff of legend at Carrow Road and rightly so, maybe even more so than the final which followed it. A tight first leg at Portman Road had seen Ipswich come away with a 1-0 victory, courtesy of a Mich D'Avray goal after just six minutes. It might, might have opened the goalscoring floodgates for the men in blue and white, nowhere near the footballing force they had been a few years previously but still, with quality players such as George Burley, Terry Butcher, Jason Dozzell and Eric Gates in their line-up, a more than decent team capable of, on their day, wielding a lot of damage. So it was vital that Norwich held firm and resisted the storm. Which they did and magnificently.

It wasn't without a scare or two. Romeo Zondervan looked to have scored a second and, quite possibly, decisive goal only for referee George Courtney to adjudge it had not fully crossed the line, a decision which made immediately made Mr Courtney the most popular man in Norfolk and least popular in Suffolk – at exactly the same time, quite an achievement. Fortunately for Norwich they held firm in the face of repeated Ipswich attacks and, whilst the 1-0 reverse wasn't perfect, it did, at least, give City something to realistically work on in the second leg at Carrow Road. And work on it they did in front of one of the most vocal and passionate crowds seen at the ground for many year. With the game Ipswich's third in only five days, the chance was there to get at them from the off, which Norwich most certainly did, heartened, no doubt, by the early exit, due to injury, of first leg goal-scorer D'Avray. Not that D'Avray was replaced by an inferior player. His replacement was Alan Sunderland, a man who not only knew what it was like to play in major Cup Finals (one League, three FA and one European Cup Winners Cup Final) but who was also a more than capable goalscorer. He was, thankfully, kept well under wraps by the Norwich defence throughout, as were his teammates and it came as both no surprise and some relief when Norwich went a goal up and made the aggregate score 1-1 when John Deehan scored, his shot going in via the unfortunate Ian Cranson's knee. Lucky Norwich? Maybe. And maybe the Canaries had also been lucky in the first leg when Zondervan's goal had been ruled out. But you take whatever you can get in big matches, semi-finals against your biggest rivals most definitely. And now Norwich had the ascendancy, their confidence and conviction eventually being rewarded with just three minutes to go when a Mark Barham corner was powered past Paul Cooper and into the Ipswich goal by the majestic Steve Bruce, yes, Steve Bruce, the man whose own goal in the opening game of the season against Liverpool had led to people questioning his ability just two minutes into his career as a Canary. Now, here he was again, with just two minutes of a game left, the man who had sent his new club to Wembley. No one was doubting him now. A quirk of the fixture list meant that, a week before Norwich were due to meet Sunderland at Wembley, the two sides were set to meet in a League game at Carrow Road with Sunderland getting the all-important psychological advantage by winning 3-1. The game itself, regardless of the result, seemed inconsequential. Hearts and minds were on Wembley and, with top-flight status seemingly assured for another season, no one was too bothered about the defeat, no one, that is, apart from Ken Brown. His line up for this game would almost certainly have been the one, barring the missing Steve Bruce, he would have selected at Wembley – strong and dependable defensively with pace on the flanks and no little guile on top of all that with Mike Channon and Asa Hartford as valuable to the team on the day for their big game experience and nous, two calm and wise old heads who would, if the occasion needed it, be able to calm things down, be it on the training pitch, dressing room or wide open spaces of Wembley. Keith Bertschin had, by then, moved onto Stoke City but, with Channon and John Deehan more than capable of playing together and with ex-Sunderland striker Gary Rowell held in reserve, Brown knew he had all positions covered and would have been more than ready for the big day.

Except of course, that things in life never go quite to plan – and even less so in football where an incident that lasts for no more than a few seconds can change a players life or even the long term future of a football club. For Greg Downs, that league game against Sunderland, his 201st appearance for Norwich, was the one that changed both his life and career, both in the short and long term. He had been the veritable model of consistency for the club ever since his debut for the Canaries in a League Cup game at Burnley in 1977 – when his teammates had included Kevin Keelan, Doug Evans and Duncan Forbes. Downs had started his Norwich career as a striker, indeed, he'd worn the Number 9 shirt for that game. Yet Mel Machin had seen something in his pace and the way he could read the game that suggested he could be better used as an attacking full back which was, in time, the position he made his own at Carrow Road, even winning the club's Player of the Year award in 1982, quite an achievement when you consider who he would have been up against that season for the popular vote, namely the far more high-profile figures of Keith Bertschin, Dave Watson and Chris Woods.

Yet, on that day, with Wembley just over a little week away, Greg Downs didn't have the best of games. Hardly a capital offence. After all, there hasn't yet been a footballer born who has gone through his entire career without having some. Even the greats had their off days. Pele would have done, likewise Johan Cruyff and Diego Maradona. Likewise the great and the good of Norwich City, there would have been days when they had the proverbial stinker. Martin Peters, Ted MacDougall, Dave Watson. How about Steve Bruce and his own goal, scored just minutes into his debut? Yet he'd recovered from that to score the goal that earnted his team their place at Wembley. Having a bad game didn't matter. What did was how you came back from it and that was what made you stand out as a player.

But Downs wasn't given that chance by Ken Brown to do that. Not this time.

He'd found himself out paced and out muscled by Ian Wallace as the fast and aggressive striker put Sunderland ahead. 1-0 to Sunderland and to Wallace who Downs, just as he was on this day, would have also been expected to keep a watchful eye on a week later. Twenty minutes later Downs mistimed an attempted defensive clearance, sending the ball into his own net in the process. Game over for Norwich – and, for the unfortunate Greg Downs, his chances of playing at Wembley for, out of the Norwich team that lined up on that day and collectively underperformed, he was the one man missing at Wembley, failing even to make the substitutes bench on the day with Brown giving the Number 12 shirt to the versatile John Devine. Downs did, at least, make the match day squad and took his place on the Wembley pitch pre-match, clad, alongside Gary Rowell and all of the other players in their light grey suits including Dennis Van Wijk, the man many thought would have been the one to miss out in order for Steve Bruce to return to the side alongside Dave Watson at the heart of the Canaries defence.

The match itself was not a classic and one which didn't really come to life until early in the second half when a hopeful pass down the Sunderland right was met by David Corner, a late replacement for the injured Shaun Elliott. Leaving Corner in his wake, Deehan swiftly passed the ball into the penalty area where Mike Channon, attended to by Sunderland defenders, was only able to contribute to the ball deflecting away and behind him where it was met by Asa Hartford, a player as grizzled and hewn in the rigours of the game as Corner was green and fresh. Grizzled or not, for Hartford, the sudden chance of individual glory was quite irresistible and his actions were immediate as he attempted to bend the ball around Chris Turner in the Sunderland goal only for his shot to take a deflection off the static figure of Gordon Chisholm before rebounding into the goal, much to the delight of the watching Norwich fans who promptly detonated in a yellow and green technicolour cloud of delight as an overjoyed Deehan turned and looked them squarely in the eye, his fist clenched in communal and triumphant solidarity. It was Norwich's third League Cup Final and whilst they still hadn't a goal to call their own at Wembley, they were as sure as hell going to take this one, an own goal or not. After all, it had been another own goal, the one that came off the knee of Ipswich's Ian Cranson, that had helped get them here in the first place. And Deehan had been the architect behind that as well. Maybe, just maybe, the footballing fates were smiling on Norwich City this time and the omens were in their favour. But then again, maybe not. This is, after all, Norwich City Football Club. There has to be some drama, hearts have to leap into mouths, heads must be raised to the heavens in despair. It's the law. Those more long in the tooth Norwich fans can see it coming, one proclaiming, to anyone who'd listen that 'it hint over yet' – and it most certainly is not. Sunderland break, fast and true, its Barry Venison, a footballing Bee Gee advancing with the ball, cutting into the Norwich area with only Chris Woods between him and immortality, that is, until he is thwarted by the Flying Dutchman, one Dennis Van Wijk. His tackle was clean but inconclusive. Venison remained a threat and Van Wijk went to ground, all looking lost, at least from his perspective, so, in desperation, he promptly stuck out an arm and palmed the ball away.

It was as clear and obvious a penalty as you will ever see.

Sunderland instantly rejoiced as Woods, head in hands, danced a jig of despair in his penalty area. There had only ever been one penalty miss in a Wembley final and that one doesn't really count as Ray Graydon had, a decade earlier, scored seconds after Keelan's initial save. But it was still a penalty miss. Against Norwich. At Wembley. And at the same tunnel end. Hope springs eternal. Yet Walker is as good a penalty taker as there is in the game. He promptly took ownership of the ball and prepared to go through the motions, the red and white devotees gazing at him in adoration as they also prepared, this time for ecstasy. But this is the cunning ecstasy, its darker brother that becomes despair. Walker has fired the ball fractionally wide with Woods even looking as if he might have got a touch to it. He momentarily bows his head as Van Wijk, the most relieved man in the stadium, trots past him in relief, his moment of footballing madness forgiven if not forgotten.

Norwich, of course, held onto to win the game via that solitary goal and the sight of Dave Watson lifting the trophy aloft from atop the thirty-nine steps is one that the Norwich fans there on the day will never forget, even if the soundtrack to that moment was a rousing chorus of 'Blaydon Races' coming from the defeated yet still content Sunderland fans. The pre-match bonhomie continued as both sets of supporters decanted from the stadium and made for their coaches, with scarves, rosettes and other souvenirs being exchanged amidst the football chat and camaraderie at the end, much to the astonishment of the Met's finest who found their steeds being offered as many Polo mints as they could ever wish to have as both sets of fans mingled together in the late afternoon gloom. It was, for many, as good a feeling as the match and its result itself, proof positive that football did have its good side and good people within it, people who had, on that afternoon at least temporarily (for there would be more horrors to come) patched the open wound that was English football in the 1980s. The afore mentioned game against Coventry City that followed a week later was treated in the celebratory manner that would might expect of a club not used to success, one signified on the pitch by the magnificent match that Mark Barham had as well as the two goals scored by Mike Channon, his last for the club at Carrow Road. The Cup was joyfully paraded before the fans pre-match and, in the wake of an exciting week and all that happened, not least the promise of, for the first time in the club's history, qualification for European football the following season, the Canaries might have been forgiven for easing up and playing the season out with a Cup won, top flight status assured and a European adventure to come. Yet football, for all the glories and joy it can bring you is one of the cruellest of mistresses, and there was yet to be a bitter denouement to all things, with, of all clubs, Coventry City, the post-Wembley sacrificial lambs, yet to play a very significant part indeed in how the season would end and, for them, a case of the club that plays last is the one that laughs the longest. Which is exactly what the Sky Blues ended up doing.

Following that win over Coventry, things began to settle down at Carrow Road. Ken Brown had done a few press interviews saying how proud he was of his players, adding that, with a major trophy won and with the allure of European football to come, he would look forward to bringing some real quality to the club that summer. Which is exactly what anyone would have expected him to say. The club now had, in what it had done and what was yet to come, a very real and substantial foundation from which they could build on and if that meant some old faces leaving in order to make way for new ones, that was completely understandable. For the mainstays in the side, people like Chris Woods, Dave Watson, Steve Bruce and John Deehan, it was an exciting time. But how might some of the other members of the squad felt at that time? Plus there was Mike Channon and Asa Hartford. Invaluable they might have been, but they'd be thirty-seven and thirty-five respectively during the season to come, could they be expected to play their part in what would be a long season comprising of a full league programme and three cup competitions? It seemed unlikely. There also seemed to be, at least in glorious hindsight, a sense in and around the club that, as far as the 1984/85 season was concerned, it was 'job done' and that, consciously or not, people started to go through the motions with, maybe, an eye on either the campaign to come or their own futures.

That seems to be the one of the most likely explanations for a run of form that saw Norwich win just two of their remaining twelve league games, a dreadful run of form that, at one point, saw them suffer five consecutive league defeats. By the time of the fifth of those, a 3-1 reverse at Carrow Road to a Leicester City side inspired by Alan Smith and Gary Lineker, Norwich fans were, for perhaps the first time that season, casting nervous glances at the Division One table. The Canaries had, post-Leicester, now played thirty-six league games and were 16th in the table, just four points ahead of Luton Town who occupied the first of the dreaded relegation places. There was some immediate relief three days after that result when the Canaries headed out to already relegated Stoke City and won 3-2 (with Keith Bertschin scoring against his former club) but any platform that might have given Norwich to make good their Division One status in their following games was wasted as just one point was gained from a possible twelve, meaning the Canaries were all set to go to Chelsea for their last game of the season needing a win to give themselves a more than reasonable chance of staying up.

And win they did, on a near waterlogged pitch, Asa Hartford and Steve Bruce scoring in a much needed and totally deserved 2-1 win. It was a performance much more akin of the 'old' Norwich, the one that had so impressed earlier in the season, a committed team effort and victory against a side that was then in the top six. It meant that Norwich finished their Division One campaign with forty-nine points, only two fewer than they'd got the previous season, and, seemingly safe in 18th place, a point ahead of West Ham, who had one game in hand, but, crucially, eight ahead of Coventry City who still had three games to play, one of which was against Champions elect Everton. In order for Norwich to go down therefore, the Sky Blues, yes, the same Sky Blues who had looked so insipid at Carrow Road on the weekend that followed those Wembley heroics, needed to win all of their last three games. A feat they'd hadn't achieved all season and one which they had only done once the previous campaign – when their opponents had been Stoke City, Birmingham City and Queens Park Rangers. Whereas this time around it was Stoke City, Luton Town and Everton. Coventry may well beat Stoke, Norwich fans reasoned. They may even beat Luton. But they wouldn't beat Everton. And yet there remained, for all the unlikelihood that a struggling club would defy the odds and win three games in ten days, one of which was going to be against the best team in the country, a sense that it exactly what Coventry City would do. And they did, their 4-1 win against the Champions twelve days after Norwich had played their final game, sending Norwich down to Divison Two, a point adrift of Queens Park Rangers who were on fifty points. It was a sickening feeling, a relegation that felt as if it had been taken out of the club's hands and that they, able only to watch Coventry have the time and games needed to overhaul them at the death, had been at a disadvantage, something which the Football League ultimately recognised, ensuring that , in due course, every club in all four leagues would play its final fixture at the same time on the same day, a ruling that remains in place to this day. Norwich may, of course, still have been relegated no matter how those final fixtures of the 1984/85 season had been played, indeed, the grim reality behind the details was that they'd lost twelve of their remaining twenty fixtures, gaining just sixteen points out of a possible sixty which is, however you chose to look at it, the results and form of a team that is going only one way. Down. And that was Norwich City, their third top flight relegation in just over a decade.

It was a much more familiar feeling. And most certainly not a good one.

CHAPTER FIVE

# Just Passing Through

*It seemed, therefore, that, in this instance at least, Norwich had been fortunate
not to have signed the player in question.*

Relegation at the end of the 1984/85 season had hit Norwich City hard. Board of Directors, management and coaching staff, players, administrative and financial staff and the fans. Everyone and anyone connected with or at the club in fact.

The club's first relegation, back in 1974 had been disappointing, of course it had. But it had never been regarded as a disaster, more a sign of perhaps needing to take a step back in order to take two forward, an indication of how the club was moving on, growing and adjusting to the game and what it had become. Then there was the presence of John Bond; the best possible manager the club could have, someone who could not only take the club back to the First Division but keep them there. Relegation or not, the summer months of 1974 were exciting times.

Once Bond had left and the club had, again, in his wake, slipped out of the top flight, there was still a sense that things were not as bad as they might have been portrayed. Furthermore, with Ken Brown now at the helm, a popular and respected man; one who represented the continuity that is so important in football, the club had an outstanding chance of repeating what Saunders and John Bond had done before them and come straight back up again. You certainly wouldn't have been blamed for thinking so, especially with the squad that Brown had been steadily building up, one that included players like Mark Barham, Dave Watson and Chris Woods, three players who would go onto play for England whilst they were still at Norwich.

Kipling had mused that if you should meet with triumph and disaster, then those twin imposters should be treated in exactly the same way. Which is exactly what Norwich City had done. Be it glorious or desperate in nature, the resolve had been grim, the countenance steady. Don't over-elaborate success and don't over dramatise failure. Just do whatever needs to be done. It was an approach which had its rewards. Three promotions, two relegations. And two immediate returns to the elite in the wake of each of those relegations.

Yet, come the summer of 1985, and Norwich's third relegation from that elite league at the top of the English game, it was a lot harder to generate any optimism for what was to come. The sheer joy of winning at Wembley had been extinguished by the relegation that followed. Even the added anticipation of UEFA Cup football as a small consolation now swept away from a blameless Norwich by the events that happened at the Heysel Stadium prior to the 1985 European Cup Final. The Canaries had dropped out of Division One and had now been kicked out of Europe, club and fans tarred with the brush that deemed all English football supporters to be hooligans. From a lap of honour at Wembley, regular visits to Highbury, Anfield and Old Trafford and the chance to play, for the first time, in some of the great stadiums of Europe to Second Division football again and the visit of Oldham Athletic on the first day of the new season.

It had been Liverpool just twelve months earlier. Liverpool, Tottenham, Chelsea. The East Anglian derby. Now it was Oldham, Grimsby Town and Carlisle. Whilst Ipswich, who the Canaries had so enjoyed knocking out of the League Cup the previous season would be looking forward to all the trips and the moments that Norwich would now be doing without. The question was, therefore, did the club have the resolve to follow up another relegation with, for the third time of asking, an immediate return to the top flight and the level of football which the Canaries now felt was their rightful place rather than one they occasionally occupied as honoured guests.

Could they do it? There would have been doubt and doubters, of that, there is no question.

To the surprise of some, Ken Brown was the man who the club's board was best able to deliver another promotion. In these days of knee-jerk managerial decisions and sackings precipitated by what might be about to happen, rather than what has happened, it seems curious that a man who had now two relegations on his CV should be given the opportunity to right the footballing wrongs a second time. Yet, that is exactly what was expected of Brown and there was little danger of him going anywhere that summer. And that made sense. He was, for all that had happened, the best man for the job. He knew the club well, he knew his squad of players and what they were capable of. And they knew, liked and respected him. More to the point, many of them would have felt that they had let him down with some of their performances the previous season and that they wanted to put things right by him and the club as a whole. This attitude was best illustrated in the fact that all of the club's leading players stayed put and committed themselves to getting the club back into Division One. No one would have been surprised if the likes of Mark Barham, Steve Bruce, Peter Mendham, Dave Watson and Chris Woods had moved on that summer, indeed, the club would almost certainly have had enquiries about the availability of some of them, enquiries which they would have felt duty bound to let the player in question know about. Enquiries which, in return, the player in question would have felt equally duty bound to turn down. Loyalty in football, whatever next?

This may not have been the case, of course, had Sir Arthur South and the club's directors chosen to dispense with the services of Ken Brown after relegation was confirmed. But they stood by him and were rewarded when all of their leading players, in turn, stood by the club and their manager. By electing to do nothing at all, the men at the top of Norwich City had done the very best thing they could have done in order to give the club every chance of renewed success.

There were, of course, some exits. Two were expected, those of Mike Channon, who, ever the character, chose to join Portsmouth, the deadliest rivals of his first club and main footballing love, Southampton, an act akin to Martin Peters suddenly turning up at Portman Road. Channon, initially signed on a short-term deal from Bristol Rovers, ended up making 112 appearances for the Canaries, more than he had for Manchester City, scoring twenty-five goals, proving, in his near three and a half year spell at the club to be an invaluable presence and character at Carrow Road, on and off the pitch, a man who left the club with the best wishes of everyone connected with it. As far as Hartford was concerned, it was a slightly different story. Whilst Channon had been expected to leave, efforts had been made to get him to sign a new one year contract at the club, one he politely declined in order to take up an appointment with Bolton Wanderers as player/coach. Another departure, maybe not quite as expected, had been that of Greg Downs, dropped for the League Cup Final in favour of Dennis Van Wijk and a man who had played in just five of Norwich's games following the Sunderland exit. He joined Coventry City, the team that had so dramatically sent Norwich back down to Division Two for only £40,000, going onto make 146 League appearances for them, deservedly winning a FA Cup Winners medal with them in 1987.

In total, eight players who had featured for the Canaries in at least one competitive game during the 1984/85 season had left,[1] some long since and others only ever short term loanees, when Ken Brown and Mel Machin commenced preparations for another promotion campaign, six of which were strikers. Norwich had tried and mostly failed with a succession of potential goalscorers, some of whom, such as David Fairclough and Gary Rowell, were more than proven at the top level of the game but, for one reason and another, those signings had not worked out and the players had since moved on. With Channon also gone, it was therefore imperative that the club signed a reliable strike partner for the ever-reliable Deehan; drawn out efforts were even made to sign Trevor Senior who had a prolific scoring record with Reading only for them to come to nothing. Not that it mattered too much as the Canaries had, much to the surprise of quite a few other teams who had been tracking him, already managed to sign Kevin Drinkell from Grimsby Town. Drinkell was an excellent signing, a strong and brave centre forward who'd scored eighty-nine goals in 272 league appearances for the Mariners, but had missed, due to injury, the chance to play against the Canaries in the club's League Cup meeting the previous season.

Drinkell had certainly been a wanted man over previous seasons, hence the surprise that it was Norwich who had eventually signed him when clubs such as Middlesbrough, Leeds United and Manchester City were all said to have been previous suitors with offers of £300,000 for him having been suggested – and turned down flat by Grimsby who reportedly wanted a lot more for their best player. It should not, therefore, have come as too much of a surprise for the Norwich hierarchy when their reported bids of £140,000, followed by one of £165,000 weren't as much as turned down by their peers at Blundell Park as laughed at. The whole matter eventually went to a transfer tribunal with Drinkell, who wanted to join Norwich and had made no secret of the fact he wanted to, stating his case and that for his potentially new club at that tribunal. The fee was eventually set at just £105,000, lower than the amount Norwich had first offered and less than half of the amounts they had reportedly turned down from Leeds and Manchester City.

Norwich's new centre forward was immediately impressed at both his new surroundings and the calibre of player he would be playing alongside, admitting in his autobiography that the club had, despite relegation, remained upbeat and ambitious, the evidence of that being the quality of the squad that they had kept together for their season back in Division Two. It boded well for Norwich that Drinkell and his new team mates were so determined to do well, determined and confident that they would do so. The vibrancy that he says was very much present at Carrow Road at this time would almost certainly have been noted by the club's other signings as well, namely Mike Phelan who arrived from Burnley; David Williams (Bristol Rovers); Garry Brooke and Ian Culverhouse (Tottenham) and Wayne Biggins who arrived from Burnley that October. The Canaries opened their 1985/86 Division Two campaign against the afore mentioned Oldham Athletic and were workmanlike at best in a scrappy match which they won 1-0, Peter Mendham scoring with Garry Brooke missing an opportunity to make the score a little more respectable when his penalty hit the Oldham post. The fact that four players (Phelan, Drinkell, Brooke and Williams) were making their debuts in the game explains why City didn't open up their season with the convincing victory and free flowing football that many had expected to accompany it, yet, for all that, Oldham were a massively competent side who would, in time, reach Divison One themselves under their manager, ex-Canary Joe Royle. They also had, adding a little bit of interest to the day, a further three ex-Canaries in their team that day, namely Willie Donachie, Mick McGuire and David Fairclough, the one-time Liverpool 'super sub' now doing it again for the Latics with Fairclough making his appearance off the bench in place of the unfortunate Brendan O'Callaghan who tore his abductor muscle so badly at Carrow Road on that opening day, he never kicked a ball again and was forced, on the advice of his doctors, to retire from the game.

It hadn't been pretty but it was a win and that was all that mattered.

Four games without a win followed, four games that saw three defeats, including a 2-0 reverse at early leaders Portsmouth, for whom, typically, Mike Channon was outstanding, on 31 August. He'd set up Nicky Morgan for Pompey's opener and was influential throughout. Yet, despite their slow start, no one at Norwich was panicking, least of all Ken Brown who played a virtually unchanged starting XI for all five of those opening games,[2] confident that Norwich would come good. Which they did in their sixth fixture, an emphatic 4-0 win over Sheffield United, a game that saw Drinkell lead the line superbly, capping a tremendous individual performance with two goals, his first for the club, with Paul Haylock and Steve Bruce the other scorers. Norwich were up and running, winning fifteen of their next twenty-one games, a superb run that, at one point, included ten successive league victories, the whole impressive sequence including convincing wins over Carlisle (4-0), Blackburn (3-0) and Millwall (6-1).

That run of form, one of the best and most convincing in the club's history to this day, saw the Canaries ease themselves into first place in the Division Two table a week and a half before Christmas, courtesy of a 3-1 win at Oldham. It was a position they held until the end of the season, compelling football from a side that knew only one way to play the game – and that was to attack. Take that 6-1 win over Millwall for example. Norwich had been so dominant on that day, that they were 4-0 up by half time, more than enough to earn them a standing ovation as they went off.

Unfortunately, as good as things were on the pitch, an ongoing row at boardroom level had been overshadowing the great work that Ken Brown and Mel Machin were doing with the team. Things had come to a fractious head back in September when Director Jimmy Jones quit in response to the board's decision to award the £1.5 million contract to build the new main stand to a company that he felt should not have been given the work. It further transpired that the successful company was one which Chairman Sir Arthur South did have personal links with, although, fair and scrupulously correct in his dealings at all times, South had already withdrawn from the voting process because of this link. But the row wouldn't die down, especially when it was revealed that there had been some procedural errors at the meeting held in order to decide who would get the contract which was alleged to surround proxy voting. Those errors were acknowledged and put right at the earliest possible opportunity, but it was still too much for Jones who, angered at the fact that such errors were even made in the first place, felt he had no option to propose a vote of no confidence in the board. This choice was well within Jones remit at the club. He had a successful amusements arcade in Great Yarmouth and held a 20 per cent shareholding in the club, so he was a powerful figure at Carrow Road and one who had to be listened to. The vote would have been made in December but, after an emergency meeting held on a Sunday evening, the existing board decided to pre-empt the vote and resigned, as one, en-bloc. This meant a temporary board of directors would need to be elected so that the club could continue to be effectively ran until a brand new seven man board of directors could formally be created and put into working place.

It is to Ken Brown's immense credit that, despite all that was going on behind the scenes; he, his staff and the players were able to focus on footballing matters and not allow themselves to be distracted. The club had, at the height of the in-house arguments, played five games in September, winning three and drawing two. In one of them, the steadily growing depth and quality of the squad was illustrated when Robert Rosario, in for the injured John Deehan, scored in the home game against Hull City. It was around this time that the Canaries interest and bid for Trevor Senior came to a head with Reading, having accepted Norwich's offer for the player, giving Norwich permission to talk to the player with regard to personal terms. These were long and protracted and eventually collapsed with no agreement even, it would seem, even coming close to being agreed. Sceptics could have pointed to the boardroom unrest at the club having an adverse effect on the deal but, given that Senior, having turned down the chance to join Norwich even after his club had agreed the fee, ultimately stayed with Reading for another two years, it would appear that the player, quite simply, did not want to move from Reading and had taken the opportunity to place himself out of Norwich's reach financially in order to ensure that he stayed put. He eventually joined Watford but, after a short and not particularly fruitful spell with them, followed by another brief period with Middlesbrough, he re-joined Reading a year after he had first left them. It seemed, therefore, that, in this instance at least, Norwich had been fortunate not to have signed the player in question.

With regard to the ongoing furore at board level, a small group of shareholders, presumably annoyed at the manner in which Jimmy Jones had acted then tried to prevent him from getting a place on the club's new board of directors. They were, however, easily outvoted and Jones took his place on the club's new board, one which was to be chaired by former director, Robert Chase. Sadly, this now signalled the end of Sir Arthur South's tenure at the club, an unfortunate conclusion to his time at the helm of the club he loved. His life and business interests had also included time spent as the senior partner of the Norwich Fur Company as well as a year spent as Lord Mayor of Norwich plus sitting as a Labour councillor. He was an active and genuine man who, throughout his time at Carrow Road always tried to do what he thought was right for the club and who didn't, as Ron Saunders would attest, suffer fools gladly. The club eventually named its South stand after him,[3] and, to this day, there is a Sir Arthur South lounge in the River End stand, a lasting tribute to a true servant of the football club.

Regardless of how events off the pitch had been developing during those early months of the season and the inevitable settling in period for the new board and Chairman that followed, the Canaries' attempts at a swift return to Division One continued unabated. By the time Norwich travelled to Shrewsbury Town for a league fixture on 8 February, they were on a run of nine consecutive away games without defeat, one that, inevitably, reached double figures with a convincing 3-0 win at Gay Meadow, Kevin Drinkell scoring two of the goals with Mark Barham grabbing the other after a typically well-crafted pass from David Williams. The Welshman, who'd signed from Bristol Rovers during the previous Summer had, surprisingly for the fans if not for Brown, turned out to be one of the Canaries most consistent and classy performers that season, not a bad return for a player who most Norwich fans would have admitted to never had previously heard of when he arrived. He was, during his spell in charge of Bristol Rovers from 1983 to 1985, been the youngest manager, at only 28, in the entire football league, eventually swapping to that to become the Canaries' oldest player when he joined the club. He was a stylish and creative midfielder, a player who always seemed to have time on the ball and who was never rushed in whatever he did, playing the game and conducting himself in the calmest and most professional manner at all times. He made thirty-nine league appearances for Norwich during the 1985/86 season, scoring eight goals but crafting many more, a player whose efforts were perhaps overshadowed that campaign by the free scoring efforts of Kevin Drinkell and rock-solid defensive partnership of Dave Watson and Steve Bruce, but who, nevertheless, made as important a contribution to the club's eventual title success that season as anyone.

The visit of Sunderland to Carrow Road on 9 April gave City the chance to clinch promotion if they could beat the team that they had not only come down with at the end of the previous season, but beaten at Wembley in the League Cup Final. Sunderland had struggled ever since, needing points in order to avoid a second consecutive relegation and they successfully kept the Canaries at bay as the game tamely fizzled out into a 0-0 draw, despite Kevin Drinkell and John Deehan having efforts cleared off the line. The Canaries starting line-up for the game reflected the changes that had been going on at the club and had been necessary in the wake of their relegation the previous May with only six players featuring who'd also played against Sunderland at Wembley. One notable absentee was Paul Haylock who had lost his place in the Norwich side to Ian Culverhouse. He'd played in all but one of Norwich's league games the previous season but, with Culverhouse immediately impressing as soon as he had been given his chance at Norwich, it was always going to be difficult for Haylock, a different type of right back to the poised and less energetic Culverhouse, to recover his place in the Norwich side. He had, like David Williams, arrived at Carrow Road as a virtual unknown, a player who was always, to quote Canaries historian Mike Davage, one who would be '... playing for the side rather than the gallery', a quote that could equally well be said about Williams.

The Canaries finally clinched promotion with a 2-0 victory against Bradford City at the Odsal Stadium three days after the Sunderland game. It wasn't one of football's great arenas, indeed, it wasn't even a ground that had been meant for football in the first place, but, given the way that Norwich had set about returning to Division One, no one was bothered about that. Fittingly, the goals came from two of the seasons new arrivals, Kevin Drinkell and Wayne Biggins, the latter arriving as an alternative to the once coveted Trevor Senior and proving to be a more than able alternative to Drinkell and Deehan in attack as he contributed seven goals in his twenty-eight starts but, again, like David Williams, proved himself an invaluable member of the squad when it came to working hard and creating chances for other players. Because Biggins was the classic centre forward, the man who came in, took the knocks, made the chances and got down and dirty in the company of opposing defenders. That was, and remains, the unglamorous side of a striker's game, the ability, indeed, the desire to be the maker rather than taker of goals. In John Deehan and Kevin Drinkell, Norwich had two great goal-scorers, players who would, given even a half chance, put the ball into the back of the net. But who created those chances in the first place? A player like Wayne Biggins, that's who. He'd be the one to make a nuisance of himself in opposing teams penalty areas, to put himself about and attract not just the attention but the occasional ire of defenders, leaving them to perhaps pay a little more heed to him than they should have done, leaving, as they did so, time and space for the likes of Deehan and Drinkell to finish the job off. Thus, as either of the two of them would celebrate a Norwich goal with arms aloft and fans chanting their name, there would be Wayne Biggins, taking himself back to his own half for the restart, shirt torn, skin grazed and job, as usual, done to perfection.

The Canaries 1985/86 season had also pretty much been done to perfection. That 2-0 win at Bradford clinched promotion with, a week later, the Division Two title confirmed as results elsewhere, combined with Norwich's 1-1 draw at home to Stoke City (for whom former Canary Keith Bertschin scored the opener) meant that Norwich's lead at the top of the table was now out of reach for both Charlton and Wimbledon, their nearest rivals. Two defeats followed, perhaps not surprisingly but, never the less, disappointing ones at Grimsby and Hull, the former tainted by fighting between opposing fans, shameful behaviour at what should have been a time of celebration that led to nine arrests and a half time appeal by a clearly shocked Ken Brown for some calm and order amongst the 3,000 travelling Norwich fans. But, at least the season ended on a high with the visit of Leeds United on the last day. Norwich had, the previous May, looked on in shock and no little anguish as three wins by Coventry City in their last three games had sent them down, now, following a 4-0 stroll against the once feared men from Yorkshire they were back-and as Champions. Norwich, admittedly, needed an own goal to settle the nerves on their big day but, once Brendan Ormsby had headed past Mervyn Day for the opener, it was one-way traffic and a party all the way with Kevin Drinkell, Steve Bruce and David Williams completing the route with Drinkell ending up being named as the club's Barry Butler Player of the Season, thanks to his twenty-two league goals from forty-one starts.

Slick and professional on the field and starting to look that way off it as well. With all the furore from the long running Boardroom dispute well and truly at an end, the new board took the opportunity to spend the time travelling to Bradford to hold a board meeting en-route with new Chairman Robert Chase explaining, 'No other businessman would spend four hours travelling without doing any work. So why should we?' There was no answer to that – just as no other club in the division has come even remotely close to finding an answer to the Canaries dominance throughout much of that Divison Two campaign. It that had seen the club go on an unbeaten run of eighteen league games from October to February with, perhaps the only low spot of the season, at least from a footballing point of view, being the club's defeats in both their league games against Wimbledon – and, on both occasions, after having taken the lead. City would, at least, have the chance to put that right at some point during the 1986/87 season as Wimbledon, red of both tooth and claw in their never say die attitude to the game, had been promoted in third place, eight points behind Norwich with ex-Canary John Fashanu, who'd joined the Dons from Millwall in March 1986 playing his part in the final stages of the season with four goals in their nine remaining league games.

The Canaries had, of course, missed the opportunity to test themselves in European football that season. Pre-match events involving the supporters of Liverpool and Juventus prior to the 1985 European Cup Final ultimately led to a sine die ban for all English clubs in Europe from the 1985/86 season onwards, something which then, as now, seems a disproportionately unfair punishment on both the clubs and their support who missed out on European football as a result. In an attempt to soften both the footballing and commercial losses suffered by the clubs affected, the Football League developed and introduced a new knock out competition, one that was initially known as the Football League Super Cup. That competition, which upon securing a televised sponsorship deal, became known as the Screen Sport Super Cup was originally intended to be held on an annual basis for the duration of the European ban on English club and competed for between the clubs that would, under normal circumstances, have been playing in European competition that season.

Far from being the success that the Football League felt it might be, the completion was, from the start, a dismal failure, both in terms of the interest given to it by both its participating clubs and their spectators alike as well as potential sponsors, with fledgling sponsor Screen Sport only agreeing to sponsor the final rather than the entire competition. All of the six clubs invited to take part in the completion, hopeful that their doing so would provoke some interest from their support and, through supposed prestige matches being held at their home grounds in lieu of European ties, generate some sort of income, at least through attendances. Norwich therefore found themselves in a qualifying group alongside Everton and Manchester United whilst Liverpool, Tottenham and Southampton made up the second group, the top two in each going through to the semi-finals stage.

The Canaries acquitted themselves well in the competition, beating Everton 1-0 at Carrow Road (Peter Mendham scoring the goal in front of just 12,021 spectators) alongside two 1-1 draws,[4] home and away against Manchester United, a 1-0 defeat to Everton at Goodison Park being their only group defeat. It was enough for the Canaries to reach the semi-finals by virtue of finishing second in their group, three points ahead of Manchester United, going onto face Liverpool over two legs before bowing out of the competition 4-2 on aggregate to a chorus of shrugged shoulders and general indifference all round, the same reaction, pretty much, that all the participating clubs had held for the competition from its outset. It had, at least, given the Canaries the opportunity to test themselves against three clubs from a higher Division and three, of course, who they wouldn't normally have played that season. Six games therefore of two apiece against Everton, Liverpool and Manchester United which, for the three home matches attracted a total attendance of 42,444; an average of 14,148 per game as against a seasonal average for the club's twenty-one league games of 14,527.

A worthwhile exercise? Logistically and commercially, probably not and that was almost certainly the case for all six competing teams, a fact not lost on the Football League who decided that the competition did nothing to help an already crowded fixture list and abolished it. As a footballing exercise however, it was almost certainly worthwhile for the Canaries. Those six games had given them a reminder of what playing top opposition was like as well as handing an opportunity for players who had yet to play at that level, the likes of Kevin Drinkell, David Williams and Mike Phelan, to test themselves against some of the best players in the game. The fact that they, and the club, exited the competition, one that they would have gone into as underdogs come whipping boys, with a record of P6 W1 D3 L2 shows that even though the Canaries didn't set the competition alight (but then no club did) with their football and results, they certainly did not disgrace themselves either and that the way they'd coped against the three top level sides they'd faced boded well for the future. This was, of course, providing you conveniently forgot the club's third match up that season against Liverpool, an FA Cup third round tie at Anfield that resulted in a heavy 5-0 defeat in a game that was played in a constant blizzard, weather conditions and an icy pitch which Norwich never seemed, on the night, to get to grips with, literally or figuratively. It was, however, a one off icy blip in an otherwise near perfect season.

Such was the lack of interest Everton manager Howard Kendall had for the competition, his now famous team talk prior their game at Carrow Road took up just ten words – 'What a waste of time this is. Out you go'.

The ban which had been handed out to all English clubs post-Heysel was eventually amended to allow clubs to travel overseas for friendly i.e. non-competitive matches in the close season. The Canaries took advantage of this during the summer of 1986 by undergoing a five match tour of Sweden, coming home unbeaten with one of those games, against IFK Härnösand, ending in a convincing 9-0 victory. Four domestic pre-season friendlies back home followed, none of them at Carrow Road as Norwich completed their preparations for the 1986/87 season with games against (Norwich City score first) Southend United (0-1); Cambridge United (3-0); Colchester United (2-1) and Lowestoft Town (4-1). The club had good reason not to arrange any pre-season games at Carrow Road as they were busy finishing off and preparing the new main stand open in order for it to be officially opened at the club's first home fixture that campaign, one that, following a request to the Football League for not only their opening game league to be an away one but for them to be omitted from the usual round of midweek league matches that followed.

After the euphoria of that convincing Division Two title success the previous season, the excitement and positive anticipation for the new season was very much dealt a setback for the Norwich support when two of the club's leading players chose to move to pastures new that summer. Chris Woods was the first to leave, signing for Rangers on 1 July for £600,000 with captain Dave Watson following just two days before the start of the season, the Canaries' inspirational captain, described as the club's 'jewel' by Ken Brown, returning to Merseyside in order to sign for Everton for £1.23 million, a record fee for Norwich. Both players would, of course, be enormously missed and their departures meant that, again, the club had two glaring holes to fill in crucial positions, just as they had when Kevin Keelan and Duncan Forbes had eventually left the club. Yet, in fairness to the players, they could have left the club in the immediate aftermath of relegation a little under eighteen months earlier – and would certainly have had the opportunity to do so. Yet they didn't only feel obliged to stay at Norwich in order to play their part in getting the club back to Division One, they wanted to, a wonderful sense of both loyalty to the club and commitment to putting something right which was as rare in the game then as it is today.

So there were few arguments or recriminations when Woods and Watson left. Sadness yes. But that was as far as it went. The club had made an effort to keep Watson for another year and there could even have been talk of a new contract but he had decided he wanted to move on, later admitting that, 'I wanted to get higher up; I wanted to win the FA Cup; the League Championship. I wanted to go on winning things and, no disrespect to Norwich, we weren't going to win the Championship.'[5]

The Canaries were now a little over £1.8 million to the good in terms of transfer fees received – not bad going against an original outlay of £275,000. But suddenly having all that money in the bank was all very well and good-and it at least gave the club the option of adding some new players to the squad in order to fill the sizeable gap left by the departures of the two players. But, and, again, this echoes the thoughts of those at the club when other Canary luminaries had moved on in recent years: how on earth do you go about replacing two players as important and as good as Chris Woods and Dave Watson? The club had struck gold in signing them both – but could lightning strike as fortuitously a second time?

In terms of finding a new defensive partner for Steve Bruce, the Canaries ended up signing a fellow Northumbrian for their new Captain by signing Sunderland captain Shaun Elliott for a fraction of the money they'd received for Watson. Elliott would almost certainly lined up against the Canaries in the League Cup Final just under eighteen months earlier had he not been suspended and had ended up being a player who Sunderland missed on the day just as much as Norwich would have missed either Watson or Steve Bruce had they not been playing. Elliott was now a teammate of Bruce, taking his place alongside his new Captain in the Norwich side that met Chelsea on the first day of the 1986/87 season at Stamford Bridge. Bruce was now the only survivor from the Norwich team that had beaten Sunderland at Wembley on that memorable day, a sign of just how quickly and effectively Ken Brown had been rebuilding his Norwich side since the club's relegation at the end of that same season.

Elliott was joined by two other new signings in West London, Ian Crook who had arrived from Tottenham for just £80,000 and fellow midfielder Trevor Putney who had arrived from Ipswich as part of an exchange deal that had seen John Deehan head in the opposite direction. The club's decision to offload Deehan seemed a puzzling one at the time, he was still only twenty-nine when he left Norwich and, with a club record of seventy goals from 197 League and Cup appearances, would, have in all likelihood, been more than capable of adding to that total and maybe even going onto score a century of goals for the club. He had, however, found it increasingly difficult to displace Kevin Drinkell and Wayne Biggins as the club's first choice strike partnership and, despite his versatility meaning he could play in most outfield positions (including a spell at left back) he was, first and foremost, a centre forward, so the opportunity for him to join a club where he would be first choice in that position was, eventually, one he felt he couldn't turn down.

The signing of Crook turned out to be yet another astute piece of business by Brown, one to rival the acquisition of Martin Peters by John Bond for half the amount the Canaries paid for Crook. Well, almost. If no one has come close to matching the class, elegance, inventiveness and sheer footballing artistry of Peters as a Norwich player, then Ian Crook comes mighty close. He would, no doubt, have gone onto be a regular first team player at Tottenham, that and, in all possibility, an England regular as well, had it not been for the fact that a plethora of midfield talents stood in the queue ahead of him at White Hart Lane. Glenn Hoddle and Ossie Ardiles for example. Even if Crook had been the third best midfield player in the country whilst he was at Tottenham, the fact that Hoddle and Ardiles were probably the top two when they were at their artistic peak means he still have been a player on the fringes of the first team. His rise to prominence with Norwich was like his game – calm and measured. And, although the midfield quartet he was part of for Norwich's first game of the 1986/87 season was completely different, in both terms of personnel and playing style to the one he graced from 1992 to 1994, he never looked out of place and forever offered a graceful and technically adept alternative to the traditional midfield terriers he often played alongside or against.

The first of a series of ball winning and energetic midfielders that Crook played alongside at Norwich was Trevor Putney who'd arrived at Carrow Road in part exchange for John Deehan. With Putney an ex-Ipswich player there was, as you might expect, some apprehension from parts of the club's support with regard to his arrival at the club. But nothing serious. Ex-Ipswich players arriving at Norwich were regarded in much the same way as you might regard a spider or a snake, in that you are conditioned from birth to neither like it nor trust its origins, yet, after a gentle introduction and some handling, you learn that they are infact a miracle of nature and a sight to behold. Now Putney was not exactly a miracle of nature. But then very few footballers are. But his competitive style of play together with the sheer *joie de vivre* he exhibited whenever he was on a football pitch immediately endeared him to the club's fans, just as previous Ipswich Town players who'd seen the light had done the same in their deeds and words. Peter Morris, Johnny Miller, Clive Woods – the latter a self-confessed Norwich City fan even when he was playing for Ipswich. They'd all known a great opportunity and a good club when the chance came. And Putney was no different. His cause was helped by the fact he was, and remains, one of the great characters of the game, someone who Jeremy Goss later described as 'one of the funniest blokes I've ever met'. That, plus his ability on the pitch would have swiftly soon held Putney in very high regard at Carrow Road, both amongst the clubs support and his playing colleagues. And especially Ian Crook, the magician who Putney was brought in to complement, the steel to his silk and his extra pair of legs.

The opening fixture of the 1986/87 season meant a trip to Stamford Bridge to play Chelsea, the second top flight in succession when the Canaries first opposition had also been their last of the previous season at that level. Back in May 1985, the Canaries 2-1 win at Stamford Bridge had given them very genuine hope that they had, with that win, done enough to stay in Division One. That was, of course, before Coventry City had gone on that previously unfeasible three game winning run that had dumped Norwich back into Division Two. But now they were back and determined, right from the outset, that they'd never have to go into the last few games of either this, or any other season, with the threat of relegation hanging over their heads again.

Ken Brown's line-up for the Chelsea game showed ten changes from the side that he'd picked for that ultimately fruitless win at the same stadium fifteen months or so earlier, with Steve Bruce the only survivor. Upwardly mobile Norwich also showed a change on the day in their shirt sponsors, with the homely and locally known name of Poll Withey being replaced by multinational brewing giant Fosters. For those Norwich fans who preferred the taste of traditionally brewed real ale as opposed to that of a mass-produced lager, it was a bit of a sop to their personal tastes, both sartorially and literally, but, such was the growth and commercialism in the game at that time. Any company or business that was willing to pay the club large amounts of money in return for having their name on the front of the shirt was, albeit with some misgivings, going to be reluctantly accepted.

With Chris Woods now in Glasgow with the blue half of the Old Firm, the daunting task of replacing him was handed to his one-time deputy Graham Benstead who'd made his debut for the club in a 2-0 defeat at Arsenal in April 1985 but had not featured since. Benstead, like Woods, had originally signed from QPR on loan the previous month as much needed cover for Woods who had already missed some games that season, his place then being taken, for three games, by another loanee, Joe Corrigan. Yet, Benstead, who went onto sign for the Canaries permanently for just £10,000, was not seen as merely cover for Woods at that time, but as a genuine rival to him for the number one shirt and, potentially, his long term replacement. The reputation that he'd brought with him to Carrow Road certainly seemed to merit it. He'd been playing for Wimbledon in a Southern League floodlit game against QPR and had impressed Tommy Docherty so much that he promptly arranged for Benstead, then just 17, to sign for them as an apprentice. Docherty was relieved of his managerial duties a fortnight later but it didn't take long for his successor, Terry Venables, to sign him on professional terms with the proverbial icing on the cake for Benstead coming in September 1981 when he played for the England youth team against their Austrian counterparts in Umag, a game England won 3-0.

Impressive credentials for a player who the Canaries had supposedly signed as cover. Norwich were not, of course, intending to sell Woods at the time Benstead signed, nor he shown any signs of wanting to leave the club. But the Norwich management team were aware that, given his ability and seemingly endless potential, he wouldn't be a Norwich City player for the rest of his career. Signing Benstead was therefore a wise move, a chance for the player to bed into the side and the club as a whole, learn from his initial role as Woods' understudy, fill in for him incase of injury or suspension and, as and when required, step into his place as the club's new first choice goalkeeper. It was sound long term planning by the club, had only cost them £10,000 and meant that Benstead was more than ready to step into the first time for the opening game of the new season.

He impressed on what was only his second league start for the club as did debutants Elliott, Crook and Putney. Bruce was the new club captain and started as he meant to go on, forever cajoling and encouraging his defensive partners – as well as praising them when the occasion demanded it, especially when Benstead made a couple of point saving stops from Kerry Dixon as Chelsea pressed forward, desperate to see the new boys off in front of a small but vocal Stamford Bridge crowd. The resulting 0-0 draw might not have done much for the football purists and it would doubtless had been last on *Match Of The Day* had it been played a quarter of a century later, but no matter. Norwich had, with a new goalkeeper and captain as well as three new faces weathered the brief Chelsea storm and done a thoroughly professional job. The Canaries' defence was a little bit more charitable in their next match a week later against Southampton, conceding three goals, one of which was a 30 yard strike from Mark Dennis, a man with a reputation built on his hard man image rather than a tendency for the spectacular. But it mattered not. At least, not that much, as Norwich scored four of their own, securing their first win of the season in a thrilling manner, the goals being nicely shared out as part of the process with Kevin Drinkell, Dale Gordon, David Williams and Steve Bruce all getting the better of Peter Shilton. The game also saw, as planned, the official opening of the new stand although the attendance of just 15,205 was again, very disappointing. At least those who were there were the very first to see a certain Matt Le Tissier in action, the Southampton player making his senior club debut on the day.

By the time the Canaries travelled to Luton on 11 October they had put together an impressive run of six wins in their opening ten league games, a sequence that had included a massively impressive 4-1 win over Aston Villa at Villa Park, a game that saw future Norwich Captain Ian Butterworth make his debut for the club having signed on loan from Nottingham Forest. The game at Kenilworth Road was unremarkable by comparison, save for the fact that the result, a 0-0 draw, took Norwich to the top of the table. The club's record over those ten games certainly made for impressive reading and no one could, at that point, form and results withstanding, argue with them being there.

P10 W6 D3 L1 GF18 GA11 GD +7

What was also pleasing about that run was that those eighteen goals so far scored had been spread around eight different players. Kevin Drinkell was, and remained, the focal point of the Canaries attack and would have been expected to score at least 15-20 goals that season. But it was as important for his teammates to get their fair share of goals as well and take some of the burden away from him, something which made the fact that seven other Norwich players had also scored at least one in the league after just ten games especially satisfying for Ken Brown and Mel Machin.[6] They didn't, of course, expect Norwich to match, or even come anywhere close to scoring the eighty-four league goals they'd scored in winning the Division Two title. Yet, at the same time, they would have expected to improve on the forty-six scored during the relegation season.[7]

Ever mindful of the need to have reliable goal-scorers in his team that season as well as having an alternative if there was a worst case scenario of long term injury for Kevin Drinkell that season, Ken Brown pulled off another of his minor transfer coups in the summer in signing striker David Hodgson from Sunderland on a free transfer after he had been released by Sunderland where, despite his obvious talent and goal-scoring ability, he had scored only five goals in forty games. His was a clear case of a potentially stellar career going off the rails. He hadn't exactly been a prolific goal-scorer at Middlesbrough, his first club, yet there had still been something about him that led to a big money move to Liverpool where, right on cue, he demonstrated that, in a good team, he had an eye for goals, scoring four goals in his first six games for the club and positively thriving playing alongside Kenny Dalglish and Ian Rush, ending his first season with them on nine goals from thirty-seven matches, a reasonable return for a player whose outstanding pace meant that Liverpool manager Joe Fagan saw him as a natural fit for the position of right sided midfielder in his Liverpool team.

Hodgson saw himself first and foremost as a striker and demanded a transfer when Liverpool signed Michael Robinson from Brighton. But the move to Sunderland had never worked out and now, four years after signing for Liverpool (where he won two League Championship medals) he was a free agent desperate for a chance to rebuild his career. He had been on the verge of signing for Swedish club side IFK Gothenburg before Brown stepped up his bid to add him to his pool of strikers and, rather than shy from the obvious challenge of competing with Kevin Drinkell, Wayne Biggins and Robert Rosario for a place in the Norwich team, Hodgson signed, grateful for another chance in Divison One, worked hard and waited for his opportunity. It duly came with his full debut in a League Cup 3rd round tie at home to Millwall on 29 October, a debut that players can only normally dream about as he proceeded to score with his first touch of the ball before going onto claim a hat-trick in Norwich's 4-1 win, his pace a perfect match for Kevin Drinkell's (who, inevitably, scored the other Norwich goal) strength and ability to hold the ball up in order to make chances for others. It seemed, however momentarily, as if Ken Brown had discovered a potential strike match that could have been forged in footballing heaven.

Unsurprisingly then, Hodgson retained his starting place for the Canaries' next league game which was at, of all places, Liverpool, the club where he had tasted so much trophy winning glory. He extended his scoring run at Anfield as well, making it four goals in just two games for his new club but, sadly for both Hodgson and Norwich, his 8th minute strike was no more than a late consolation as Liverpool won 6-2, Paul Walsh scoring a hat-trick of his own in the process in a game that, ultimately, was the beginning of the end of the unfortunate Graham Benstead's career as a Norwich City player.

In many ways, Benstead's career at Norwich had mirrored that of one of his predecessors in the Canaries Number one shirt, namely Roger Hansbury. He had acted as a more than willing back up to the seemingly immovable and almost irreplaceable Kevin Keelan, appearing in a game or two whenever Keelan was missing but, for the most part, being content to bide his time and wait for the chance to make that position his own. It had come following another heavy defeat for the Canaries against Liverpool, the spectacular 3-5 reverse at Carrow Road in February 1979. That had turned out to be the last of Keelan's 659 League and Cup games for the Canaries as the evergreen keeper set out for a career in the USA that continues to this day, leaving Hansbury with sixteen league games remaining that season to make the number one position his own. Yet neither Hansbury or Clive Baker were able to do so, leaving Ken Brown little option but to look further afield for a replacement for Keelan, a search that ultimately led to the arrival of Chris Woods at Carrow Road. And, whilst Woods was never going to be a bigger name or more constant presence in the Norwich goal than Keelan had been, he'd still done enough in his own five year spell at Carrow Road to make himself almost as daunting a figure in terms of replacing as Keelan had done before him. Thus, where Hansbury and Baker had not been quite able to step out of Kevin Keelan's shadow at Norwich City, neither was Graham Benstead quite able to do so with regard to Chris Woods. All three players were good goalkeepers and professionals in their own right as their later careers went onto prove (Benstead went onto win promotion to Division One with Sheffield United in 1990 before winning a Third Division title winners medal with Brentford two years later) yet were never able to fully meet the demands and expectations forced upon them at Carrow Road for no other reason other than they were 'guilty' of following in the footsteps of a couple of Norwich City legends.

The Canaries had been actively searching for a new goalkeeper long before Benstead's nightmare game at Liverpool that November. However, the man that Ken Brown and Mel Machin had in mind had, as far as the summer of 1986 was concerned, just headed off on his holidays, having celebrated, along with his Aberdeen teammates, their 3-0 win over Hearts in that year's Scottish FA Cup Final – even though he hadn't been playing. Twenty-two year old Bryan Gunn did, however, have his mind set on a move to another club at the time, and, with his chances of a regular first team place at Aberdeen made unlikely by the presence of Scottish international Jim Leighton there, had half an eye on a move to Glasgow

Rangers that summer. That particular dream had been shattered as, whilst he was on holiday, Gunn was flicking through a copy of the Scottish Daily Record which claimed that Rangers, the club he, and his manager, Alex Ferguson, felt he was about to join, were in the running for the signature of England goalkeeper Peter Shilton who was then at Southampton. The next morning, half dreading reading a report in the same newspaper that Shilton had indeed signed for Rangers, Gunn saw that Shilton was staying put – but that Rangers had, in his place, signed another England goalkeeper, namely Chris Woods from Norwich.

Gunn's initial reaction was, not surprisingly, one of huge disappointment. He felt that he had more than served his learning time at Aberdeen under the twin tutelage of Alex Ferguson and Jim Leighton, time that had now prepared him to move on and challenge for a first team place himself somewhere. And who better than Rangers? Celtic had Pat Bonner and Peter Latchford, so there wasn't likely to be an opportunity at Parkhead soon. And that was even if either he or, for that matter, Celtic would be interested in the first place. The fact was that, with Rangers now having signed Woods, Gunn was stuck between the proverbial rock and a hard place, at least as far as continuing his career in Scotland was concerned. After Aberdeen, there was Celtic, Rangers and – well, that was it. Yes, both Dundee United and Hearts were doing well. But neither of them were as big a club as Aberdeen, let alone Rangers. It seemed, therefore that, unless the unthinkable happened and Aberdeen sold Leighton, Gunn was destined to spend more time as Aberdeen number two, something he was now not prepared to accept. Gunn sought out Ferguson as soon as he's returned home from Scotland. Ferguson, as straight as they come, admitted that he hadn't seen Rangers signing of Woods as ever happening. Yet that move could still work to Gunn's advantage as Ferguson added, 'Ken Brown is very interested in you and they'll look to take you at Norwich on my recommendation.' Unexpected news for Gunn but pleasing all the same. He maybe hadn't considered moving down to England but this sounded like a good opportunity. Norwich had just been promoted, he'd even see them on television a few times so it sounded a possibility worth taking further. He threw himself into pre-season training with Aberdeen with his usual commitment and enthusiasm before, just as thoughts of heading south and a meeting with Ken Brown came to mind, Jim Leighton suffered from a slight injury, meaning Gunn was needed in goal – but for Aberdeen. It did, however, give Mel Machin the chance to take a look at the Canaries prospective new goalkeeper in action which is exactly what happened as Brown's trusted number two flew north to watch Gunn playing for Aberdeen in a Scottish League Cup second round game at home to Alloa Athletic on 20 August – three days before the Canaries opening day fixture against Chelsea which, up to now, Graham Benstead was down to play in. Ferguson introduced Gunn to Machin before the game and, as the teams went out for the game, Gunn noticed Machin standing by the tunnel looking on. He knew then that he needed to have a good game on the night, but, as luck would have had it, with the game against lowly opposition, one that Aberdeen won 4-0, he had a very quiet match indeed, later recalling to me that he had perhaps needed to make one late save in the game but, by then, grateful that he'd used his pre-match warm up as an 'audition'.

He'd done enough. Machin was suitably impressed and, by the time Leighton was fit again, the move to Norwich swiftly went through with Brown meeting his new goalkeeper at Norwich Airport on 15 October 1986, that meeting recorded for posterity by a photographer from the *Eastern Daily Press* with the paper running the story in its next day edition. Gunn was big news but, even so, he knew he would have to bide his time and wait for his league debut.

That opportunity came a week after that heavy defeat at Liverpool, Benstead being ruled out after he sustained a shoulder injury early on in that game which meant that Gunn the one and only change to the Norwich starting XI for the home game against Tottenham a week later. He played exceptionally well against a strong Spurs side which featured strikers Clive Allen and Belgian international Nico Claesen as well as Chris Waddle.[8] Norwich's first goal was scored, fittingly against his old club, by Ian Crook, right place and right time to finish off a sweeping move that had involved most of his teammates. And, although Claesen managed an equaliser, it was a short lived joy for the away side as, just four minutes later, Shaun Elliott towered above everyone else on the pitch to head the winner, courtesy of a typically precise Crook free kick past Ray Clemence, the ex-Liverpool and England goalkeeper making a point of seeking Gunn out at the final whistle to shake his hand, telling him, 'Well done. You made a couple of great saves out there today', those few words having a deep impact on Gunn as he later revealed in his excellent autobiography,[9] admitting that 'It was a dream come true, my hero telling me how well I'd played. Fantastic.'

It had been a good debut. It might even have been called an outstanding one with Norwich's new man in the number one shirt, the latest custodian of a role and proud tradition that included other fine goalkeepers such as Woods, Kevin Keelan, Sandy Kennon, Ken Nethercott and Harry Dukes. He had, in a sign of what was to come over the coming years, made a last minute save that belied his youth and lack of experience at the top level in England, saving a header from Claesen that had looked goal bound from the moment contact had been made. But not this time, not against this goalkeeper. He had, and would, turn out to be yet another inspired signing from Brown, a manager who seemed to have the sort of eye for a player that few of his contemporaries had. It was serving the Canaries well.

Three more players made their Canary debuts in the coming weeks, one of whom was destined to become a prominent figure in the club's first season in the Premier

League six years later as well as the subsequent run in the UEFA Cup in 1993. The player in question here was Ruel Fox who made his first appearance for the club in the 2-1 win over Oxford United on 29 November, the much liked Foxy stepping up to replace the injured Mike Phelan with the managers son, Kenny Brown junior also making his debut in that game, coming off the bench in order to replace the injured Wayne Biggins. The Canaries had also brought in Mark Seagraves on loan from Liverpool, the highly rated left back filling in for another injured player in Tony Spearing. Things didn't get much better for the injury ravaged Norwich after the win against Oxford United either with more players having to drop out for various reasons, so many infact that, by the time City travelled to Goodison Park to play Everton on 6 December, nine first team players were unavailable due to injury, including Tony Spearing, Mike Phelan, Shaun Elliott and Wayne Biggins. The circumstances at least gave Ken Brown the opportunity to give some of the club's fringe players a chance to impress with Jeremy Goss and Robert Rosario both coming in for their first games of the season at Goodison. For Goss, part of the Canaries side that had won the FA Youth Cup at the same venue back in 1983, it was his first league start since the visit of Southampton on 12 January 1985-78 games previously with only Steve Bruce, yet again, the link between Brown's previous side. The ever patient and resilient Goss did well on the day, a shining, biting member of a Norwich side that, clearly weakened all over the pitch was swept aside to the tune of 4-0 against the eventual Champions, the second big defeat the Canaries had endured on Merseyside that season. Unfortunately for Goss, it was a cameo appearance for him only as, having gone seventy-eight games without a league start and he now was forced to wait another forty games before he would get another opportunity, albeit under a different manager.

It was, at least, a happy Christmas for Canary fans everywhere, celebrated with a deserved 2-1 win over Nottingham Forest at Carrow Road, Ian Crook and Robert Rosario both scoring in a frenetic four minute spell ten minutes after Stuart Pearce had put Forest ahead – and in front of a wholly satisfactory attendance of 22,131, not far short of 10,000 up on the loyal souls who had been there for the Oxford United game a month earlier. Ken Brown was, by now, playing a 4-3-3 formation in the Canaries games, one that saw Ian Crook at the centre of a midfield trio with Mike Phelan and Dale Gordon on either side of him just ahead of an forward line of Wayne Biggins, Kevin Drinkell and Robert Rosario. As an attacking trio, the three of them were certainly a handful for any defence; all were physically strong, good in the air and able to hold the ball up for one another, qualities that meant the pace and trickery of Dale Gordon, a first team regular by now became an added worry for opposing defences. The four of them played in 127 league games between them during the 1986/87 season, the twenty-eight goals they scored more than half the Canaries end of season total, testimony to both their importance to the side as well as their effectiveness, especially at home where the Canaries lost just two league games all season (to Watford and Everton), with only Everton and Nottingham Forest losing fewer.

Norwich eventually finished the 1986/87 season in fifth place, the club's highest ever finishing position. Admirable evidence of all the hard work Ken Brown had put in at the club, work and relative achievements that had turned him into the most successful manager in the club's history. A particular highpoint had been the trip to Old Trafford the day after that win over Nottingham Forest with the Canaries getting an impressive Christmas 'double' with their 1-0 win, their ever in the league at the ground. The decisive goal had been another typical moment of magic by Kevin Drinkell, stretching into a diving header from the more and more impressive Ian Culverhouse with ten minutes left. That win lifted Norwich to fourth in the table, one point short of second place. A disappointing run of thirteen league games with only two wins to call their own followed for Norwich, a sequence that did, admittedly, see only two defeats. However, too many of those games, eight in all, ended as draws and it is interesting to speculate where, given a few more wins from that run, where Norwich might have ended up in the table with just an extra four points from the twenty lost during that spell being enough to have seen them finish the season in third place. One notable achievement for the club that season was the fact that in five league games where the Canaries had originally fallen behind in the game, they had been able to bring themselves back into the game and win it, a sign of the sort of belief and personal resolve which Ken Brown had instilled into his team. The five in question were the games at Carrow Road against Southampton, Leicester, Nottingham Forest and Liverpool, plus the away fixture at Charlton. Out of those five, the win against Liverpool was the most impressive. After all, it not only served to emphasise Liverpool's domestic superiority at the time but also what a prolific goal-scorer Rush was. Prior to the 1987 League Cup Final against Arsenal, Rush had scored 144 goals for Liverpool, all of them in games that they hadn't lost. Impressive. That is, at least, until they came up against Charlie Nicholas at Wembley that year. Rush had given Liverpool the lead in the game (to an inevitable chorus of, '... and of course, Liverpool never lose a game in which Ian Rush has scored a goal') meaning that, to all extents and purposes, the game was now over and it would be just as well if Lester Shapter blew his whistle there and then in order to let everyone get away earlier than usual, including Liverpool with the trophy. But not so. Arsenal not only had the temerity to play on, they also won the game with two goals from Charlie Nicholas sealing both the win and the end of that most oft quoted footballing statistic. Or at least you would think so. Almost in retaliation to the reaction that the record had gone, Liverpool fans redefined it, pointing out to anyone who'd listen (or those who would rather not, but were given no choice in the matter) that

Liverpool still had yet to lose a league match that Ian Rush had scored in and that the league was far more important than any cup and, with that in mind, the stat in question could, and would, not unlike a piece of tumbleweed skipping its way across the footballing horizon, still be trotted out for all the world to hear. Which it was when, after thirty-seven minutes of their first match following that final, a league game against Norwich at Carrow Road, Rush put Liverpool ahead. That's Liverpool who had never lost a league match in which Ian Rush had scored in.

The Canaries were about to do football and favour and consign, once and for all, the matter to the record books. Drinkell set up Trevor Putney for the first before hitting the winner himself from an acute angle with no more than a couple of minutes left. Liverpool had lost, their Championship aspirations were now looking remote at best – and football's most quoted stat had, finally, been laid to rest. Except of course the one that said Liverpool had never lost an FA Cup match in which Ian Rush had scored. But then Norwich could say the same thing about the FA Cup and Paul Haylock.

That win against the reigning league champions was probably Norwich's best performance of the season. Not only because it was against Liverpool but because of the fact that Rush had scored to put them ahead and had done so shortly before half time. That was classic Liverpool. Take the sting out of the opposition early on, wear them down, score in or around a ten minute window before the interval and then take command in the second half. They were masters at it as Norwich knew only too well. But not on this occasion. The Canaries didn't, as the script usually dictated, simply roll over and give in, they fought back. Belief and momentum, the latter something that they had maintained pretty much since the beginning of the season saw them rise to the challenge and win the game, despite all the odds that suggested that they wouldn't and couldn't. That it was Liverpool. And Ian Rush. Plus the fact they'd been heavily beaten at Anfield. This Norwich weren't there for the taking, they were there to win the game. And win it they had.

Drinkell's winning goal was his fourth in six games and eighteenth of the season in League and Cup. He'd proved, yet again, the near genius that Brown had when it came to identifying a player who would come into his side and improve it. Two players that he'd signed during the course of that season plus one who he brought in for the beginning of the 1987/88 campaign ultimately became pivotal members of the side that Mike Walker so memorably took to third place in the first ever season of Premier League football, the 1992/93 season. Indeed, of the side that took part in that game against Arsenal, seven were players who were either bought or given their Canaries debut by Ken Brown.[10] These were players that both Walker and his immediate predecessor, Dave Stringer, would have been more than grateful to make pivotal members of their own Norwich teams; a fact that is sometimes forgotten when the plaudits are being handed out for Walkers side and its achievements that season – his achievements were partly down to Brown's players and the spirit and belief that he brought to both them and the club.

Norwich's final league game of that season resulted in yet another impressive win, this time at Highbury where, prior to kick-off, Arsenal had lost just three league matches all season. That, their reputation and the fact it was the last game of the season, a time when most players' minds are drifting towards distant beaches and sun loungers mattered not and the Gunners were added to an impressive roll of honour for the season as regards victories over more illustrious opponents, joining a list that included wins over Aston Villa, European Champions only five seasons earlier (4-1); Tottenham (2-1); Manchester United (1-0) and Liverpool (2-1). Yet, frustratingly, given those and other notable wins throughout the campaign, Norwich had slipped up when it came to those games that they might have been expected to win. Frustrating results and performances included games against Watford (lost 1-3); Luton Town (Kenilworth Road, drew 0-0); Wimbledon (Plough Lane, lost 2-0); Charlton Athletic (home, 1-1); Wimbledon (home, 0-0); Luton Town (home, 0-0) and Coventry City (Highfield Road, 1-1). There is a danger, of course, of over-analysing results, performances and 'what ifs?' and I have already gone too far into it here. So it stops now. It is, nonetheless, interesting to look back and think, in hindsight, what the club could have achieved during that season, and others, if they had not been quite so inconsistent when it mattered. Norwich certainly slipped up a few times in exactly that fashion during the 1986/87 season. Yet, as can also be seen, they also won their fair share of matches when it might have been more reasonably expected that they would come out of them with nothing more than pride in a good showing. Football has, as we have all seen and now easily expect, a habit of balancing things out in the end and that campaign was one which proved just how it did that for the Canaries whose finishing position of fifth was, on the whole, what they deserved and one achieved on a balance of the usual run of good results when they weren't anticipated and bad ones when the opposite was assumed. Just ask fans of Everton. Their season had included defeats to Charlton and Watford and disappointing draws against Coventry City, QPR and Oxford United and they ended the season as Champions, nine points clear of runners up Liverpool.

There had been some low spots during the season, not least missing out on a trip to Wembley. Norwich had, despite the distraction of the ill-fated Screen Sport Supercup the previous season, opted to take part in another new knock out cup competition known as the Full Members Cup, another attempt by the Football League to offer some kind of alternative to those clubs which had qualified for European football but, through no fault of their own, now found themselves banned from competing in each of the (then) three competitions they had otherwise qualified for.

The Full Members Cup did, unintentionally at least, illustrate the attitude the 'powers that be' had towards their competing clubs at the time. Those participating clubs, including Norwich, who played in either the First or Second Divisions at the time were granted full voting rights within the league structure whilst those in the Third and Fourth Divisions were mere associate members who were shuffled off towards their own competition, the Associate Members Cup which survives to this day as the Johnsons Paint Trophy. Back in 1986, Norwich entered the Full Members Cup at the 2nd round stage, beating Coventry City 2-1, thanks to two goals from, who else, Kevin Drinkell who, far from ever being rested at any stage of the season, started in every single one of the Canaries fifty-three League and Cup games, scoring in the League, FA, League and Full Members Cups in the same season, an impressive achievement. The tournament failed, however, to capture the imagination of the Canary support with only 6,236 in attendance at Carrow Road for the game against Coventry. Norwich went as far as the semi-finals after subsequent wins over Southampton and Portsmouth but even the chance of a Wembley place on offer to the winner in the semi-final at Charlton was a turn off, with just 5,431 there to watch the home team beat Norwich 2-1 after extra time.

A more significant blow to the club's future aspirations came at the beginning of May when Assistant manager Mel Machin quit Carrow Road in order to accept the managerial job at Manchester City. Machin had been a hugely popular player as well as an influential and highly capable Coach in his time at the club, one who had a reputation for his bark not being half as bad as his bite, yet, despite that, players liked and respected him and coaching and tactical acumen. It wasn't as if going to Manchester City was an offer Machin couldn't refuse either. They were in the process of dropping out of Division One under a deadweight of unsustainable debt and a large and, for the most part, wholly unremarkable squad of players. A club light-years away from the multi-billion pound behemoth that astrides the world game today. Then there was John Bond, the former Norwich manager who he'd also played for at Bournemouth, the man who had a 'job for life' at Carrow Road but who had given that up for trying to do the impossible in Manchester. His high profile role and ultimate dismissal had, after a brief spell at Burnley, saw him take charge at Birmingham City who'd spent much of the season fighting against relegation from Division Two. The once mighty had fallen a long way. Yet, had he resisted the overtures coming from Manchester, might he, even now, still be at Carrow Road, either as manager or even as a member of the board? The grass was not always greener on the other side in football yet the prospect that it might have been was irresistible to Machin who, like Bond, had a job for life at Norwich if he wanted it. That, plus the very strong possibility that whenever Ken Brown chose to move on himself, Machin would be in pole position, indeed, quite possibly the only contender in the race, for the top job at Carrow Road himself. Machin didn't even get a warm welcome at his new club, at least not from the Manchester City support who questioned the appointment from the start, with the influential fanzine *Blue Print* depicting him as something of a country bumpkin,[11] producing a faux managerial column from him in their publication called 'Farmer Mel'.

No reason at all for him to want to leave then. Yet he not only felt compelled to go, but did so with three games of the season remaining for Norwich, an abrupt and unexpected departure which, you feel, might, under normal circumstances, have waited until the end of the season. But no, Machin wanted out and he wanted to do so with time left to save the club from the relegation that had seemed likely since the previous autumn – and almost certain since a 4-0 defeat at Leicester City on 28 March had sent them to the bottom of the table. Could he do it? Well, if he did, he'd have immediate hero status. But if he didn't? Well, he'd only had three games to try and save them, one of which was at Everton. It was a win-win situation for Machin whose sudden departure from Norwich had been precipitated by uncertainty over his long term future at Carrow Road and the lack of commitment from the club to him over a new contract.

One of the reasons behind Machin's decision to move on may have been the rise and rise, at Carrow Road, of David Williams. The cultured midfielder, a virtual unknown when he was signed by Brown for the start of the 1985/86 season had been outstanding during his first season at the club with only a severe injury to his Achilles restricting him to just twelve league appearances during the 1986/87 campaign. His class on the pitch was unquestionable, his expertise and reputation as a coach swiftly growing. He had, after all, prior to joining Norwich, spent two years as player-manager of Bristol Rovers and, at thirty-two, was a decade younger than Machin. He was also a fan of the more technical approach to coaching whereas Machin might have been more dedicated to the traditional, old school methods. Whatever. The fact was, Williams, who had been a Brown signing whilst Machin was one of Bond's players, was very highly rated and regarded within the club and it dies seem as if that, whilst the Canaries didn't want to lose the services of Machin and would never had made moves to precipitate his departure from Carrow Road they weren't going to make much effort in trying to get him to stay if an offer came in from elsewhere.

It was hardly surprising then when, in the wake of Machin's departure to Maine Road, Williams was immediately appointed as Norwich player-coach, a different title to that of Machin's of assistant manager but, nevertheless, one that saw him step up and become number two to Brown.

Brown, Williams and their players certainly had a lot to think about as they all went their respective ways for a few weeks holiday after the Canaries had wrapped up all of their end of season formalities. As usual, they had seen a number of friendly and post-season obligations met, including two domestic friendlies (at

Southend, drew 1-1, and at Bournemouth, lost 4-2), before the club jetted off to the USA for a gruelling end of season tour that saw them play matches on both the east and west coasts. The Canaries played four games in total, the first against a Bravert Co Select XI (won 7-1) before three games against established US teams, starting with the Orlando Lions (lost 4-2); before games against Seattle Storm (lost 2-0) and the California Kickers (won 4-1). That victory against the Kickers was the last game of a busy season that had commenced almost a year ago in Sweden and had now concluded on the west coast of the USA seventy games later. No rest, it would seem, for either the wicked or the professional footballer. Moreover, it was all due to start all over again, with the Canaries returning to Sweden, just seven weeks later as serious preparations for the 1987/88 season got under way.

It would turn out to be a pivotal season for the club, even if it didn't exactly turn out as expected.

# CHAPTER SIX

# Brown and Out

*The Canaries lost 2-0 in a game where their performance was so abject that those Canary fans who had been in attendance collectively waved white handkerchiefs in the air as a symbol of both their side's surrender and their growing discontent at the club's decline.*

Sweden was, once again, the favoured pre-season destination for Norwich City as the club's plans for the 1987/88 season began to take shape in its favourite new summer hideaway. The trip to the USA which had served as the conclusion to the previous season was more of a commercial duty, one undertaken to give the club visibility in a part of the world where, as always, the game always seemed to be just about to take off. And, regardless of whether it was or was not, that was enough for Norwich City to be there. Just in case.

For, even then, commercial tie ins, contacts and the need to promote the club – or, as the marketing men and women would have said, 'the product', was becoming more and more important in the game. And the USA, the nation that was soon to be entrusted with hosting the 1994 World Cup, was too enticing a prospect for the Canaries not to want a prospective stake in all of the new possibilities a soccer crazy nation would have offered to the world. After all, under what other circumstances would you haul a large squad of players, management and coaching staff plus numerous other personnel across not just the Atlantic Ocean but the whole of the North American continent, east to west, a matter of weeks after they had played the last game of a demanding season. The previous season had seen its leading players play in excess of sixty games – including friendlies that were played during the league season, one of which involved a near 3000 mile round flight to Morocco to play Raja Casablanca just five days before the league fixture against Everton at Goodison Park – which, perhaps not surprisingly, given their travelling exertions in the days leading up to that fixture, the Canaries lost 4-0.[1]

The pre-season trip to Scandinavia in August 1987 was part of a slightly less intense schedule for Ken Brown and his players. Six games, three of which were to be played in Sweden, one of which just happened to be against Lulea, the club Jeremy Goss had spent two summers playing for on loan from the Canaries. Goss found himself in the Lulea side on that day playing against his parent club and teammates, confessing that the fitness and strength of the Norwich players, even at that fledgling stage of the new season put that of many of his teammates to shame. Norwich won the game, the last of their tour 3-1 and, despite their wanting to sign Goss permanently from the Canaries, it ended up marking the beginning of the end of two very happy summers spent in Sweden for Goss who has since admitted that, given the chance he would have considered signing for Lulea permanently, confident that he would, in time, have been noticed by one of Sweden's leading sides, for example, Malmo or IFK Göteborg.

Lulea were not the only club interested in signing Goss at the time, Mel Machin, the former Norwich Assistant manager was now in charge of Manchester City and also wanted him to be one of his first signings at Maine Road – and his offer was a tempting one. With Goss given permission from Norwich to travel up to Manchester to speak to Machin about the move, the former Norwich man sold his vision of the club and what Goss's role would be. Goss was to play in the centre of midfield as a ball winner, a player able to win possession before passing the ball to one of the Sky Blues creative players, someone like Paul Lake or David White. Did the prospect appeal to Goss, even though it would have meant dropping a division? Hell yes. Personal terms were soon agreed and Goss was all set to quit the Canaries and Norfolk for his new life in Manchester before, with no warning, Peter Swales, the Manchester City Chairman and Robert Chase, his counterpart at Carrow Road fell out and the deal was off. Goss returned to Trowse in time for the start of the 1987/88 season still very much a Norwich City player – but wondering if he would ever get a chance to prove himself as one.

He certainly was not in Ken Brown's plans at the beginning of the 1987/88 season. Brown opted for a midfield quartet of Dale Gordon, Mike Phelan, David Williams (now the club's player coach, the number two to Brown and heir apparent) and Trevor Putney for the trip to Goodison Park to play Everton with the unlucky Ian Crook named as substitute. A workmanlike team that gave a similar sort of performance on the day, lots of effort and energy but precious little in the way of quality in a match that Everton won 1-0 thanks to a first half goal from Paul Power. It was the first time the Canaries had lost their opening fixture since 1982 when they had lost 2-1 to Manchester City for whom Power also scored for on that day.

A disappointing start to the season then but by no means a disaster, especially with three of Norwich's next four games due to be played at Carrow Road. Things didn't go immediately to plan though, as that first home game of the new season, against Southampton ended in another 1-0 defeat for Norwich with a rather more disappointed and disjointed performance to go with it. There was, at least, the chance for the Norwich fans to see a new face make his Canary debut on the day, the player in question being former Tottenham defender Mark Bowen who'd signed for just £90,000 earlier that summer, evidence yet again of Brown's mastery in the transfer market.

Following the Southampton defeat the normally perky Brown appeared downbeat, admitting to reporters that he and his players still had 'a lot of work to do' if they were to get their season properly underway. It seemed a strange thing to say at the time, especially for someone as positive and optimistic as Bond. Yes, the club had lost their opening two fixtures (for the first time since 1976) but this was still pretty much the same squad of players who had, only the previous May, achieved a best ever league finish of fifth place. Seven of the players who'd been part of the team that sealed fifth place had played in the Southampton game together with Ian Culverhouse, an 'upgrade' (in the kindest possible sense) on Kenny Brown, the previous incumbent at right back. Brown senior had kept his squad together and added Mark Bowen to the Canary ranks. The squad was strong, the club was coached well and the players were, alongside the fans, confident of improving on the previous season's displays and league finish. Some people were even suggesting that Norwich might be a good outside bet for the league title. If that was to be the case then, with no points and not even a goal scored after their opening two league games City desperately needed to put things right in their next league game, another home game, this time against Coventry City. They'd started the season well with two wins out of two, a club that was enjoying riding on the crest of the wave that their unexpected triumph at Wembley in the FA Cup Final a few months earlier had instigated. It was going to be a tough match against decent opposition with one man in particular keen to impress. That was Greg Downs, dropped from the Canaries League Cup final side in 1985 and sold by the club shortly afterwards. He now had a regular place back in a top flight side plus an FA Cup winner's medal, a step up from the one he'd missed out on. He'd now be looking to show Ken Brown that has career had also taken a step up since he'd left Norwich.

It was Brown, however, who walked to John Sillett, his opposite number at Coventry with the consoling handshake at the end of the game rather than the latter offering his sympathies at a third consecutive defeat for Norwich. The Canaries had prevailed 3-1 and, if the manner of their victory wasn't exactly convincing, the fact that they'd won without really hitting the heights the fans had regularly enjoyed the previous season, was seen as a good sign for what was to come, the old adage about 'winning when you aren't playing particularly well' coming to mind. Star of the show had been Kevin Drinkell with two goals, his first in five games; another sign, everyone hoped, that things were coming back together again with the chance to prove that all was, after all, well at Carrow Road to come at West Ham the following weekend. Yet, again, the Canaries misfired, unable to cope with the pace and trickery of Tony Cottee who scored twice in a victory for the Hammers that was a lot more convincing than Norwich's over Coventry a few days earlier had ever been.

A run of just one win in their next six games followed for the Canaries, one that included four consecutive league defeats with just the one goal scored. The home defeat to Derby County on 12 September had been bad enough, an undisciplined display that saw Mike Phelan giving away a penalty for the Rams second and decisive goal. The nadir of that run came at the Manor Ground, the home of Oxford United on 3 October. Luckily for Norwich, there was only 6,847 present to see one of the club's worse performances for some considerable time, a humiliating 3-0 defeat that saw Oxford's second and third goals scored within a minute of one another. Ken Brown had gone into the game having made the brave decision to play David Williams as a sweeper, yet it backfired badly with Oxford cutting holes through the Norwich defence at will, so much so that the final scored could, and probably should, have been a much heavier defeat for the Canaries.

A little under a quarter of the season had now been played and there was no doubt about it now. Norwich were struggling and, inevitably, questions were starting to be asked. That capitulation at the Manor Ground saw City drop down to twentieth place in the Division One table-one off the bottom.[2] More to the point, their opposition, who had also endured a poor start to the season with just one win in their first six games, had now won three on the spin. There was, quite simply, no consolation or comfort to be found anywhere, no matter how hard the Canaries faithful looked. Ten games had been played and they'd already lost seven of them by early October – they hadn't lost their seventh league game the previous season until April and had lost only eight in total for the whole campaign.

Ken Brown was now, completely unexpectedly but inevitably finding himself under pressure, not something anyone at the club would have been predicting the previous May when there were more likely to have been fears that a perceived bigger club might have tried to tempt him away from Norwich. And with good reason. Not only had he won promotion to Division One twice during his time at the club so far – and he'd also led the club to its first ever win in a Wembley Cup Final as well as overseeing a best ever fifth place finish – something that would normally have seen the club playing in European football the following season, the second time he'd achieved that in just three years. He'd also brought a host of top class players to the club – or, put another way, brought players to the club who he went onto make top class ones. So how on earth could he be under pressure after a poor opening quarter of just one season, having previously achieved all of that? It was ridiculous. Yet also understandable, given the circumstances. He and the football club had constantly over achieved during his time in charge. Good results and performances were now seen as the standard and, because of that, Norwich had gone into the 1987/88 season thinking of themselves as possible league champions. Brown had raised the yellow and green bar to hitherto unknown heights and was now very genuinely in danger of losing his job because the club was not living up to the high expectations he had instilled at Carrow Road.

Had Norwich lost their following game, a home clash against Tottenham a week after the Oxford debacle, it is almost certain that Brown would have been dismissed. As is so often the case in the game however, manager and players managed to turn an increasingly bleak situation around with a consummate performance and result that brought about at least a temporary cessation from all the off pitch tensions and speculation with a 2-1 win that was impressive as the defeat at Oxford had been desultory. Mark Bowen, playing in a soon to be unfamiliar midfield role, set up the opening goal against his former club by finding Kevin Drinkell in space. His thunderous shot beating Ray Clemence and going in via the crossbar. So had Norwich's luck changed on a fortuitous deflection? It seemed so – for around ten minutes anyway, the time it took for Paul Allen to bring a fine save out of Gunn, only for the lurking Belgian international Nico Claesen to fire home the loose ball.[3]

Had the fates now moved against Norwich as swiftly as they had seemed to play out in their advantage just ten minutes earlier, perhaps? If luck had still been on the Canaries side Gunn's save would have been safely cleared or gone out for a corner, rather than left for Claesen to capitalise on. The match now seemed to be one that was set to not only define the Canaries season but also decide the fate of their embattled manager. All, bar one, of the Norwich players selected for the game had been brought into the club by Brown with many of them feeling that they'd come to Carrow Road with a point to prove to their previous employers.[4] Brown had given them the chance to do just that – and at the highest level of the English game. They would have felt that on this day they owed Brown a big performance and, in a thrilling second half, they delivered with Wayne Biggins thwarting both the Tottenham defence and three-time European Cup winner and former Liverpool and England keeper Ray Clemence to score the winner.

How fitting that it was Biggins who scored the winner. His modest origins in the game saw him stand out as someone who'd come into the game the hard way, even amongst most of his Norwich teammates, let alone the star studded Tottenham side. He'd started his career with Lincoln City in 1980, playing just eight games for them in Division Four before, at just nineteen, being released. Being shown the door by Arsenal, Liverpool or Manchester United was one thing. But by Lincoln City? Not only would that have hurt, it would, for the vast majority of young players have led to them quitting the game. But not Biggins. He spent a season with Matlock Town before drifting even further into the depths of non-league football by signing for Kings Lynn, then in the Northern Premier League, combining his continuing love of football with working as a hod-carrier on local building sites. That work made Biggins as strong physically as he undoubtedly was mentally and, after some good performances for the Linnets, he ended up back at Matlock Town before being offered a route back into the full-time game at Burnley, then in Division Three. Grateful for the opportunity, Biggins impressed, scoring four goals in his first four appearances for them, including a hat-trick against Lincoln City, the club that had rejected him. How satisfying must that have been? He went onto score twenty-one goals for Burnley during the 1984/85 season, a total all the more impressive by the fact he did so in a struggling team with Burnley ending the season in one of the relegation places, dropping down to Division Four for the first time in their history. He scored four goals in their opening twelve games of the 1985/86 season, his never say die attitude and physical strength were enough to convince Brown that he had what it took to mess with the Division Two defences that Norwich were up against that season. He did that in some style, scoring seven goals in his twenty-eight appearances for the Canaries while making many more goals and opportunities for strike partner Kevin Drinkell.

Now Biggins and Drinkell had scored the goals that gave Ken Brown that temporary reprieve from the pressure he was under at Carrow Road. The Canaries next game was against Manchester United at Old Trafford, one they might have been expected to lose anyway. They did, Biggins opening the scoring with a classic turn and shot after half an hour. But, again, the relief was temporary. Peter Davenport made the most of a defensive mix up between Ian Culverhouse and Bryan Gunn early in the second half to make the score 1-1 before winning a penalty which Gunn saved from Brian McClair. Had the balance turned in Norwich's favour again? It hadn't. Ten minutes remained when Bryan Robson, showing a typical disregard for his own well-being opted to heavily collide with a post as the pay-off for his brave header which won the game for United, that latest defeat, Norwich's fifth in six games, sending the Canaries back down to eighteenth place in the table. A single-goal defeat against Sheffield Wednesday at Hillsborough followed, only a second win of the season for the Owls who'd been struggling up until then but had, in that game, been dominant throughout. Yet, somehow, Brown hung on.

Three days later Norwich went out of the League Cup after a 2-1 defeat at Stoke. A result and performance that provoked Brown into promising major team changes over the course of the next few games. He made good on his threat as well, dropping five members from the side that had started against Stoke with Ian Culverhouse, Shaun Elliott, Kevin Ratcliffe, David Williams and Mark Bowen all paying the price, their places being taken by Kenny Brown junior, Ian Butterworth, Trevor Putney and Ian Crook for the home league game against QPR on 31 October. Brown also, at this time, enquired about the availability of former Canary Justin Fashanu only to discover that he was still struggling to regain full fitness, having had surgery on the knee he'd badly injured during his time at Brighton and was therefore unavailable.

It's easy to speculate now as to whether or not the enquiry about Fashanu was a move that Brown thought would not be favoured by the club's support but also go some way to galvanising a squad that was low on confidence. Fashanu had been a massively popular character during his time at Norwich, outward going, extrovert and friendly, the sort of personality you could use to calm feelings of disquiet anywhere. But these were not his only good qualities. He was also a battler on the pitch, someone who would rough up opposing defences from the first minute of the game to the last. And, had Fashanu been fit, it might have been an inspired move, as so many of Brown's had been. But he was not fit, in fact, he was far from ready to play football again at any level, let alone ride down to Carrow Hill in the style of the US cavalry, always there to save the day at the last moment. Fash eventually opted to continue his career in the US with the Los Angeles Heat whilst Brown managed to buy himself some more time after that game against QPR ended in a 1-1 draw, Wayne Biggins (the man whose place might have been most under threat had Fashanu returned) scoring the Norwich goal, his third in four games.

The end for Brown came after the club's next fixture, away at bottom of the table Charlton Athletic. The Canaries lost 2-0 in a game where their performance was so abject that those Canary fans who had been in attendance collectively waved white handkerchiefs in the air as a symbol of both their sides surrender and their growing discontent at the club's decline. For many, the protest and discontent was aimed solely at the club's board and chairman Robert Chase in particular rather than Brown, a view that was shared by the senior professionals at the club, all of whom liked and respected Brown and wanted him to remain as manager.

Nonetheless, Robert Chase wasn't, on this occasion, going to take soundings from the players or the club's fans. And, after what have must have been one of the most hastily arranged board meetings in the club's history, Brown was promptly sacked. Amongst the first to learn the news were the players. They had turned up for training as usual on the Monday morning following the Charlton game, only to be informed of the dismissal by Brown himself, there to pack away his belongings and take his final leave of all things Norwich City after fourteen years with the club that had become his life. To a man, the players were against the decision as were the very great majority of Norwich supporters who chose to express their discontent with the club and Robert Chase in particular at the Canaries next game against Arsenal at Carrow Road, one that ended in a not all together unsurprising 4-2 defeat. For once, however, the result and performance on the day played second fiddle to the emotions of those who felt that the decision to dismiss the universally liked and respected Brown had been made too hastily and with little thought or consideration for what he had already achieved at the club – didn't he deserve a little loyalty in return for all of that? Seemingly not. The outcry at Brown's dismissal was taken up by the media with even the popular tabloids condemning it, their leader articles going onto point out Brown's achievements with Norwich, further pointing out that it was still only November which left plenty of time for the Canaries to get themselves clear of danger and up the table. Normally the popular press would have been focusing on who might have been his successor at Carrow Road, with gossip and idle speculation filling the column inches rather than articles in support of him and critical of the club's board. It was, to say the least, a time when no person connected with the club welcomed the prominent place it now had in the sports news. Prominence driven by a decision that had not gone down at all well throughout all of football.

Looking back at that unhappy time for the club and its support, it seems clear that the shock departure of Machin to Manchester City was the catalyst that ultimately led to the turmoil that followed. Brown and Machin were very much a typical footballing double act, two men who were ultimately stronger when they had the other working alongside them. Brown's role at Carrow Road had seen him cultivate a reputation for being a fine manager, someone who related well to professional footballers and the ups and downs of their lives and careers. He would focus on being the face of the club and a widely respected and popular one at that, someone who his players trusted and wanted to work for. He was also a great judge of footballing talent as that part of his Canary CV clearly shows. Time and time again he would identify and sign a new player for the club with the captures of, for example, Dave Watson and Steve Bruce being typical of his ability to identify diamonds in the footballing rough. But if he brought them to the club Machin was then the man who worked with them on the training pitches at Trowse, the man who made them better players and, in some instances, internationals. Machin's capabilities as a coach were unheralded at the time but you only need to speak to any of those players who worked under him at Norwich to understand just how highly he was regarded during his time at Carrow Road. He and Brown complemented each other perfectly with Brown all too often playing good cop to Machin's bad cop. Good cop and bad cop – maybe. But good football manager and a good coach, who made a great team between them? Definitely. The initial approach for Machin from Manchester City in May 1987 had not been rejected by the club and it is their readiness to let Machin move on, maybe because there were aspects of his fiery character that certain members of the board felt uncomfortable with, that was, ultimately, to blame for the club's 1987/88 season to have been the great disappointment that it was. Had the board fought to keep him and, in turn, given their full backing to him and Machin instead, I have no doubt that the club would have had every chance of surpassing their achievements in the campaign that followed rather than flirting with relegation and being rightly criticised throughout the game for firing a much respected and capable manager.

Robert Chase swiftly appointed Dave Stringer as Brown's replacement, albeit on a temporary basis only. Stringer had enjoyed success during his time in charge of the club's youth team, including guiding them to a League and Cup double in the 1982/83 season so, as far as having a trusted and reliable hand at the tiller whilst the club looked for a permanent replacement for Brown was concerned, it was an eminently sensible decision made by a board that had realised it had a lot of work to do in order to gain the fans approval again. There would certainly have been no shortage of applicants, despite the club's lowly league position. Yet, for whatever reason, it seemed as if David Williams would not be one of them. He'd been working alongside Brown since Machin's abrupt departure and, having already had managerial experience with Bristol Rovers might, rightly, have strongly fancied his chances of being offered the job. The fact that he had been overlooked in favour of Stringer suggests that the board didn't feel he was yet ready for the top job, at least not yet. One of the first applicants for the post was Mike Channon who publicly announced that he was so keen to enter club management that he would, at least for a short period, work for nothing. His application may have been a serious one and it is interesting to speculate what sort of football manager he might have been. Certainly if he'd brought the same sort of success to the club as he did to the racehorse owners for whom he was been a trainer, then Norwich City might have done very well. But the board did not take his application seriously. Other candidates for the job might have included John Docherty who was impressing at Millwall; Denis Smith who was in the process of leading Sunderland to the Division Three title and the double act of Alex MacDonald and Sandy Jardine who were collectively raising eyebrows in Scotland with a Hearts team that was very clearly challenging Celtic and Rangers for the Scottish title. All of them intriguing possibilities in their own way. Yet, for all of those possibilities, there seemed little doubt that, once he was given the job in time for that trip to Arsenal, Dave Stringer was always going to get the role.

He certainly made an impact prior to the kick-off against Arsenal, despite the fact the Canaries lost that game, giving a first start of the season to midfielder Jeremy Goss at the expense of Simon Ratcliffe whilst Wayne Biggins made way for Robert Rosario; Shaun Elliott replaced Tony Spearing and Dale Gordon came in for Ruel Fox. It was the game that saw the first pairing of Goss with Ian Crook in the centre of the Canaries midfield, a combination that would go onto more than prove its worth in seasons to come with Mike Walker, in particular, benefitting from the duos respective qualities to full effect in both the 1992/93 and 1993/94 seasons. For the unfortunate Simon Ratcliffe, Stringer's choice of Goss for one of those central midfield roles ultimately meant his time at Carrow Road had come to an end and, although he remained at the club until January 1989, he failed to make any more first team appearances and eventually joined Brentford for £160,000, a club record fee for the Bees at the time.

In making those changes, particularly in giving Goss his first start of the season, Stringer had made a very firm statement of intent. He was in charge now. He wouldn't be trying to perpetuate what Brown had started nor try to copy him with regard to how he approached games and team selection. This was to be his team and his players. Goss had never been a player that Brown had seen as a first teamer. Stringer thought otherwise. Likewise, Brown had signed Simon Ratcliffe from Manchester United and selected him for eight of the ten games that followed his arrival from Old Trafford,[5] seeing him, no doubt, as a first pick in most of his Norwich teams. But Stringer disagreed and, as we have seen, Ratcliffe was dropped for the Arsenal game, Stringer's first, and never made a first team appearance for the Canaries again. Another player who felt the chill wind of change that accompanied Stringers arrival was Wayne Biggins. He'd made ninety appearances for the club under Brown but, following Stringer's appointment, he was relegated to the side-lines, making only seven more appearances between the game at Highbury and the end of the season, five of which came from the bench. It came as no surprise to anyone therefore, when he asked for a transfer and even less of a surprise when Stringer agreed to that request with Biggins signing for Mel

Machin at Manchester City in June 1988, Machin saying at the time, perhaps with reference to how Biggins had been treated by Stringer, that he'd always had a high opinion of Biggins and he expected that the young players that he had in his squad would learn a lot from his experience in the game.

Another player who didn't last for very long under Stringer was Kenny Brown junior, the previous managers son. And maybe, as with Simon Ratcliffe, Stringer would have preferred him out of the side straight away. But he didn't, with Brown junior remaining in the Norwich starting XI for the game against Arsenal as well as the two fixtures that immediately followed. Did Stringer retain Brown in the side because of how it might have looked if he'd immediately dropped Ken Brown's son after his Fathers decision? It seems unlikely. Stringer is, like Brown, a thoroughly decent man and, rare then in the game, let alone now, a gentleman with it. Yet it wouldn't have stopped him doing what he thought was best for the football club and at all times. Not for himself and not for either of the Browns. So there was no room for sentiment with him. But then no one would have expected it. Unlike Ratcliffe, Brown the younger was given a further three games to prove himself but, ultimately, Stringer opted for Ian Culverhouse as his first choice right back, with Culverhouse coming into the side in place of Brown junior for the trip to Luton on 5 December and ending up staying in that position for the rest of the season. As for Kenny Brown junior, he remained at the club for the rest of that season before becoming one of his Father's first signings when he took over as manager of Plymouth Argyle in July 1988, staying there for three years before a spell at West Ham, the club where his father had been a player, from 1991 to 1996.

Stringer had a mixed start to his managerial career at Norwich. The defeat against Arsenal in his first game whilst hardly unexpected, was still another blow to morale, particularly in the manner the Gunners had won the game with four goals in just twelve minutes. Memories of the win at Highbury on the final day of the previous season were now just that – memories, and rapidly fading ones at that. And things weren't about to get any easier. A week later, having conceded four against Arsenal, then the league leaders; Stringer and Norwich headed to Anfield to face Liverpool – who were second, Stringer making just the one change, with the recently recalled Goss now left out again in favour of Trevor Putney. As might have been expected, the Canaries had to weather a red storm from first minute to last with Bryan Gunn outstanding in goal throughout. The Canaries even, during one of their rare forays up field, scored, only for Crook's effort to be disallowed for handball after the referee consulted the Kop for their opinion on the matter.

He didn't of course. But visiting teams rarely got anything out of Liverpool at that time (they went through the entire 1987/88 season undefeated at home and only conceded nine goals in those 20 league games) so, in the end, the 0-0 draw that Norwich managed to secure was hugely impressive, a result and performance that must have convinced the board that their appointment of Stringer had been the right one, leaving only i's to dot and t's to cross in terms of the formalities of confirming he was indeed set to become the new, permanent manager of Norwich City Football Club.

Yet it so nearly all fell back to earth again the following week. Because, having travelled to Anfield and won a deserved point through a battling and well organised display, Norwich then had the chance to get their first win in seven games against Portsmouth, one place ahead of them in the table. But it was not to be, the 1-0 defeat and miserable performance that accompanied it being highlighted by renewed vocal attacks on the board from the Norwich fans including chants of 'What a load of rubbish' and, for perhaps the first (but by no means the last) time, accompanying cries of 'Chase out', the Norwich support continuing to let the board know, and in no uncertain terms, who they held solely responsible for the mess the club was in. It was hardly the sort of atmosphere that Stringer would have wanted in his early days. He and the players would, quite rightly, have felt that, with so much criticism being meted out to the Chairman and his board of directors, support and backing for the team itself was lacking, especially at Carrow Road which, increasingly, became a very depressing place in which to watch and play football, something which Portsmouth had seized upon and taken full advantage of with their win.

As a result of that, the trip to Luton on 5 December almost came as a relief to the team, strange as that might seem. Away from Carrow Road and all the attendant gloom and doom, they would, at least, be able to prepare for, and play in a game where they would determine the prevailing atmosphere in and around the club rather than the home support. But not only that. The club's away following has always seemed to be rather more tolerant and supportive to the team and less inclined to criticise and condemn at the drop of the proverbial hat so at least the very small band of Norwich fans who were able to circumvent Luton's unpopular ban on away support were vocally supportive, managing to make themselves heard amongst the attendance of just 7,002. As far as the game is concerned, things didn't look good, again, for Norwich after just twenty minutes when Brian Stein opened the scoring for the Hatters. It could, and maybe should, have been the cue for more Luton goals, playing, as they were, against a team low on confidence and a Captain whose mind was clearly elsewhere, with Steve Bruce having been informed on the night before the game that Manchester United had made an offer for him, one that the Norwich board had immediately rejected. And you can understand why, on this occasion, why a club that had always said it would not get in the way of any of its players desires to move onwards and upwards providing a good offer was made had, for once, turned one down. They would have been mindful that selling one of their best and most popular players at that time might just have sent the club's increasingly restless and disillusioned supporters over the edge.

Not that club politics would have made any difference to Bruce once he knew that Manchester United were interested. He would have wanted to go – and who could have blamed him? He'd left Gillingham in order to join Norwich for all the right reasons at the time. Norwich were a bigger club, one that played at a higher level of the game, one that would see him not only joining a squad of better players but playing against better players every week as well. He'd done well at Norwich and had been as good for the club as the club had been for him. But now it was time for him to move on again and for all the same reasons that had seen him join the Canaries in the first place. But first they, and he, had a game to play in. And, on this occasion, it rather looked as if Luton felt that Stein's opener meant the game was over. So they sat back a little, relaxed and maybe, just maybe, got a little careless and complacent, something which Stringer would have been quick to pick up on. His half-time team talk would have focused on just that, how their opponents thought the job was done, how they were taking it easy, even taking the proverbial out of Norwich. Were they going to accept that, were they going to just roll over and submit? Again?

It was a pivotal moment for Stringer and his team, including Bruce who, for forty-five minutes, vowed to put all thoughts of Old Trafford to the back of his mind. Norwich came out for the second half a changed team and with that mixture of renewed confidence and anger that Stringer had imbued in them, a little of the old green and yellow magic that had been missing for so long came back again and Luton had no answer to it. The only real surprise was that it took fifteen minutes for Norwich to equalise, but they did, through Dale Gordon before, with just two minutes to go, Ian Crook hit the winner with a beautiful lob that had Les Sealey beaten and helpless, giving Norwich their second away win of the season and, more importantly, their first league win in eight attempts.

Steve Bruce would have been happy to leave on a win. He still wanted to leave the club however, and, following some reportedly heated discussions with regard to his desire to do just that with Robert Chase, got his wish with United paying £900,000 for his services, surely one of the Red Devils best ever signings in the modern age?

With his inspirational captain gone, Dave Stringer knew that he needed a replacement centre half – and fast. The man he chose to fill the considerable gap left by Bruce's departure was John O'Neill, a relative veteran of 313 league appearances for Leicester City, many of which would have been in Division One as well as a Northern Ireland international who'd been part of their World Cup squads in 1982 as well as 1986 when he'd lined up for them against Brazil. His contract with Leicester was due to expire in the summer of 1987 and, after a short spell with QPR, O'Neill joined Norwich on 16 December, making his Canaries debut playing alongside Ian Butterworth in the game against Wimbledon at

Plough Lane. And, like Steve Bruce, his notable predecessor in the Number 4 shirt, O'Neill had a Norwich debut to remember, albeit and sadly, for all the wrong reasons when he suffered a serious knee ligament injury following a tackle from Don's centre forward and ex-Canary John Fashanu. Norwich lost the game 1-0 but, not unnaturally, teammates and fans alike were more concerned about the well-being and a hoped for quick recovery for their new man but it was not to be, with O'Neill's surgeon saying after the operation that followed that he had never seen a worse type of injury and had, even then, to express doubt as to whether O'Neill would play again which, of course, he didn't with O'Neill ultimately suing Fashanu for the tackle that ended his career. He was awarded a testimonial by the Canaries in May 1989 when a John O'Neill XI that included Gary Lineker beat Norwich 8-2.

That match and the injury to John O'Neill that will forever be associated with it largely overshadowed the debut made on the night by another new face in the Canary ranks, one who would, fortunately, have a much longer and illustrious career with the club, namely Robert Fleck, a then club record signing of £580,000 from Rangers where he'd flourished under the management of Graeme Souness, particularly during the 1986/87 season, his last full campaign at the club and one that saw him score twenty-two goals in forty-eight appearances, a total that included four hat-tricks, one of which was in Rangers' UEFA Cup game against Finnish side FC Ilves.

The question that demands to be asked therefore is, given such free scoring form and an obvious affinity with the club's support, why on earth Souness and Rangers allowed him to leave the club to go south of the border? The simple answer to that was, as good a player as he was, Fleck was still not guaranteed a starting place every week, such was the wide array of expensive talent that was in Rangers squad at the time, players like Ally McCoist, Trevor Francis and Mark Falco all competed for the two places in the Rangers attack, but, with McCoist playing in every game he was available for, Fleck was left to fight it out with Francis and Falco for the right to play alongside McCoist. So, as adept as he was, Fleck didn't always play, at least, not as much as he thought he should have. And all he wanted to do was play. But, with Souness unable to promise him the number of games and status at the club he wanted, Fleck ultimately felt that, albeit with regret, that he would have to look elsewhere in order to be regarded as a team's first choice striker. Which is where Norwich came in.

The Canaries weren't the first club in England to express an interest in him. The club that first made contact with him about a move was Watford. Fleck travelled down to take a look around the club as well as have a chat with their then manager, Dave Bassett, but, as much as he wanted to move and play games, he felt that Watford would not be the right club for him. Dave Stringer followed up

Watford's enquiry with one of his own, a move on the Canary managers part that prompted Fleck to have a quiet word with Rangers former Norwich goalkeeper, Chris Woods about the club. Woods had no hesitation in putting in a good word for Norwich City, championing both the club and the City, more than enough for Fleck to welcome the opportunity to meet with Stringer and Robert Chase who both travelled up to Glasgow to have initial talks with him there. And they must have impressed him, for, at 7.00 a.m. the following morning, Fleck joined them on the first flight back down to Norwich from Glasgow in order to sign for the Canaries. Fortunately for Fleck, he already knew Bryan Gunn well and it was the Canaries popular keeper who took the time out to welcome him to the club, bringing along a few of Fleck's new teammates with him as well as, eventually, becoming his flatmate as the two of them shared lodgings together for a while.

He must have wondered what he had let himself in for at first! His last game for Rangers, which was a 2-2 draw against Dunfermline at Ibrox Park watched by just under 32,000 people at one of the great stadiums of British football. Now, here he was, scrapping it out against Wimbledon at Plough Lane, a ground that was everything Ibrox wasn't and in front of an attendance fractionally over 4,000. Not only that but in a game soured by a career ending tackle on one of his new teammates and the prospect of a relegation battle to come for the second half of the Canaries season. No one would have blamed Robert at that stage for taking a step back and wondering just what he had let himself in for. But it would only have been a tiniest of doubts. Because Robert Fleck was a battler, a scrapper, someone who'd give every inch in every game and do whatever he had to in order to help his side win, qualities that, alongside his undoubted talent as a footballer, had made Dave Stringer keen to sign him in the first place. Fleck's spirit and character would, he hoped, be a lift for both the fans and the players already at the club, helping give everyone the lift that they so desperately wanted. A line had therefore been drawn. Twenty games played, twenty to go with, of all clubs, Wimbledon set to be the Canaries opponents in their last game of the season. Stringer wanted a very different Norwich to face them on the day, a very different one indeed. Fleck soon made his presence felt in a Norwich shirt, scoring the opener in the Canaries next game, a 2-1 win over Derby at Carrow Road on Boxing Day with Dale Gordon getting the winner after Mark Wright had briefly brought the Rams back into the game. It was a second win in three games for Stringer, both of which had come in away games. Could he win over Carrow Road with another three points in the game against Chelsea at Carrow Road two days after the Derby match? Chelsea were not the team they would eventually become courtesy of one man and his personal fortune but they were still, even then, a decent enough team that featured some very capable players, ones who, on their day were as good in their positions as any player in the country, for example, Tony Dorigo, Steve Clarke, Pat Nevin,

Roy Wegerle and Gordon Durie. Yet, for all that, they were, under manager John Hollins, extremely inconsistent.

They'd won, for example, seven out of their opening ten league games, lifting themselves up to second place in the table in doing so. They then won only two of their next ten, but, even given that, their fine start to the season still saw them comfortably sat in the top ten. By the time they travelled to Carrow Road, the Blues had drawn their previous three games so were, unsurprisingly, seeing the game against Norwich as a good opportunity to get back to winning ways in the league.[6] Yet, frustratingly for both their manager and supporters (but thankfully for Norwich) the Chelsea that turned up on the day wasn't the free scoring and winning Chelsea from the start of the season but the inconsistent one that alternated with it. Poor old Chelsea. You had to feel sorry for them. Well, maybe not. One week they'd be brilliant, as they had been in convincing wins over Portsmouth (3-0), Nottingham Forest (4-3) and Watford (3-0), the next they'd be dreadful as defeats against QPR (3-1), Everton (4-1) and Southampton (3-0) clearly showed. They most definitely added to that latter roster of poor displays with their performance at Norwich who, much to the delight of a crowd that neared 20,000, proceeded to turn them over with some aplomb, winning 3-0 with goals from Ruel Fox, Jeremy Goss (his first for the club) and a Kevin Drinkell penalty.

That win, the Canaries' third success in four games was enough to persuade the board to confirm Dave Stringer as the club's new permanent boss with David Williams, maybe surprisingly, given he'd been overlooked after Ken Brown's dismissal, named as his number two. Given the upturn in form and results since Stringer had initially taken the helm, the decision was greeted with approval by the club's fans. But it wasn't enough to soften their attitude to the board. Far from it in fact with a vote of a 'no confidence in chairman' motion proposed by the club's shareholders, his lack of popularity now amongst both some of the shareholders and many of the fans something which neither of his predecessors had encountered during their tenure, at least, certainly not with such vocal and visible opposition. But Robert Chase was a very strong willed and single-minded businessman who wasn't going to be easily distracted by outside criticism. His plans for the club went far beyond what happened on the football pitch every week. His vision for the football club was that of a business that offered more than just, well, football. Offering football as the standalone product in the fast growing commercial world at the time, one where diversification was increasingly being seen as all important, was a business plan that, in his eyes, would have been limited. The club needed to explore its options, see what else it could offer commercially and, as part of that, the ground itself would have to be improved and made more appealing to visit. That would cost money. There was also the need to work on the existing facilities at the ground designed to cater for disabled fans and families, the overall objective of that being to increase the demographic of City supporters who wanted to come along to the club's home matches. It all made sense. Improve the ground, upgrade the facilities, and get more people through the gates on a match-day. It wasn't as if the club were turning people away from home games. Attendances at Carrow Road had been constantly disappointing over the last few seasons. During the 1987/88 season for example, Carrow Road's official capacity was 26,812 – yet the average home attendance for the whole of that season was 16,397 – a drop on the average for the record breaking campaign before that which had been 17,564. It was all very well investing money in players and looking to push Norwich up the league as those spectators that did come to games were now expecting only to object when it didn't happen. Yet, at a time when clubs like Norwich were massively reliant on the income generated by attendance, the club simply couldn't afford to do this. It was why Kevin Reeves had been sold, it was why Chris Woods and Dave Watson had been sold. It was also, earlier that season, why Steve Bruce had been sold. Because the club needed the funds from those transfers to continue to exist as a business, a stark but, none the less, unpalatable fact. Robert Chase now had the problem of dealing with the pressures and expectations from those who either couldn't, or wouldn't, accept that fact, that, in order to survive, Norwich City were, and would probably always be, a 'selling club'.

The first of those big name departures, Kevin Reeves, had left the club right at the start of the decade, joining Manchester City for £1 million in March 1980. There had been a protest then, one that had included the iconic banner stretched out in the Barclay Stand that pronounced 'No Reeves, No Future, No Fans'.[7] With Bruce's departure bringing in much needed funds to, again, help keep the club afloat, you might have excused the board for pointing out the reality of the situation back to the club's dwindling support by unfurling a banner of their own, a juxtaposition of the original that stated 'No Fans, No Future, No Bruce'. For that was the reality of the situation, the reason Bruce had to be sold and, ultimately, the reason the club had been unable to build on the relative success of the 1986/87 season. Because they were broke. Which is where Robert Chase and his modernising of the football club and its overall business model came in, that need to do more to make the football club an attractive place to come, a venue that could offer more than just football, a modern stadium that could be hired out for any and all sorts of reasons and occasions that didn't necessarily involve a game of football. It was hardly a new concept. Even back in 1943, the ground had been used as the venue for a rodeo show that had been put on by members of the United States Army Air Corps whilst in June 1984, the ground had been used as the location for a four day visit and mission from US evangelist Billy Graham, something which not only raised the profile of Carrow Road throughout the non-footballing loving public but would also have made the club some money. Interestingly, however, the club's board at the time were still seen to put the football first, stating that no one at the events was to walk onto the turf and that Graham's platform had be cantilevered above it, rather than sat directly upon it. All enquiries and conversions had therefore to be done on the area of dusty running track that surrounded the pitch,[8] the club placing a value and level of care over the vital playing turf then that now seems not to matter at all, given the state of the pitch at, for example, Wembley, when football matches are played there a few days after a non-football event. So football was changing, expanding, seeking new opportunities and expanding its horizons. It's all too easy to say that the day football in England changed forever was on the opening weekend of the first season of Premier League football in 1992. The truth of the matter was that it had been changing and, inevitability, veering away from its roots and traditions for some time before then, it was just that the state of change and progress had been so slow, people had, for the most part, missed it. But commercial sponsorship was not new and didn't arrive with Sky Sports and its myriad partners or even with the appearance on the front of the Norwich City shirts the name of Poll Withey Windows, the club's first shirt sponsor in 1983. As far as the Canaries were concerned, it made its first appearance as far back as in March 1976 when Dunlop Tyres sponsored the home game against Liverpool. It was, of course, one they'd probably picked because of the fact that Liverpool, the eventual champions were in town and that, as part of the 'gig', attending Dunlop bigwigs would have the opportunity to meet and have their photographs taken with the likes of Ray Clemence and Kevin Keegan afterwards. Match sponsorship, even sponsorship of the ball and individual players is very much taken for granted in the modern game and this seemingly incidental involvement from Dunlop at Carrow Road nearly forty years ago was one of the very first indicators of what was to come in the game, something which, as its influence grew, Robert Chase was keen to see the Canaries involved in both on and off the pitch. And as much as possible if income opportunities were to be realised.

He and the still relatively new board at Carrow Road has not exactly been side-tracked by their new and ever increasing responsibilities. But it had seemed, nevertheless that, at a time when the club's footballing momentum had slightly fallen away, as it clearly did during the first half of the 1987/88 season, that their collective eyes had, pun intended, been taken off the ball, actions, or, rather, perceived inactions which had led to the disquiet and protest. They had given the responsibility of getting the footballing side of the business back on track to Dave Stringer and were confident that he would do just that with his understanding of the club, its philosophy and culture and standing in both the City and Norfolk second to none-and certainly superior to any of their own. And it was, ultimately, an inspired decision which not only put the football club back on the map for what it was achieving on the pitch, it also bought Chase and the board time to plan the remainder of their long term projects at Carrow Road.

The Canaries made it three wins out of three over the festive period on New Year's Day when they crushed West Ham 4-1 at Carrow Road, despite going behind to a first half goal from Tony Cottee. Whatever Dave Stringer might have said to his charges at half time certainly did the trick as goals from Dale Gordon, Kevin Drinkell, Mark Bowen (now playing at left back after an initial spell in midfield) and Robert Rosario sealed the win and another three points-a total of twelve now from a maximum of fifteen, enough to lift Norwich up into fifteenth place in the table. That win precipitated a continued run of fine form that saw wins at Newcastle United (3-1) and Tottenham (3-1) as well as further comprehensive wins and displays to go with them at Carrow Road over Manchester United (1-0) and Oxford United (4-2). The win against an Oxford side that would eventually finish bottom of the table was one that lifted the Canaries up into the top ten for the first time that season, into ninth place to be exact and three points behind Tottenham-with two games in hand, a truly remarkable turnaround for a club that had seemed, following their 3-0 defeat against the same opposition the previous October, absolute certainties to be relegated. That run of good results and the fact that it had convinced the board that the club's top flight status was now secure meant that Dave Stringer was even given a little money to spend which he did very wisely, finally sealing the gap in the centre of the Norwich defence left behind after the departure of Bruce and enforced retirement of John O'Neill by signing Andy Linighan from Oldham for just £300,000, Linighan having been recommended to Dave Stringer by his old defensive teammate Duncan Forbes who Stringer had the foresight to bring back to Carrow Road as chief scout.

After such a dramatic renaissance on the pitch, the club's form as the season drew to a close was disappointing. Charlton Athletic were easily beaten 2-0 at Carrow Road on 2 April but that was it as far as league wins were concerned that season as the Canaries ended an eventful season with three draws and three defeats from their final six league games, ending the campaign in 14th place. There was still some dissatisfaction amongst sections of the crowd, especially during the last game of the season at home to Wimbledon, one that had not only seen the club's lowest attendance of the season (11,782) but very vocal and constant chanting from those who were there aimed at Robert Chase.[9] But at least the season was, finally, and thankfully over. All that mattered now, and for everyone at the club, from its much criticised chairman downwards was how the club would respond after a disappointing, sometimes bitter and occasionally rancorous campaign. Yes, it had been gilded by the fine recovery work undertaken by Dave Stringer and Dave Williams. Yet that ongoing supporter discontent, further boardroom unrest and the placing on the transfer list of six players who had been part of the previous regime at the club under Ken Brown meant that there was a lot of work to do in order to re-establish the trust of the club's support and commitment of the players.

The speed at which Stringer did manage to turn things around, as it turns out, came about in a swifter and more impressive manner than even the most optimistic of Norwich fans would have believed possible.

In a strangely perverse way, the origins of that spectacular turnaround could partially be attributed to a Norwich player who made his last appearance for the club in the game against Wimbledon. Their winning goal, courtesy of Terry Gibson, had come about as the result of an uncharacteristic error on the part of Canaries right back Tony Spearing whose weak back-pass towards Gunn was intercepted by the always alert Gibson who made sure that he and Norwich were punished as a result. Spearing had been one of six Norwich players transfer listed by the club even before that Wimbledon game was played, an indication of how, even before one season had ended, Dave Stringer was preparing for the next one. Of those six players destined to be on their way, Kevin Drinkell would certainly have been the one from that list who Stringer would have preferred to keep at the club, but Drinkell was now an established and respected top flight forward and was, inevitably, attracting both the interest and money of several rather more financially well-heeled clubs in need of a good striker.

The fact that more than one club was interested in signing him came as financial manna from heaven to the Norwich board who, mindful that ready funds would be needed by Dave Stringer for the close season, chose to get as high a price for Drinkell as they could, inviting and then rejecting bids from Tottenham and West Ham before Rangers, who already had an ex-Canary in their squad in Chris Woods entered the bidding. The usual brinksmanship ensured with Norwich asking for far more money than Rangers thought Drinkell, good player as he was, was worth, with Rangers, in return, offering Norwich an amount far below what the Canaries would even have thought about considering. Drinkell had already seen that little charade played out between Grimsby and Norwich when he originally signed for the club, now it was happening all over again. He was, however, in a position of strength. He'd informed Robert Chase, and in no uncertain terms, that he was going to move to Rangers with the added suggestion that he wouldn't play for Norwich again if he didn't get the move he wanted. A mercenary attitude? Perhaps. But no more so than that of clubs in their dealing with players, especially the ones they don't want. Or, in this particular case, a manager they didn't want. Ken Brown had brought Drinkell to Norwich, not only that, he had built and developed the team that he and his teammates had prospered in, winning promotion and finishing fifth in the Division One table at the end of their first season back in the top flight. Ken Browns' team, his players, his footballing culture. Yet the club had dumped him as soon as things didn't quite seem to be going their way. Brown's dismissal had, for Drinkell, amongst others, to question whether they wanted to be at the club any longer and whether they should look out for themselves first rather than be in the same position themselves one day; discarded when no longer needed and without a second thought. Rangers would have been a tempting prospect to him, indeed, at that time, to any player. The fact that he felt his affinity with the Canaries had been sourced by the actions of one man made it all the easier for him. The clubs eventually settled on a deal of £600,000 and Drinkell headed north with no regrets other the bitterness he felt towards one particular man and the actions he had taken that ultimately had led to his leaving the club.

He wasn't the only player to leave the club in what turned out to be an eventful few months with players either departing from the club else arriving in such numbers that the old joke about a football club having to install a revolving door at its main entrance to cope with all the comings and goings would have been more than appropriate. The footballing world is truly a giant stage on which those that are privileged enough to play the game all have their exits and entrances. Drinkell's departure to Rangers was one of six from the club over the coming weeks and months with those joining him including Graham Benstead who joined Brentford; Wayne Biggins (Manchester City); Kenny Brown junior (Plymouth Argyle); Shaun Elliott (Blackpool) and, finally, the afore mentioned and unfortunate Tony Spearing who signed for former Ipswich and England defender Mick Mills at Stoke City, his and the other players departures,[10] some of which might have been a little more acrimonious than they could have been, ending up as the spark that lit the first fires of the footballing revolution that Dave Stringer was about to instigate at Carrow Road.

The money raised from Drinkell's sale as well as the other exits was invested wisely by Stringer who wasted no time in showing that he had as good an eye for a player, and, indeed, a bargain, as his predecessor. One of the first to arrive had been Paul Cook, a busy and skilful left-sided midfielder who joined from Wigan only a few days after the Wimbledon game. He was later joined by striker Malcolm Allen who signed from Watford and, just two days before the start of the season, twenty-five year old midfielder Andy Townsend,[11] a surprise signing from Southampton. A surprise signing? Most certainly. Townsend was steadily establishing himself as a first team player with the Saints having initially broken his leg whilst playing for them in a pre-season friendly against Weymouth. Having fought his way back to full fitness, Townsend was a virtual ever present for Southampton during the 1987/88 season, part of a competitive and effective midfield alongside Jimmy Case and Glenn Cockerill, his ability to get forward made possible because of the protection he was afforded as he did so by the two of them. He'd played against the Canaries in both league games the previous season, indeed, it had been his corner that had been headed past Bryan Gunn for the only goal in the Saints 1-0 win at Carrow Road, a game which also saw him hit the bar from a free kick. So there he was, almost the complete midfielder, a lesser striped

Bryan Robson almost. Townsend was comfortable on the ball, good in the tackle, liked to get forward and was an excellent option at set pieces. What's not to like? He clearly impressed the Norwich hierarchy on the day but, even so, you get the impression that the club were somewhat surprised that they'd got him so easily and relatively cheaply at £300,000.

For all that, Townsend didn't feature in the club's opening game which was a 2-1 win over Nottingham Forest at Carrow Road, Malcolm Allen making his debut for the club as a second half replacement for Robert Fleck who'd opened the scoring after just fifteen minutes, with Mark Bowen adding a second just two minutes later. Norwich were always in control from that moment onwards and, despite a second-half reply from Steve Chettle, the win was never in doubt. A potentially tricky trip to Middlesbrough followed a week later and, with it, another win, 3-2 this time in what was an entertaining affair in the Teesside sunshine which saw Robert Fleck score twice with the other coming from Robert Rosario, a player who the ever popular Fleck has since cited as one of the best and most unselfish he ever played alongside in his career: praise indeed!

By the end of September, the Canaries were top of the league having played four games and won the lot, victories over QPR (1-0) and Newcastle (2-0) following the Middlesbrough game. Those four consecutive wins made it the best ever start to a season by any Norwich side, one that was highlighted by Fleck's four goals in four games as well as the burgeoning defensive partnership between Ian Butterworth and Andy Linighan at the centre of the Norwich defence, a perfect combination of the cultured and ball playing type of centre back that Butterworth was with Linighan's physical presence and ability in the air-whatever was thrown at him he always, invariable, sent it straight back again. There has long been talk of a good teams needing a strong spine that runs all the way through it, supportive, supple and able to cope with anything and everything that comes its way, well, that Norwich side had the spine of a velociraptor. With Gunn an imposing presence in the Canaries' goal and Butterworth and Linighan providing that immovable barrier in front of him, Dave Stringer then had as central midfield pairing of Andy Townsend and Ian Crook with, at the top of his attacking 4-4-2 formation the option of Robert Fleck alongside Robert Rosario, the latest in a long line of successful striking partnerships at Carrow Road, a roll of honour that included Terry Bly and Errol Crossan for Archie Macaulay; Jimmy Bone and David Cross for Ron Saunders; Ted MacDougall and Phil Boyer with John Bond (so successful together that they eventually put on their double act at four different clubs) whilst Ken Brown had enjoyed success and goals with Keith Bertschin and John Deehan.[12] Fleck and Rosario were now continuing that fine tradition.

Norwich's great start to the 1988/89 was more than good enough to lift them into 1st place in the Division One table after the win against QPR in their third game, one they consolidated after the victory at Newcastle a week later. Top place in such esteemed company wasn't quite a new experience for the club but it was certainly one that no one thought would last for very long with those supposedly 'in the know' about such things seeing the natural order restored after Norwich suffered their first defeat of the season at home to Charlton on 1 October,[13] one that saw them slip down to second place even if, with that defeat, the natural order of things wasn't quite restored as their successors at the top were newly promoted Millwall who had held Norwich to an entertaining 2-2 draw at Carrow Road on 24 September.

Had football taken leave of its senses? First of all it had been Norwich at the top of the league – then, as if that wasn't bad enough, Millwall had replaced them. Football's establishment took a deep breath, made itself a nice, calming cup of tea and waited for Liverpool to reassume their rightful place at the top of the table and, in doing so, put together a run of results that would see them in their traditional place at the summit in time for Christmas with Norwich. And, as luck would have it, the league leaders were indeed at Anfield on the weekend before Christmas. Only it wasn't Liverpool who were in their customary position by then as everyone had expected but Norwich who had a sequence that included a 3-1 win over Tottenham, Paul Gascoigne included, at Carrow Road and, in a hugely impressive follow up to that win, a 2-1 victory over Manchester United at Old Trafford which not only saw United take the lead but, following that, Bryan Gunn repeat his feat from the previous season of saving a penalty from Brian McClair. It was a stunning win for Norwich, one made all the more impressive due to the fact that their two goals both came in the last five minutes of the game, with Mike Phelan's spectacular first time shot from outside the area to level on 84 minutes a candidate for any goal of the season award. But worse was yet to come, for both United and ITV's despairing man at the game who, as Andy Townsend won the game for the Canaries with another shot from distance denounced the cross from Dale Gordon that led to it as 'hopeful' and Townsends match winning shot as 'half-hearted'; the contempt in his voice for that goal and the Canaries win as easy to detect now as it was that evening at the end of News At Ten.

Norwich's surge to the top of the table had certainly done Robert Chase a favour. With dissenting voices against him temporarily quelled by the club's rise and rise up both the Divison One table as well as into the hearts and minds of the watching, mostly disbelieving, public, he made his first moves to raise his own profile in the game in much the same way as his team had done, standing against and, unbelievably, given the stature and popularity of his opponent, Bobby Charlton, for a place on the Football Leagues management committee. Another victory for the underdogs. It was turning into rather a good season for all concerned, one that just got better and better, for, following a 2-0 win against Wimbledon on Bonfire

Night, Norwich's lead at the top of the Divison One table had been extended to seven points. Mike Phelan and Andy Townsend's dominance and no little amount of skill and technical ability between them completely outclassed the usual ale house approach of Messrs Fashanu, Jones, Wise and company, proof positive for a grateful audience, that good football played by good players will always triumph over the kicking, elbowing, tugging and tripping of a team of flat track bullies. The Canaries truly showed Wimbledon up that night for what they really were, and, because of that and the manner in which they did it, that victory stands out as one of their most impressive of the whole campaign. It also increased the Canaries lead at the top of the table to an astonishing seven points. But back to Liverpool at Anfield. Because if they won there, it would eclipse everything else the club had so far achieved that season.

Prior to kick-off on that chilly Saturday afternoon, Norwich led Division One with 30 points from their 16 games played, followed by Arsenal (28 from 15); Coventry (26 from 16), and Liverpool with 25 points from their 15 games. A Liverpool win would, therefore, have put them just two points behind Norwich and with a game in hand. And no messing about by the Reds on such a big day either as they named a full strength side, one that included Peter Beardsley, Ian Rush and John Barnes. And, predictably, they dominated the game. But, for all of their efforts and the pressure Liverpool put on the Norwich defence, one that was missing the injured Ian Butterworth into the bargain, the Reds could not score. And, as their frustration grew, so Norwich's confidence, already high, soared to ever greater heights with the steadily increasing Canary attacking forays eventually paying dividends, an uncharacteristic error under pressure from Ronnie Whelan giving Andy Townsend a chance from close range that he fired past Mike Hooper with considerable relish.

Norwich had won. Again.

It was scintillating stuff as well as a scintillating time for the club. The Canaries, so often the subject of the footballing joke that says that, every Christmas they go down at the same time as the decorations were now preparing for the Christmas and New Year period at the top of the table, eight points, read that again, eight points clear of Liverpool, the title favourites and, by far, the best team in the country. This was, remember, the same Norwich City that had, a year earlier, sunk to twentieth place in Divison One, twenty-nine points behind the team they now led by eight points. As footballing turnarounds and changes of fortune go, it was spectacular and, in all honesty, at least if you were a Norwich fan, a little surreal.

What on earth had Dave Stringer done to precipitate such an astonishing upturn at the club? His players had no doubts at all about what had led to that remarkable upturn, with Mike Phelan, in particular, citing the confidence that comes in both knowing exactly what you are going to do and what your game plan is by saying,

'We set the pattern right from the off and the confidence came within a matter of three or four games and it showed in all the performances.' Andy Townsend felt the type of football the club was playing was so effective, it meant that, played well, you'd always have a chance of winning the games you were playing, admitting that, '... we just play football, there's no hard and fast secret to our game, we just knock it about and as long as you do that, you have a chance'.

He makes it sound as if it was easy! David Williams explained in more detail the gist of what Townsend was saying, explaining that, 'If we play eleven man football, then it is going to be attractive because the ball is going to be passed around quite rapidly, at times, one, two touch football (and) people are going to be involved in all areas of the pitch. This is what we've tried to promote amongst the players, and they've realised the responsibility they have in trying to keep the ball, moving, and keeping the play flowing from end to end.'

And you know what? Other people were, at last, beginning to take notice of Norwich City. When asked if he felt that Arsenal were Liverpool's biggest challengers for the league title, Peter Beardsley's reply was as refreshing as it was, for many, surprising.

'No disrespect to Arsenal, Arsenal are a good side but I think the biggest problem we've got at the moment is Norwich. I think everyone writes Norwich off but they're a good side and when they've had a bad result, they'll always bounce back and win the next one.'

It wasn't the first time that Norwich had been live on television. Their first time had been during the BBC's coverage of the 1985 League Cup Final. This was, however, the first time they had appeared live in a league fixture.

Another big moment came for the Canaries two days after Christmas when they featured, for the first time on a live Division One fixture, ITV having chosen the festive match against West Ham at Carrow Road for live coverage. Norwich won 2-1 in a game that wasn't anything like a classic. But their next appearance on TV most certainly was. That was their league visit to the Den to play Millwall on 22 January, a remarkable game that saw the Canaries go 2-0 up in the first seven minutes through goals from Ian Butterworth and Mark Bowen, only for the Lions to level the score by halftime with goals from Tony Cascarino and Jimmy Carter. Millwall then proceeded to apply the most extraordinary pressure on the Norwich goal for much of the second half, a forty-five minute period during Bryan Gunn probably had the best match any Canary keeper has ever had, making a series of astonishing saves, some from almost point blank range with one in particular from Terry Hurlock defying any sort of conventional analysis-it was, quite simply, world class.

Norwich memorably won the game in the last minute of the game, courtesy of a remarkable volley from Robert Fleck, his first goal in twelve league games for the

Canaries, his presence in the side throughout that run a tribute to how much Dave Stringer and David Williams valued him for how he contributed to play overall rather than just settling, in himself, for being a goal-scorer. Fleck in his Norwich prime was an absolute joy to watch, he was that rare player who, as well as being the sort who will run all day and give it his absolute all from first minute to last, was also gifted with the skill and technique that you'd more likely expect in a playmaker and there is no doubt that, had he been picked to play in the Number 10 shirt and play the role, Fleck would have excelled. He was a superb player who is, to this day, revered amongst Norwich fans of all ages, as well as being a total and utter gentleman with it. As if their good form in the league wasn't enough to get the fans of the club over excited, the Canaries also broke with long term tradition in having a more than decent run in the FA Cup, a competition which, during the preceding ten years had seen them only get at least as far as the 5th round on three separate occasions. With that in mind, there was some cause for concern after a little over half an hour of their third round tie at Port Vale, when, on a quagmire of a pitch and in typically wet and wintry conditions, Alan Webb put the home side a goal up, leaving some of the long suffering Norwich fans at the game fearful that Port Vale would soon be added to the lengthening list of lower league teams who had toppled the Canaries at that stage of the competition over the years, adding their name to the list of not so greats who had already done just that; Orient (1978); Wrexham (1970); Bristol Rovers (1964) and, horror of deepest ever horrors, non-league Bedford Town in 1957 who hadn't just beaten Norwich in the 1st round in 1956, but did so, at Carrow Road to the tune of 4-2! Fortunately for Norwich, Andy Townsend, who was already having a superb season scored two goals which, alongside a typical predatory effort from Fleck saw Norwich win the game 3-1, a comfortable enough victory in the end. Comfortable, that is, until the draw for the fourth round was made, one which saw another non-league club due at Carrow Road in the guise of Sutton United who had already caused a sensation in the competition by beating First Division Coventry City in their third round game at their Gander Green Lane.

With Norwich second in the Division One table on the day that the match was due to be played and being, well Norwich City, the tie attracted even more than the usual attention that had been made to similar perceived mismatches over the years. Some pundits even predicted that Sutton had a good chance of repeating their feat from the previous round, citing any and all footballing clichés in support of their argument: they had nothing to lose, they'd already beaten another First Division side and, to add insult to injury, if they beat Norwich then surely, surely they'd get the dream tie against one of English football's big clubs, '... the game they so richly deserve'. It was the sort of attitude and near expectancy that writes a managers pre-match team talk for him. The BBC were certainly in on the act, choosing to feature the game as their main feature for that nights FA Cup *Match Of The Day*, hoping, no doubt, that commentator John Motson would have another Ronnie Radford moment at Carrow Road even if, in the event of an unlikely Sutton win, their supporters would not only be liable for arrest if they invaded the pitch in the manner of that of the Hereford fans in their famous win over Newcastle United in 1972, but, rather than wearing parkas, would be more likely clad in leg warmers, fingerless gloves and shoulder pad assisted jackets.

Sutton did not, of course, win. In fact, they were put to the sword swiftly and with little mercy by a rampant Norwich side that won 8-0 with Malcolm Allen scoring four of the goals. Joy for the Canaries then but gloom across the rest of the footballing nation, deprived a Saturday night giant killing by Dave Stringers side, one which was acknowledged by a clearly disappointed Motson who said, after Allen's first goal, Norwich's second that '... it looks as though the Sutton Cup dream may be over as early as the sixteenth minute'. A surprise, therefore, that no one contacted the BBC to demand a refund on the cost of their licence fee. 8-0 to the First Divisions side? Where was the romance, where was the 'magic' of the FA Cup in that? The game was a procession, a one sided cakewalk for the Canaries that, at most, earned the vanquished Sutton players a sympathetic round of applause as they walked around the pitch at the end of the game, a bitter sweet memory for them to take to their old age.

Easy as the win might have been for Norwich, it was also one of their most important and significant of the whole season, one that was right up there with the victories over Manchester United and Liverpool? Why? Because it had been, as so many before it, a game that Norwich might well have slipped up in and fallen, all too easily, back into their bad old ways. We've already seen the evidence for that. Remember Orient, Bristol Rovers, Wrexham and Bedford Town? Precedents had been set. Which is why the BBC were present. No one was actually predicting that Sutton United would win the game, at least, not publicly. But there were those that thought, and with some justification, that Norwich might find it a difficult game to win. Regardless of their league position at the time. The fact that Norwich not only won, but did so in a thoroughly professional, merciless and efficient, controlled manner spoke the sort of volumes you only normally encounter at a Motorhead concert. This was a team that meant business. And one with a manager who knew that business better than most, despite his humble origins.

That win over Sutton United and the 3-2 win over Sheffield United that followed in the fifth round of the competition finally saw the Canaries twin assault on both the League and FA Cup that season be taken seriously as odds on the club doing the fabled League and Cup double began to be offered by the nations bookmakers.[14] They were, admittedly, as high as 80/1 at one point and, no doubt, a few hopeful punters put a fiver on the unthinkable happening. High odds, yes.

And an impossible dream? Probably. Yet, again, it was a sign of the continuing rise and rise of the Canaries fortunes that season. And, if doing the Double, something which, after all, had only been achieved five times in the previous 100 years was, as it was for most teams, going to be beyond Norwich, good as they were, then surely, hopefully, maybe they'd at least manage to tie a yellow and green ribbon around one of the cups at the end of that season?

It was not, of course, to be. Things were, admittedly, still looking good at the end of February, a month that at least saw Norwich confirm one 'double', that of league wins over Manchester United home and away with a 2-1 success at Carrow Road. Three games against West Ham in the space of ten days in March followed, a 0-0 draw in the FA Cup quarter final at Upton Park that led, gloriously, to a 3-1 win in the replay four days later and a first FA Cup semi-final for thirty years as a result, goals from Malcolm Allen (2) and Dale Gordon sealing the win with Allen's goals taking his total in that year's competition to seven, the first time a Norwich player had scored that many in one season of the competition since Terry Bly had in 1959, a year which, like this one, had also seen Norwich beat Sheffield United en-route to get that far. By three goals to two. At Carrow Road.

If you believed in omens then it was beginning to look as if it just might be the Canaries year in that seasons FA Cup. Had their name been written on the trophy from the start? And, with that in mind, had thoughts of Wembley in May become a little bit of a distraction to the players? It might, at least, be a reason why, following the third of those games against West Ham that March, a 2-0 win at Upton Park, the Canaries league form suddenly, and without warning, spluttered before going into freefall with the club failing to record a victory in any of its subsequent six league games, a massively disappointing run that was capped by a 5-0 defeat at Arsenal on May Day, the club's heaviest defeat for eight years occurring in the same season as they'd also recorded their biggest victory in fifty-nine years.

Typical Norwich where triumph and disaster inevitably always meet on the same page. By the time of the defeat at Highbury, the Canaries were also out of the FA Cup, losing a close fought encounter against Everton at Villa Park 1-0 thanks to a fortuitous goal from Pat Nevin. It was a painful defeat, one that signalled the end of any hopes of silverware, rather than plaudits, accompanying the end of that season. Yet, as the tragic events at that days other FA Cup semi-final showed, football was, after all, only a game and that, ultimately, there are far more important and precious things to worry about in life and to grieve over than losing a match.

The Canaries met Everton again at Carrow Road on 6 May for their final home league game of the season, ending it on a high with a 1-0 win, newly crowned Player of the Season Dale Gordon scoring the only goal with just two minutes left. The win maintained the Canaries hold on 3rd place, one they were not quite able to confirm by the end of the season after a defeat at Luton Town (1-0) and draw at a suitably subdued Hillsborough in a delayed final game of the campaign, Robert Rosario and Robert Fleck responding to an own goal by Andy Linighan and 82nd minute effort from David Reeves. It was perhaps fitting that it was Fleck who topped and tailed the Canaries season, it was his goal against Nottingham Forest back in August that had got the season off to a flier for Norwich and now, nearly nine months and sixty-nine League and Cup games later, he was bringing the curtain down on City's season with the club's seventieth and his fifteenth of that eventful campaign.

What a season it had been. The Canaries had ended it in their best ever top flight finishing position of fourth. They'd also topped the Division One table for three months and, in combining that with a superb run in the FA Cup, had maintained their chances of an unlikely League and FA Cup double right up until April. They'd also recorded their best ever win in the FA Cup with that 8-0 success over Sutton United as well as racking up an impressive six successive away wins in the League from the start of the season.

A season of superlatives. Yet one that, ultimately, ended in disappointment. Which was a good thing. Because it meant that the club had wanted more, that City were not content with their achievements that campaign and thought they should have done more, won more and taken a trophy with it. Or maybe two. The 1988/89 season remains, I think (and I know there will be disagreement!) Norwich City's best ever in their 113 year history, a memorable end to an equally memorable decade that saw two promotions, two relegations, a first £1 million departure, a first win at Wembley, three managers, two Chairmen and a 'goal of the season'. Amongst quite a few other things. Because life with Norwich City is never boring. It can be joyful. It can also be bleak and, seemingly without hope. But we could never be without them.

And, as things turned out, life at Norwich City and football in general was about to get even more eventful. But that's another tale for another book.

On The Ball, City.

And Never Mind The Danger.

# Acknowledgements

As ever, and, I hope, will be the case again, my huge and never-ending thanks to everyone who has helped, indulged, coaxed and cajoled, else gently encouraged or even slightly bullied me along the way whilst I've been writing this book.

You'll all know which of apply to you, so I'll leave it to you to decide which one applied.

To Tom Furby, Jenna Whittle and all at Amberley Publishing.

Peter Rogers and everyone at Norwich City Football Club.

Mick Channon for so kindly writing the foreword. Loved that windmill celebration. The original and the best. You can read all about what Mick is up to these days at www.mickchannon.tv.

Chris McGregor. Thanks for the insights and stories. Especially the ones I couldn't use! Also to James Woodrow, Rob Butler and Chris Goreham at BBC Radio Norfolk, Peter Mendham, Paul King, Gary Gowers, Jeremy Goss, Russell Saunders, David 'Spud' Thornhill and Mick Dennis.

To Rick Waghorn, author of *12 Canary Greats* – an invaluable resource. Also to Rob Hadgraft, author of *Norwich City –The Modern Era: A Complete Record* and Mike Davage, author, alongside John Eastwood of *Canary Citizens* and sole author of *Glorious Canaries – Past and Present*, recommended reading for any Norwich fan.

Other books read again (and enjoyed!) as part of the planning and writing of this one were *Drinks All Round* by Kevin Drinkell with Scott Burns (Black and White Publishing, 2010), *In Where It Hurts* by Bryan Gunn with Kevin Piper (Vision Sports Publishing, 2006) and *Forbidden Forward – The Justin Fashanu Story* by Nick Baker (Reid Publishing, 2013).

If I've forgotten anyone – and I probably have – then please accept my apologies.

I hope you enjoyed the book. It isn't meant as a definitive history of the club at that time, nor is it a comprehensive or all-encompassing account of every player, match, goal, transfer and incident. I'd need around a million words to even start to do something like that.

One day maybe.

Edward Couzens-Lake

# Notes

## Chapter One

1. From 5 January 1957, Norwich's league record in Division Three South read as P20, W3, D5, L12-the Canaries finished bottom of the table and had to apply for re-election to the Football League.
2. Baker, Nick *Forbidden Forward: The Justin Fashanu Story* (Reid Publishing, 2013).
3. Bond junior ended up winning the club's Player of the Year trophy that season, quite an accolade when you consider the quality of the 'opposition' in the Canary ranks who might also have been expected to be in with a chance. A detailed interview with Kevin Bond features in previous book to this one, *Norwich City: The Seventies*, also by Amberley Publishing.
4. It would be a further fourteen years before Norwich spent a million pounds on a player.
5. Couzens-Lake, Edward, *Norwich City: The Seventies* (Amberley Publishing, 2013).
6. Bobby Moore was one of the Canaries first choices for the job as manager when Bond eventually left for Manchester City in October 1980. He had, at that time, recently taken over at non-league Oxford City, turning down the offer from Norwich in order to stay loyal to the club that had given him that first managerial role in his career.
7. Imagine the teams Coach driver being so much a part of the match day routine of a club that he was free to join the staff and players in the changing room before and after a match, as well as sitting in the dugout during the game-and ever having a kick around on the pitch before kick-off. They wouldn't be let anywhere near any of those areas now-that's even if clubs take a Coach in the first place. Both Chelsea and Arsenal drew widespread criticism during the 2012/13 season for flying to Norwich from Gatwick Airport in West Sussex to Norwich, rather than taking a Coach from London, a journey of just 120 miles.

## Chapter 2

1. Muzinic ended up wearing seven different numbered shirts during his time at Norwich – 9, 7, 4, 3, 8, 5, and 12.

2. Irwin subsequently joined Swansea for £340,000, becoming their record signing. With that fee in mind it seems almost certain that Norwich would have had to have paid more for Irwin than they had for their own most expensive player, the floundering Muzinic.

3. The direct journey from Liverpool Lime Street to Norwich takes just under five and a half hours, including fourteen stops en-route.

4. Waghorn, Rick, *12 Canary Greats* (Jarrold, 2004)

5. A game that saw Glenn Hoddle go in goal for the visitors after an injury to Milija Aleksic.

6. O'Neill is one of just seven players who have been selected for a European Cup Final as well as playing for Norwich City. He was on the bench for Nottingham Forest against Malmo in 1979, as was Chris Woods, whilst David Fairclough played for Liverpool in 1978; David Hodgson featured on their bench in 1984, Jan Molby in 1985 and Peter Crouch in 2007 with Ryan Bertrand playing for Chelsea in the 2012 Final, thus completing the current septet. Paul Lambert, the Norwich City manager from 2009-2012 won the tournament whilst he was with Borussia Dortmund in 2007.hans

7. On the day of that Manchester City game, Hansbury signed for Hong King based club side Eastern AA.

8. Quite possibly – When Coton eventually left Birmingham to sign for Watford in 1984, the fee paid by the Hornets was only £300,000. He eventually supplanted Wealands in the Birmingham goal in the 1982/83 season so, had Norwich been interested, it seems plausible they could have done a deal.

9. The Canaries playing squad list, as given by the Rothmans Football Yearbook in 1981, consists of thirty-seven players in total, of which ten were born locally.

10. Beckham famously had a trial for Norwich in 1987, politely turning down Kit Carson's offer of a deal with the club by admitting he had already agreed to sign for Manchester United.

## Chapter 3

1. Gray went on to be a pundit and match summariser with Sky Sports until the company sacked him in January 2011 for 'unacceptable and offensive behaviour'.

2. Baker, Nick, *Forbidden Forward: The Justin Fashanu Story* (Reid Publishing, 2013).

3. Gronigen played in Holland's Eredivisie. Goble briefly rejoined the Canaries in 1984 but didn't make any first team appearances and eventually returned to Holland with Volendam before joining FC Utrecht.

4. Eastern Athletic were based in Hong Kong. Roger returned to England with Burnley in August 1983.

5. Keith moved after the start of the season but did not make any first team appearances during the very short time in the 1981/82 season he was still at the club so have regarded him as, like the others, a pre-season departure for that reason.

6. Brown had now spent £950,000 on five players-a sum roughly equivalent to just under £3.5 million in the spring of 2015.

7. The QPR goal was scored by Glenn Roeder, not the first time he would be the subject of anguish and debate amongst Norwich City fans.

8. Both Wynton and Shane played for Norwich in their friendly against the Fort Lauderdale Strikers at Carrow Road on 30 September, the game ending in a 2-2 draw.

9. Including Nikola Jovanovic (Manchester United), Raddy Antic (Luton), Dragoslav Stepanovic (Manchester City) and Ante Rajkovic (Swansea).

10. Twenty-three appearances for New Zealand, three of which were in a World Cup finals plus domestic club honours at the highest level in Europe as well as games and goals in the 1993/94 Champions League.

11. The Manchester City team on the day contained six players who had either previously been with Norwich (Kevin Bond, Kevin Reeves and David Cross) or would later have spells with the Canaries before the end of that decade-Joe Corrigan, Åge Hareide and Asa Hartford.

12. Phil Alexander, Mark Metcalf, Mark Crowe and Louie Donowa.

13. Waghorn, Rick, *12 Canary Greats* (Jarrold, 2004).

14. Goss, Jeremy (with Edward Couzens-Lake), *Gossy – The Autobiography* (Amberley Publishing, 2014).

15. The Stoke City team on the day included Dave Watson (the former Sunderland and Manchester City version); George Berry and Brendan O'Callaghan – seasoned, experienced and as tough as they come!

16. All of the scorers have connections, past and future, with the club they scored against. Manchester City's scorers were David Cross (x2, former Norwich); Kevin Bond (former Norwich) and Asa Hartford (future Norwich) whilst the Canaries consolation goal was scored by Martin O'Neill (former Manchester City-who he joined from Norwich!). The Manchester City manager of course, was John Bond-former Norwich whilst the Canaries Åge Hareide was-yes, another former Manchester City player.

17. A Jimmy Case goal for Brighton had knocked Norwich out of the FA Cup in the teams quarter final tie.

18. The Canaries last two league games of that season saw them draw 2-2 at Nottingham Forest before bringing it to a conclusion with a 2-1 win over Brighton at Carrow Road on the final day.

## Chapter 4

1. There are, of course, some notable exceptions to this rule. Terry Bly for one, sixty-seven games and thirty-eight goals. Dave Stringer is another. Then there are the anomalies, those Norfolk born players who either made it in the game after they left Norwich e.g. Danny Mills (derided throughout his short career at Norwich but a player who was England's first choice right back at the 2002 World Cup finals) or those that, for one reason or another, totally escaped the attentions of the club e.g. Barry Bridges, Peter Simpson (who won the League and Cup 'double' with Arsenal in 1971) and Trevor Whymark.

2. Goss, Jeremy (with Edward Couzens-Lake), *Gossy-The Autobiography* (Amberley Publishing, 2014).

3. Norwich won all four of their games on this first of their two trips to Norway in that close season, including 17-1 and 11-2 victories over Karnes and Sortland respectively.

4. Like O'Neill, Walford left the club extremely close to the beginning of the new season, hardly a good time, joining the Hammers on 23 August 1983 with the Canaries first league fixture due to be played on 27 August.

5. The other five are Paul Clayton (15), Jon Rigby (10), Daryl Godbold (2) plus Mark Crowe and Mark Metcalf (1 apiece).

6. Bennett's foot injury in the 2-1 defeat at Leicester the previous week signalled the beginning of the end of his career in football, he made no more appearances for the Canaries and, after a brief spell playing in the Netherlands, retired from the game at just twenty-five.

7. Greg Downs was the other ever present for all fifty-three of the club's matches that season

## Chapter 5

1. Keith Bertschin, Mike Channon, Joe Corrigan, Greg Downs, David Fairclough, Mark Farrington, Jon Rigby and Gary Rowell.

2. Eight Norwich players appeared in all five of those opening fixtures when it might have been easier for Ken Brown to make wholesale changes, given the club's slow start to the season. They were Chris Woods, Paul Haylock, Steve Bruce, Mike Phelan, Dave Watson, Peter Mendham, Kevin Drinkell and John Deehan. Mark Barham, David Williams and Garry Brooke were the other starters during that spell of games.

3. A popular misconception about this stand was that it was named after the direction it faced – it actually faces an approximate north-west direction!

4. Such was the lack of interest Everton manager Howard Kendall had for the competition, his now famous team talk prior their game at Carrow Road took up just ten words – 'What a waste of time this is. Out you go.'

5. Waghorn, Rick, *12 Canary Greats* (Jarrold, 2004).

6. Kevin Drinkell (4), David Williams (3), Dale Gordon (3), Mark Barham (2), Wayne Biggins (2), Steve Bruce (2), Shaun Elliott (1) and Mike Phelan (1).

7. Which they did, ending the season with fifty-three goals. Norwich's away total of league goals scored, 26, was the fourth highest in Division One that campaign.

8. Future Norwich manager Chris Hughton also played in this match.

9. Gunn, Bryan, with Kevin Piper, *In Where It Hurts* (VSP, 2006).

10. Bryan Gunn, Ian Culverhouse, Mark Bowen, Ian Butterworth, Ruel Fox, Jeremy Goss and Ian Crook.

11. Fanzines were, pre-internet, a popular and imaginative way of a club's supporters getting their views about their clubs across to their fellow fans in print, some of which ended up being extremely well produced and polished whilst others were no

more than half a dozen pages of photocopied A4 paper stapled together. Amongst the more respectable ones produced by Norwich fans were Ferry Cross The Wensum and Liverpool Are On The Tele Again.

## Chapter 6

1. I asked the club if they could shed any light on the origins or reason for this unorthodox mid-season friendly only to be advised the only information that they had was that 'it was instigated by the Chairman'. My thanks to Peter Rogers and James Woodrow for their help.
2. There were only twenty-one clubs competing in Division One that season.
3. Young famously hauled Paul Allen down in the 1980 FA Cup Final when the then seventeen year old Allen, the youngest player to appear in a Wembley Cup Final was clean through on goal for his club West Ham. Young, then at Arsenal, escaped punishment for his most professional of fouls.
4. Ruel Fox was the exception. Every one of the other eleven players on show had been brought to the club by Brown, including another new face, Simon Ratcliffe, who Brown had signed from Manchester United for £40,000. Yet even Fox was a Brown signing of sorts, joining the club as an apprentice in 1986.
5. Ratcliffe made his Norwich debut in the same game as Brazilian Mirandinha for Newcastle United in a 1-1 draw at Carrow Road on a Tuesday evening that saw sixty representatives from the press in attendance as well as 2,000 Newcastle fans.
6. Chelsea ended the season in eighteenth place and were relegated after losing a playoff match to Middlesbrough, who'd finished third in Division Two.
7. There were only 15,640 at the game where that banner was unfurled and the protest against the selling of Reeves took place. A month earlier, for the home game against Liverpool, the gate was 25,624. Perhaps the club might have been able to keep Reeves for a little bit longer had the gates for games such as that one against Brighton had more closely matched those for the games against the so-called 'glamour' teams?
8. No such problems at QPR's Loftus Road where, during the same year, another Evangelist, Luis Palau held similar events there. Only his devotees were able to join him and his entourage on the pitch as it was during the time that QPR had their plastic pitch-a decision that had been made with the holding of events such as this one in mind. Whether the Norwich board ever considered installing a plastic pitch at Carrow Road is unknown although it seems a fairly safe bet that Mr Chase and his board might at least have discussed the possibility.
9. It remains, to date, the lowest ever attendance for a top flight match at Carrow Road.
10. Another, much less heralded but ultimately significant departure from Carrow Road that summer was that of released youngster Dion Dublin who went onto sign for Cambridge United and ended up playing for both Manchester United and England before re-joining the Canaries eighteen years later!
11. For those that may not remember him in his playing prime with us, yes, this is the same Andy Townsend who worked as a match summariser for ITV and, for

some reason, never mentions Norwich as one of his numerous former clubs. Is he ashamed? He shouldn't be, for it was the Canaries who made him as a player and a Republic Of Ireland international. And that, for me Clive, is a crying shame...

12. As well as their time with Norwich, MacDougall and Boyer also teamed up together at York City, Bournemouth and Southampton.

13. The Canaries topped Division One for the first time in their history after three consecutive wins at the start of the 1979/80 season-against Everton (4-2); Tottenham (4-0) and Leeds (2-1).

14. No John Motson at that game for the BBC who sent along Archie McPherson to do the commentary, the first, and, as far as I know, only time the BBC Scotland man ever commentated on a game between two English league teams.

# Also Available from Amberley Publishing

FRANK MEERES

# NORWICH

## THROUGH TIME

This fascinating selection of photographs traces some of the many ways in which Norwich has changed and developed over the last century.

Paperback
180 illustrations
96 pages
978-1-84868-458-4

Available from all good bookshops or to order direct please call **01453-847-800**
**www.amberley-books.com**